Advan

What a surprising, practical form of energetic de-cluttering! The skill set Rose Rosetree teaches here definitely makes life more free and easy. If you believe in the power of consciousness, you will understand why these skills are so powerful.
— Rob Spears and Brenda Michaels,
   Hosts of "Conscious Talk Radio"

Rose Rosetree's simple advice regarding common astral-level problems can absolutely make life easier. Of course, I really enjoy all the practical applications she gives, like astrally detailing your car.
She touches on areas where few people have gone before. A must read for anyone looking to lighten up their lives by getting rid of old baggage.
— Sam Krause,
   Author of *Hey, Waiter... There's God in My Soup*

As a professional psychic, I have learned (the hard way) that cleansing my aura and my spirit is essential for me to live a calm and healthy life. Unfortunately, the very act of being psychic means that we pick up a lot of other people's energy. All psychics need to learn to keep what is energetically ours and let go of what is not.
The beauty of Rosetree's book is that she gives concrete, simple and usable methods for doing just that. I highly recommend this book to anyone who does — or wishes to do —intuitive and healing practices.
— Kathryn Harwig, JD,
   Author of *The Return of Intuition*

New help for living a healthy spiritual life! Once again, Rose Rosetree has articulated something we wouldn't have become aware of otherwise. In her latest book, Rose enables you to heal yourself using clear, easy techniques.

After you try them, you'll wonder how you managed without them.
— Jeffrey Chappell,
    Author of *Answers from Silence*

Here in Chicago I have helped thousands of clients as a hypnotist, so I know what a difference it makes when problems at the subconscious level can be released.

Never before did I consider that this subconscious level is equivalent to how human beings experience what is metaphysically known as "The astral level."

I think Rose has made a major discovery for healers with her perspective on astral-level problems like ghosts and psychic coercion. Her techniques for removing them are practical and easy to learn.
— Larry Garrett,
    Author of *Healing the Enemy*

Learning to manage our psychic life is not just a necessity for those of us who happen to be more intuitive and sensitive, but also for every human being. Of course, that requires us to maintain a clean and healthy psychic space — in the same way that if we expect to do well physically, we would need to take care of our bodies.

Use Your Power of Command for Spiritual Cleansing and Protection by Rose Rosetree offers psychic tools and step-by-step guidelines on how to apply them in your daily practice of maintaining your inner spiritual space.

Rose provides easy-to-follow instructions for each of the healing tools, simple enough for a beginner yet powerful and effective for experienced practitioners.

Her intention to empower readers shines through the tongue-in-cheek humor sparkling throughout this book.
— Michael J. Tamura,
    Author of *You Are The Answer*

Use Your Power of Command

for SPIRITUAL CLEANSING and PROTECTION

ROSE ROSETREE

Use Your Power of Command for Spiritual Cleansing and Protection

This book was manufactured in the U.S.A. 10 9 8 7 6 5 4 3 2 1

Publisher's Cataloging-In-Publication Data
(Prepared by The Donohue Group, Inc.)

Rosetree, Rose.
   Use your power of command for spiritual cleansing and protection, / by Rose Rosetree.

   p. ; cm.

   Includes index.
   ISBN: 978-1-935214-03-8

   1. Mental healing. 2. Energy medicine. 3. Spiritual healing. 4. Mind and body. 5. Self-help techniques. 6. Aura. 7. Parapsychology. I. Title.

RZ999 .R674 2011
615.8/528

Please direct all correspondence and inquiries to:
Women's Intuition Worldwide, LLC, 116 Hillsdale Drive, Sterling, VA 20164-1201. Call 703-450-9514. Email rights@rose-rosetree.com.

Interact at www.rose-rosetree.com/blog

CONTENTS

PART ONE. Become a Resourceful Healer

1. How These Skills Can Change Your Life 1
2. Gather Your Cleaning Supplies 9
3. Consciousness at Your Service 17
4. How Breathing Can Puff Away Astral Grime 25
5. Physical Self-Awareness Made Gentle 29
6. What Is an Emotion, Anyway? 35
7. Awaken Your Power of Command 41
8. Resourceful Healing 51
9. Your Date with the Divine 53

PART TWO. Clean up Everything You Own

10. Get Skills 63
11. Cut Astral Ties and Win The Lottery 67
12. Quickly Heal Stuck Spirits (Ghosts) to
    Free Both Them and Yourself 85
13. For A Free Vacation, Move Out Thought Forms 109

PART THREE. Free Yourself from Within

14. Deepen Your Power of Command 127
15. When Bullies "Should" on You,
    Defend Yourself Deftly 151
16. Prevent Psychic Attack 179
17. Experience the Ultimate Energy Makeover 199
18. Let's Party 221

Acknowledgments 243
Glossary 245
Index 247

Online Supplement at www.rose-rosetree.com

Part One.
BECOME A RESOURCEFUL HEALER

1. How These Skills Can Change Your Life

How bad does life feel when psychic-level debris clogs up your aura? Not so bad. Pretty normal, unfortunately.

What a difference it can make, cleansing that goop and moving, fast forward, up to a new state of "normal."

I'm going to teach you a complete skill set to heal ghosts, replace psychic coercion with self-authority, do aura makeovers to upgrade your social image, and more.

The entire set of techniques is called Spiritual Cleansing and Protection. Let's move forward together, one easy skill at a time. The very process of learning can bring new appreciation for five great things about yourself, especially Your Power of Command.

All this can help you feel better, as if waking up within your own life. With less astral-level clutter and more personal power, you may notice an effortless change in yourself — a new kind of confidence. Hence the name I'll be calling you from time to time, Resourceful Healer.

After learning our skill set, Resourceful Healer, there might also be *less* to you. Behold a short list of clearing accoutrements that students of mine used to need:

- "I depend on specially programmed crystals. These must be cleansed regularly."
- "I've bought some pictures of spiritual masters and saints so that they can protect me."
- "Once I took a special workshop that was supposed to cleanse my vibrations. I had to stand beneath a waterfall. At the time, this felt great. But I can hardly locate convenient waterfalls on a regular basis."
- "Smudging and burning incense — I do this every day. Once I burned so much incense, smoke filled my room. My room-mates were ready to report a fire. Even after I explained, I don't think they ever forgave me."
- "Bathing with Japanese rice wine (sake) is supposed to help. Except I didn't notice much from it. Also, that bathtub took an awful lot of sake. How expensive does cleansing your aura have to be?"
- "There's a special aromatherapy spray I'm supposed to squirt under my bed. It's all very complicated. I worry when I go visit my mother-in-law. It's hard to find a way to squirt anything beneath her bed."

Less can be so much more! If you have been trying to simplify your life energetically, I think you're going to love the results of these easy, effective techniques. Spiritual Cleansing and Protection is the ultimate in decluttering.

Besides decluttering various aspects of your human life, might you have an interest in spiritual development? How about meditation or healing; aura reading or psychic guidance; angel cards or channeling or mediumship?

Interests like these can make life more worth living. Unfortunately, interests like these can also cause a person to take on weird thought forms, draining astral ties, and psychic coercion that is downright disgusting.

At the time, do you know this is happening? Of course not... unless you learn dedicated skills for Spiritual Cleansing and Protection.

Unfortunately this skill set must be learned separately from other mind-body-spirit interests. Don't expect it to be included just because you're told, "When you learn Reiki, you're automatically protected," etc. Far from it. Professionals at energy healing, channeling, teaching yoga, etc. can be jammed up with astral debris and have no conscious clue.

Sure, techniques of protection are often included in psychic practices and energy work. Sometimes these techniques do work beautifully. I don't mean to suggest that our skill set is the only one that will work.

However, many comparable techniques are not as easy to learn, or else they take longer; some require specialized psychic training. Also some forms of protection may be taught as a formality, more a comforting ritual than a flexible, portable, practical method.

With the skill set of Spiritual Cleansing and Protection, you will gain the ability to identify and heal several different kinds of astral-level debris. If you're going to attempt this type of healing, why not do it really well?

Many of my clients and students have been pleasantly surprised to experience energetic decluttering. All it took was the same skill set I'm teaching you one technique at a time.

Yes, I want to share this amazing skill set with you, both the underlying concepts and some very specific techniques. If you find those concepts interesting — if you laugh at my jokes along the way — great! But the real point of this book is for you to *use* the techniques. Then you can discover real-life results, both immediate and cumulative.

Results

When it comes to any techniques for healing, I'm a believer in the biblical saying, "You will know them by their fruits." Plenty of techniques sound wondrous in theory. Results, however, are more like what happens when you buy gasoline for your car. You know, "Your actual mileage may vary."

Witness this story from my student Fabiola.*

"I was in a workshop where the leader asked Archangel Michael to take over. Afterwards I think everybody in the room felt nauseated. I did, anyway. Now I'm scared to even *think* the name 'Archangel Michael.'"

---

* Stand-alone first names in this book are fictitious. Sometimes it's to preserve the privacy of the speaker. Mostly it's because I don't always remember people's names. Notice, this is a how-to on "Spiritual Cleansing and Protection," not "How to Remember the Names of Everyone You Ever Meet." I can assure you, however, that every story recounted in this book is true.

A somewhat technical explanation of what happened to Fabiola will come in our final chapter. For now, let's simply use common sense. Whenever you try a new technique of Spiritual Cleansing and Protection, you will be asked to pay close attention to what?

The. Results. For. You.

- Do you feel better? Count that as good fruits. Keep reading.
- What, you don't feel much yet? (But you don't feel anything terrible, either.) *You* might not be ripe yet. Keep exploring.
- Do you feel bad results, even one? Slam this book shut. Add sound effects, such as howling, to taste.

I'm pretty sure that this third possibility won't occur. For decades I have used and taught these healings. Far as I know, nobody has suffered as a result. Perhaps a few have been bored or not noticed much, but that's different from nausea, wailing, or gnashing of teeth.

Results in my life.

In 1985, I first encountered techniques for Spiritual Cleansing and Protection. They were part of a course taught by the late Rev. Rich Bell, a minister with a group called Teaching of the Inner Christ, a.k.a. T.I.C., website at www.teachingoftheinnerchrist.com. (Note that "Christ" here simply means "Enlightened Person." While "Inner" points you in the direction of finding spiritual truth from within.)

Studying with T.I.C. brought me results that were subtle but impressive. Each type of healing helped me to feel more like me, less scattered and unsure.

So I took a second course, this one taught by Rev. AlixSandra Parness. She thought I had a knack for this type of healing. Noticing that no T.I.C. ministers lived in the Washington, D.C. area, Rev. Sandi invited me to start teaching these healings as a lay minister.

Aw, shucks! I did.

Meanwhile, in a non-flashy way, I kept gaining more clarity as a person. The spiritual healings had a lot to do with it. Within a year, I started teaching classes that, over the decades, became books and trademarked systems about energetic literacy.

In addition, I began offering sessions using a system of healing that I now call "Energy Spirituality." By 1986, things were going so well that I was able to quit my day job. Teaching plus healing became my new day job.

Eventually that day job went international. Working with clients has become an amazing, fulfilling part of my life. If I had to credit one skill set as most directly responsible for all those tasty, nourishing fruits, it would be... the verbal healings and co-creation techniques I learned from T.I.C.

Over the decades, I began adapting the healings, discovering loads of practical uses for them. As you'll soon read.

What got me teaching this skill set.

Eavesdropping started it. Friends, students, and even session interpreters would sometimes overhear me using these healings. Demand grew to learn the skills for themselves. One of the deciding factors was a request from my friend Kyoko Sakai. She told me:

"You know, Rose, other people give workshops about spiritual healing. Why not you?"

Since this didn't seem enough to motivate me, Kyoko continued:

"Once I signed up for a weekend workshop on spiritual healing and it was just horrible. As we went along, the group became weirder and weirder. Especially the teacher! He started off strange and became even stranger.

"By Saturday afternoon, the place was so extremely crazy, I couldn't stand it anymore and I left. Although I don't know exactly what happened, my guess is that we actually attracted more astral debris than we healed."

When you read further, I think you will understand why things like this happen. (For now, here's a hint. I think Kyoko's theory was right.)

So, yes, I took Kyoko's advice and started to workshops on Spiritual Cleansing and Protection. Students love it. However, I have also received numerous requests for something even more convenient and inexpensive. Something compatible with absolutely everyone's tight schedule. Something easy to understand but also thorough.

Hey, that would be an old-fashioned technology called "this book."

Ask an interpreter.

Another big motivator for me in writing this book was interpreters besides Kyoko-san. Thanks to many foreign teaching trips, I have done hundreds of sessions and dozens of workshops with interpreters. Trust me, it's a very interesting type of relationship.

Do good interpreters merely translate your words? No, they crawl inside your brain. Where they proceed to tease out what you are really trying to say.

Then interpreters figure out how to adjust your words so that people from an entirely different culture will go "Aha!"

I have developed enormous respect for the brainy *session* interpreters who will sit with six clients in a row, healing away. Moreover, many *workshop* interpreters have personalities so lively that they make my offerings seem way more interesting than if I were the only speaker.

Being so grateful to all these interpreters, did I listen when they asked me to teach them the skills of Spiritual Cleansing and Protection? Can I use a chopstick?

Okay, two chopsticks work better. Okay, sometimes I have decent skills with making a pair of chopsticks hold food. Anyway, you get the idea.

Again and again, interpreters would thank me, saying something like, "Even though we had a long day, I don't feel exhausted or weird now. How odd. I even feel good."

Apparently this was unusual.

Over the years I learned why. Many psychics and healers don't have the skill set for doing effective Spiritual Cleansing and Protection. Instead, their talents, interests, or training lie elsewhere.

Pity the poor interpreter — and maybe the client — and maybe also that talented healer doing the session in the first place. As the day wears on, air in the room gets thicker and heavier and more crammed with astral goop.

In Japan, I was working with a company called VOICE that specializes in mind-body-spirit services. Interpreters told me, after a typical day of interpreting for healers sponsored by VOICE, clients might have felt good but their hardworking interpreters would go home exhausted.

So why, after spending a day with me, did interpreters feel better than ever? How come they looked positively recharged, even glowey? It had to be the skills of Spiritual Cleansing and Protection.

Our company, VOICE, had a 28-year history of sponsoring healers like me, approximately a hundred of us every year. A couple of times I set records for the company.

Why did I wind up helping more clients than any of their other healers or psychics? All of them were highly trained professionals in their own specialties. All of them could have been way more talented than me. Only they definitely lacked one particular skill set.

Because Spiritual Cleansing and Protection isn't included in other skill sets. It must be learned on its own.

What will happen when you know these healings, too? Maybe you will go to foreign lands and wow some interpreters. Whatever your heart's desire for career, I hope that you will become more productive. Whatever your home life, your love life, why not learn to de-clutter the energies around you?

Less friction in your life. Less confusion. More you. That simple.

2. Gather
Your Cleaning Supplies

Resourceful Healer, I think you will enjoy this product line. It has been manufactured directly by God. Altogether we'll be using five products: Consciousness, Breath, Body, Emotions, and Your Power of Command.

Working with these supplies is not like ordering shiny new furniture from IKEA, where you're almost afraid to take the separate pieces out of their big, flat boxes. Because you just might screw Widget A into Flat Piece Q, wreck them both, and then scream for an hour.

Yes, you can definitely, easily, use all your God-Given Five Cleaning Supplies. No harsh chemicals will be needed. No mechanical ability, either which is helpful if you're like me, spiritually resourceful but klutzy at changing vacuum cleaner bags or similar "really hard, high-tech" human-type jobs.

Security will grow within you as you develop skill at using your cleaning supplies. No midnight trips to Home Depot. No repeat trips to Home Depot because you didn't buy all that you needed the last time. All five of your cleaning supplies have been with you always.

That is why you can do any technique of Spiritual Cleansing and Protection and be 100% successful. Every time! Effortlessly!

So, Resourceful Healer, here comes an overview of your mighty cleaning supplies.

Cleaning Supply #1. Consciousness

Whenever you're awake, you have **consciousness**. Previously you may not have known its protective power. Maybe you never thought of your consciousness in the same category as Comet, Formula 409, or Mr. Clean.

Well, consciousness is bottled within you and available to help on demand. All your thinking, feeling, touching, learning, and knowing are written in a kind of energy. Which is your consciousness.

Philosophers, psychics, even mothers of very small children — exhausted mothers who still suffer from preggo-brain — everybody has consciousness. Some make consciousness seem like a very big, complicated deal. Well, it doesn't have to be.

Back in the day, your mother got right to the basics when she told you, "Pay attention." That's the essence of using your Cleaning Supply #1.

For best results, use your consciousness effortlessly. In our next chapter, I'll supply a technique for doing that.

No need to scrub, ever. Simply pay attention. What is it like to be you, yourself in the moment, here and now?

Whatever you notice counts. And that, in itself, will count for *us* as "Using your consciousness."

Cleaning Supply #2. Breathing

For thousands of years, mystics and yogis have explored the power of breathing. As a spiritual teacher, I've experimented with breathing techniques for over 40 years. During that mere puddle of time, I've managed to discover one super-useful breathing pattern for Spiritual Cleansing and Protection.

Vibe-raising breaths can bring clarity to your experience of consciousness. Depending on what you need, this breathing pattern may help you to feel more secure or relaxed or grounded or emotionally stable. Not bad, for a simple variation on something you do already.

I'll teach you this cool breathing pattern soon, in Chapter 4.

Cleaning Supply #3.
Physical Self-Awareness

Long before you met Rose Rosetree, I'm pretty sure you managed to find some excellent uses for that physical body of yours. Welcome to a splendid new app: Physical self-awareness. Paying attention to your body can become a fabulous resource for cleansing.

Soon I'll show you how to use **physical self-awareness** as an amazing energy feedback device. Doing one healing technique at a time, you will aim your consciousness directly at your body and notice results. Comparing before and after, what changes?

Your physical self-awareness can become such a fabulous resource, once you learn how to use it. And this cleaning supply is built right into you — one of five reasons why the skill set for Spiritual Cleansing and Protection requires zero clairvoyance or far-out anything.

Note, too, that use of physical self-awareness as Cleaning Supply #3 will not require that you worry about your health. Spiritual Cleansing and Protection is not the same skill set as hypochondria.

Nor will you be bossing your body around (as usual?) with "How dare you look/smell/weigh that way?"

Instead you can develop an appreciative physical self-awareness. Think that is common among people who do self-healing?

Think again. Far too many people treat their bodies like extras in "The Night of the Living Dead."

Cleaning Supply #4.
Emotional Self-Awareness

For some of you Resourceful Healers, the greatest benefits from learning Spiritual Cleansing and Protection will involve teaming up with your emotions.

It's natural to feel better emotionally without the negative hidden interactions that so many of us have with the astral. Your own aura contains an astral component, you know.

In order for this built-in astral connection to work well, must you nag yourself? Will it help to interrupt normal life every few minutes, straining to keep that tricky thing going?

Nope. All human beings are affected by astral-level life. Your healthy connection is automatic. Unfortunately astral garbage can be deposited automatically too.

When you purposely clean up astral-level garbage, what happens? Very often a person will notice emotional shifts in the direction of calmness, relief, alignment, clarity, and one of the sweetest emotions on earth, "Feeling more like yourself."

So **emotional self-awareness** can be considered a powerful feedback device for noticing results from our skill set. Use it as Cleaning Supply #4 whenever you do a technique for Spiritual Cleansing and Protection.

Emotional self-awareness can also help you discern the need for one particular healing skill versus another.

Cleaning Supply #5.
Your Power of Command

Blah, blah, blah. Sure, people talk all the time. Talking doesn't necessarily use the Power of Command, does it? Because this power creates immediate results exactly as intended.

You were born to do more than just talk. By waking up **Your Power of Command**, the words you speak for healing can become power-packed. Resourceful Healer, you will produce the desired results immediately.

This awesome power of yours has been installed even before you knew how to talk. Learning to harness that power, you will be able to request miracles of healing. And get them. Every time.

Your Cleaning Supply #5 matters so much, it's central to our system for Spiritual Cleansing and Protection. So let's explore more deeply what it is… and also what it isn't.

What ISN'T Your Power of Command?

Moving your listener like the preacher of a hell-and-brimstone sermon? No, that isn't Your Power of Command. Tone of voice has nothing to do with it, nor will you need to gather a large congregation before you can do your best.

Neither public speaking nor religion need be involved for you to use Your Power of Command.

How about developing a stern **power voice**? Parents of young children need to develop that special, urgent, "Listen up" voice. So do elementary school teachers.

"Melissa, you will not throw Jimmy out the window. Stop right now."

Gee, I sure hope that no-nonsense voice will work on Melissa. I happen to know that particular classroom window is five stories up.

To some degree, survival of the human race depends upon the judicious use of power voice from authority figures. It can take a whole village full of these voices to keep that village from exploding due to experimenting children. Meaning no disrespect, however, power voices have nothing to do with the spiritual Power of Command.

What about **obedience training voice**, required to domesticate certain pets? Any human survivor of puppy training has my sympathy, as well as congratulations. You know about obedience training voice. When you say "Bad dog!" you had better mean it.

Save your carpet if you can. Still an obedience training voice isn't what you will need for Spiritual Cleansing and Protection.

How about **positive self-talk**? Imagine yourself dressing up for a big date. Could you improve your chances by speaking encouraging words in front of the mirror?

Maybe "Good dog"?

Please keep up those pep talks. Just don't do it out loud *during* that big date. Otherwise it could quickly become a small date.

Whether you're married or single or whatevering, sometimes a person needs extra encouragement. Positive self-talk can help enormously. Regardless, this has nothing to do with using Your Power of Command.

Telling yourself **affirmations**, does that count as using Your Power of Command? Surprisingly, perhaps, no.

Have you ever set yourself a program of using affirmations? I'm a believer in using those positive words. In fact, I have a cute set of positive statements that goes into my daily routine, just like doing my brave little pushups.

Still that doesn't count as using My Power of Command. Because those affirmations are repeated every day. Whereas the Power of Command only is used once, as needed, for a particular healing to be completely successful.

How about **prayer**? When a communication is sent out to God, sure, it can be done through words either thought silently or spoken out loud. Spoken words of prayer might have a beseeching quality, or perhaps setting the prayer into spoken words can lift up your heart, your soul, your thoughts, your will. Beautiful!

Prayer is intensely personal, never needing to be the same twice. Whereas you can use your Power of Command for specific techniques, doing something rather routine, and not necessarily heartfelt.

Say that you arrive at a motel at 2:00 a.m. , after a long traffic jam. Even if feeling totally limp, you still could clean the place up fine with some of our skill sets for Spiritual Cleansing and Protection.

Resourceful Healer, you would get results by saying and doing what's needed, not necessarily making this cleansing technique a bigger deal than flossing your teeth.

Whereas who really needs to offer God a semi-snoring, ultra-sacred prayer?

Also, prayer does not necessarily carry the strong implication that "I demand to actively co-create with you now."

So don't consider prayer synonymous with using Your Power of Command, Resourceful Healer. Otherwise you'll weaken your use of both.

Supersized power speech needs to be used only once, but it's different too. This speech of mega-power is available only when you've got high status, money, great fame, etc.

Sure, supersized power speech can get a job done. For instance, back in the day, England's King Henry VIII said the equivalent of, "I am so over that wife. Off with her head!"

You may know that this not-so-great royal husband did have to repeat himself occasionally. However, he was speaking about a different wife each time. Soon she, too, would be very dead. Like it or not, King Henry's royal supersized power of speech worked exceedingly well.

On the bright side, Your Power of Command won't require kingship or queenhood or other political power. Nor will there be any beheading. So....

What IS Your Power of Command?

Five conditions must be met in order to use Your Power of Command:

1. Your words are *aimed* precisely where a problem is
2. You know *what* to request
3. You understand *intellectually* what you are requesting
4. You are in the *presence* of the Divine, actively engaged
5. You have earned the *standing* to make your request

Yes, of course you can learn to do all this. We'll get there.

As we prepare, let's keep things in perspective. Using Your Power of Command will involve something different from all the examples I've given about supersized power speech, training puppies, etc.

Using Your Power of Command is, essentially, something private. Something that eavesdroppers won't necessarily notice.

Other people, overhearing you, might have no clue whatsoever that you are co-creating by means of a mighty inner power. Casual listeners know nothing of your internal spiritual process, how you aim your consciousness, or your discernment for choosing what to request.

Just the opposite, probably. Think of all the overheard cell phone conversations, people's lurkings at Facebook, all that twittering, the incessant watching of entertainment.

You know, electronic eavesdropping is part of everyday life today. All our movies and YouTubes and plays can be great fun. Personally, I'm a big fan of Shakespeare's plays about King Henries, the more the merrier.

Yet great performances have trained us fans to expect extreme drama. Plus special effects whenever possible.

By contrast, skills of Spiritual Cleansing and Protection are not flashy on a human level. They aren't even flashy on the astral level. More like taking your Uncle Snuffy to the bus terminal, bestowing a restrained manly hug, and sending him on his way home.

No elocution lessons would be needed for this late night trip to the bus station. Nor would you need to project your voice until it could be heard clearly throughout the bus terminal, even by that sleepy wino slumped against a back wall.

Using Your Power of Command is a *spiritual* experience. What will someone else hear in your voice? Only a voice.

Only *your* voice, to be more specific. Your Power of Command will mean your personal voice, used with magnificent spiritual awareness and human skill. Not your voice when that special power is un-activated, nor your voice when half- awake and used with no skill whatsoever.

You are the one who will know when you wake up Your Power of Command… along with the rest of your sacred and mighty cleaning supplies for Spiritual Cleansing and Protection. Then the sound will go out, making your life so much better.

3. Consciousness At Your Service

Now that our overview is complete, let's begin exploring.

Consciousness is our #1 Cleaning Supply. Remember, all your thinking, feeling, touching, learning, and knowing are written in a kind of energy. This is your consciousness.

Turn the page for a technique to help you appreciate this great asset for Spiritual Cleansing and Protection.

CONSCIOUSNESS MEET-UP

Read through these instructions first. Then do them, taking a peek as needed.

For a fancy version of this technique, record the following steps, allowing appropriate time between them. Then play back the sound recording and follow your own instructions.

Resourceful Healer, it's fine if you do a browse-through. Only stop browsing here. Skip ahead to the next chapter. When you're ready to do the slower kind of read, experiment with the technique that follows.

Do the following effortlessly, with zero expectations.

1. Sit comfortably.
2. Close your eyes for 10 seconds.
3. Open your eyes.
4. Close your eyes for 20 seconds.
5. Open your eyes.
6. Close your eyes for 30 seconds.
7. Open your eyes.
8. Say out loud what you noticed.

For example, did you hear yourself thinking? Hear silence? Feel one or more emotions? Notice sensations in your physical body? Feel energy? See colors? Whatever!

What happened?

Whatever you noticed with "Consciousness Meet-Up" was fine. And you did notice something, right?

You could have had mostly one thing or a combo. That's definitely fine.

Whatever you noticed, you can thank your consciousness. Your consciousness is what you automatically used for noticing that fine thing.

Got it? To clarify further, let's do some Q&A.

Q. I'm not sure that I even have "consciousness." What if I don't have any?

A. How sweet! Such modesty!

Enough with the compliments. Now let's get down to business. Of course, you have consciousness. That's just the effortless ability to notice what is going on inside you.

At least you have the ability to notice things happening inside of you unless you're drunk or under some other influence, like recreational chemicals or prescribed medication that really dulls you out.

If you're high on recreational substances like pot or bourbon, wait until you sober up. Never, ever do techniques of Spiritual Cleansing and Protection while under the influence.

If you're taking prescribed medication, keep taking it. Unfortunately, medication can sometimes prevent a person from having clear inner experiences.

Do the best you can. You're still using your consciousness, even if experiences aren't crystal-clear at this time. All the healings will work regardless; it's just that your inner experiences won't be as clear as they would be otherwise.

Q. What if I'm not taking medicine but still feel blank inside?

A. Then the most likely culprit is **expectation**.

Specifically, your real-life inner experiences are not matching up with your fancier ideas about "supposed to." As if that were unusual! Or an impossible obstacle to overcome!

Now hear this: Natural experiences of consciousness do not come with special effects like a big-budget movie. Keep reading our Q&As to learn about some popular expectations that are, sadly, counter-productive. You can overcome.

Q. Should I worry if nothing special happened?

A. Don't worry one bit. If anything, applaud yourself.

What if you had wild, flashy experiences every time you paid attention to your consciousness? You might paint like Vincent Van Gogh. But how well would you function outside the asylum?

Sometimes a newbie expects that true self-awareness means hearing a completely different voice inside, perhaps like Charlton Heston performing as "God" in "The Ten Commandments." During the clearest experiences of consciousness you will, actually, sound exactly like you.

Q. You have just confirmed that my consciousness isn't special. Doesn't that make me a pathetic loser?

A. So what if your consciousness isn't flashy? It can still be magnificent, wise, super-creative, even downright holy. "Special" is different from "loud," right?

Noticing your consciousness is like eating. Isn't your idea of fine dining more Four Seasons than your neighborhood Seven Eleven?

Good. I'm relieved.

Still, for practical purposes, a quick 'n tasty fast food meal also counts as food. Just as you need everyday meals to build your strength in life, most experiences of consciousness are simple and natural.

For most people, the long-term habit of accessing your consciousness is what leads to inner experiences that are equivalent to dining at the Four Seasons.

Therefore, a regular, not-terribly-flashy experience of your consciousness is perfectly fine. For gaining the skill set of Spiritual Cleansing and Protection, all you need is a simple feeling like, "Here I am."

Q. What if all I had were thoughts?

A. When I ask you to do a technique, I am asking you to simply do the technique. Nothing else. Nada.

So "Pay attention to your consciousness" does not mean "Remove anything else you might possibly notice, like your nose or your thoughts."

Honestly!

Q. **I'm still worrying. What if other people do this first exercise so much better than me?**

A. Comparing yourself to others — why do such a nasty thing to yourself? Has this ever helped you before to gain even one smidgeon of extra goodness?

The technical term for comparing yourself to others is "Ouchers!"

Let's try an experiment. Keep comparing yourself to others most of the time. Spend every waking moment comparing yourself to others for the rest of your life, if you wish. Except let's make one exception: Please do no comparing whatsoever when using any part of our skill set for Spiritual Cleansing and Protection. Deal?

Darling, try just being you for a while. A unique creation, made by God! Someone with a full set of gifts, talents, wonders, all available to explore!

Of course, if you prefer, compare away.

Alternatively you could spend the next 50 years analyzing this need to compare yourself to others. Your choice.

Q. **In the "Consciousness Meet-Up" technique I just did, can I just skip that part about saying words out loud? I hate that part.**

A. You have plenty of company. But get over it. Saying those words out loud is important for waking up all Five Cleaning Supplies. In many of the techniques that follow, I'll ask you to write down some words or record them.

You're not my first student to find this a nuisance. Why bother to find those words?

Consciousness does you no good as a cleaning supply unless you are willing to stretch your mind a small bit and find language to describe what is happening inside you.

It's worth that small amount of effort, given the many benefits of expressing your experience of consciousness. Benefits can include all of the following:

- Get in touch with aspects of yourself that you may have previously ignored.
- Access inner wisdom to become more resourceful in life.

- Decrease the amount of inner clutter, denial, and even (Dare I say it?) (Yes!) inner bullshit.
- Improve your intimacy skills for every relationship that matters to you.
- Communicate more clearly with God.
- And let's not forget this: Be able to tell when you have successfully completed a technique of Spiritual Cleansing and Protection.

Q. Look, you've persuaded me in theory. Only I still feel inner resistance to speaking things out loud or writing them down. How do I get past that?

A. Just do write those words down or speak them out loud. Whether it's fun or not.

Now, please return to our Consciousness Meet-Up Technique. This time, say something out loud, anything. If you like, start with words like "I feel stooopid."

Sooner or later, your flow of words will turn into something meaningful.

Q. What if the words I say out loud don't feel real?

A. Make something up. You're not selling these words on Ebay, are you? This is just a little personal exercise.

Connecting to deep inner experience and expressing it in words — what an achievement this will be when you have mastered it.

Sure you can. This is a kind of coordination that grows with practice.

Q. What if my consciousness doesn't give me words but images?

A. Then say words that summarize the images, like "Big waterfall, bigger rocks."

Q. Okay, I'll admit it. I'm ashamed to express what happened. It was so ordinary, like feeling a mood or two and then having my left elbow feel heavy. I mean, really, how pathetic is that?

A. Everything you notice counts. This is just our first exercise, right? Trust the process for now. Consider it a preview of what you will understand in more depth later. Incidentally, noticing things about energy or seeing images is NOT superior to having other experiences like noticing an emotion or finding a physical sensation in your body.

Q. Can I be excused from saying words out loud? English is hard for me.

A. So glad you asked! Many of you Resourceful Healers speak a first language other than English. Congratulations on being able to read English as well as you do. I admire you for learning more than one language and dealing with it as well as you do.

Now comes the very important practical point. Whenever you play with an exploration from the skill set of Spiritual Cleansing and Protection, write words in your most comfortable language.

We're not testing your English skill set here, right? We're doing Spiritual Cleansing and Protection.

Experiences with this skill set may introduce you to some of the deepest levels within. Of course it's appropriate to think about them in words from your mother tongue. You will grow fastest that way.

Q. Forget foreign languages. What about horrible in any language? What if I experienced something in this exercise and I didn't like it?

A. Not to minimize your pain and suffering but let's get real. In the grand scheme of things, what's the big deal if you groan your way through an unpleasant experience for half a second? Doing an exercise here or there… is part of a lifelong project. You're developing trust that will serve you the rest of your life.

Please don't tell me you are like my friend Brad, who went into deep depression at age 21. This happened right after a dentist drilled out Brad's first cavity. Up until then, Brad tells me, he believed he was perfect in every way.

Could be, some of the problems that have upset you for years were forms of astral-level junk. Could be, your life will change a lot when you learn to do Spiritual Cleansing and Protection.

If you're un-comfy right now, feeling bad in any way, don't fix it by taking a large dose of vodka or slamming down your Reiki hands or doing any other techniques you may have learned so far. Keep reading.

Use the skill or exercise provided in each chapter to find out what it can do.

After you finish exploring our skill sets, if you still feel lousy, sure. Turn to your usual forms of consolation. Just do them after, rather than during, the exercises here.

Actually, it is just possible that Spiritual Cleansing and Protection will not remove every problem you have in life.

Perhaps your first experience with Cleaning Supply #1 (or #2, #3, #4, or #5) will reveal some slightly uncomfortable problem. Further, what if that problem remains even after using the full skill set of Spiritual Cleansing and Protection? Would that necessarily be bad?

Experiencing something "horrible" that was in you all along might motivate you to heal it for good. Maybe you will be motivated to try out a new technique, like learning a quality method to cut cords of attachment. Or perhaps you'll decide to finally get some short-term help from a psychotherapist. (Instead of putting this off until your dying day.)

In which case you would discover a fine advantage as a consumer. After you have done a few of our healing chapters and started enjoying all five of your cleaning supplies, guess what? You can use them to evaluate other things that you do, not only techniques of Spiritual Cleansing and Protection. A very cool consumer app!

Consciousness is the ultimate, bountiful cleaner-upper. Simply paying attention, you can cut through illusions and find your truth, here and now.

4. How Breathing Can Puff Away Astral Grime

What, you already knew that your breath is very, very valuable? Breathing, our Cleaning Supply #2, does have some pretty well-known uses apart from the way we'll employ it for Spiritual Cleansing and Protection.

Consider **breath as enticement**, for instance. In the past, before a big date you might have done the puff-on-hand-in-front-of-nose trick. "Is my breath kissing sweet? Please, please, please."

Resourceful Healer, I'm happy to announce that your breath is definitely clean enough. In fact, it hereby qualifies as an official Cleaning Supply. Certain breathing patterns wake up your consciousness, helping you to notice more clearly all energetic improvement in yourself and your environment.

One breathing technique is particularly essential to Spiritual Cleansing and Protection. I call it "Vibe-Raising Breath."

Each time you take a Vibe-Raising Breath you will breathe slowly and deeply in a particular sequence.

What's the big deal about breathing this way? To find out, let's combine this particular breathing pattern with Consciousness, your Cleaning Supply #1. To start, just turn this page.

BREATH FOR CLEANSING

Browsers, please skip ahead to the next chapter. Learners, go ahead and actually *do* the following technique.

Read through all the steps first. Then do them without trying hard, taking a peek at the next step as needed.

For a fancy version of this exercise, make a sound recording of all the following steps, allowing appropriate time between them. Play back the sound recording and follow your own instructions.

1. Sit comfortably.
2. Close your eyes.
3. Notice how it feels to be you. (Which could be anything about your body, emotions, thoughts, energy, visuals.)
Find a few words to describe. Open your eyes just long enough to write words down; then close your eyes.
4. Take three Vibe-Raising Breaths in a row. For each one of these special breaths:

- Slowly and deeply breathe in through your *nose*.
- Pause for one gentle moment.
- Breathe out through your *mouth*.
- Pause again, gently.
- Return to normal breathing, in and out through your *nose*.

5. Notice how it feels to be you. (Especially notice the same kind of anything you noticed before.)
Again, write something down. Immediately close your eyes.
6. Send your respiratory system some thoughts and feelings of gratitude. Then think, "This technique is complete now." And open your eyes.
7. Look over the notes you wrote down. Now is the time to compare your before-and-after.

What Happened?

What fun it can be to use "Breath for Cleansing"! Let's bring on our latest round of Q&A.

Q. Exactly how comfortably did I have to sit?

A. What a perfect time to ask such a wise-ass question....

"Sit comfortably" is my tweet version of saying many things related to getting the best possible results from "Breath for Cleansing" or *any* technique used for Spiritual Cleansing and Protection. "Sit comfortably" means:

1. Back supported by a chair or pillow.
2. But your head is not supported (as in a recliner or lying down).
3. Legs not crossed.
4. Hands and arms not folded, not even touching each other.
5. No holding a gun. (Hey, we're not into that kind of protection.)
6. No chewing gum or cigarettes.
7. No pets in the room.
8. Have you been holding hands with your sweetheart? Let go until you have finished the exercise.

Am I strict or what? The goal is for you to have the clearest possible inner experience.

Q. Does it really matter if I write something down?

A. Yes. Most of our techniques will require something like that, at least while you're doing the part called "Explore the Results." Consider them physical supplies for getting the most from your spiritual cleaning supplies:

- Keep pen and paper handy for jotting down whatever you notice.
- Substitute a keyboard, if you prefer.
- Or use an electronic device for recording your voice.
- Use something! Don't shortcut your own experience by skipping this vital step. Record those inner experiences.

Q. Why must I close my eyes? I like the color. I bought that color on purpose; otherwise I needed no contact lenses. Whenever possible, I want the world to see those baby turquoises.

A. Your world of admirers will be so much more welcoming when you have skills for Spiritual Cleansing and Protection.

Let me tell you why it's so important to close your eyes in conjunction with using all five of your cleaning supplies.

What happens, thanks to closed eyelids? (Your eyelids also look very cute, incidentally.)

Automatically you remove about 85% of the stimulation to your brain from the external environment. This makes it easier to notice your inner experience.

Even people who are blind know what it means to toggle between "Close your eyes" and "Open your eyes."

Q. In that last exercise, what was I supposed to notice about myself?

A. Forget about "supposed to." All that matters is what spontaneously happened.

You might have noticed something physical or mental, thoughts or emotions, energy or colors. You might have felt the rhythm of your heartbeat.

Q. What if I noticed something outside me, like a smell of popcorn down the hall?

A. No tragedy there. Except this kind of noticing isn't about you directly. So go back and repeat "Breath for Cleansing." No need to concentrate hard, remember? Just simply be interested in yourself.

Sooner or later, you will notice something. About yourself. Not the hall or the popcorn. Such a treasure, in its quiet way... something that happened within your dear, personal, unique self, here and now.

Find words about that. Write it down.

Then consider yourself the proud owner of a brand new resource, Vibe-Raising Breaths.

5. Physical Self-Awareness Made Gentle

Pain is not the only reason to pay attention to your body. Orgasms are nice, but ditto.

All day, every day, your physical body sustains you. It's no more than good manners, really, to praise your body at random moments throughout the day. My friend, medical intuitive Judy Lavine, got me started saying, "Dear precious body, thank you for all you do for me."

That tiny technique alone began to upgrade my use of Cleaning Supply #3, Physical Self-Awareness. Try it.

The practical definition of Cleaning Supply #3 is simple: Choosing to pay attention at will, in an appreciative way, to your physical body.

Like all cleaning supplies used for Spiritual Cleansing and Protection, Physical Self-Awareness helps you to notice more clearly what happens energetically in yourself and your environment.

Appreciating and enjoying your body, just as it is right now? Are you used to doing that?

Do you stretch first thing each morning? Some people greet that body as though it mattered at least as much as a sunrise. Others start the grumbling almost immediately, as if greeting a much despised spouse. "Oh, it's you in the bed again? Too bad."

Marriage counseling and full body rehab are a bit outside the scope of this book. However, I can definitely help you to use Cleaning Supply #3 for Spiritual Cleansing and Protection, Physical Self-Awareness. The technique on our next page can help.

BODY MEET-UP

Read through these instructions first. Then do them, taking a peek as needed.

For a fancy version of this technique, record the following steps, allowing appropriate time between them. Then play back the sound recording and follow your own instructions.

No peeking ahead, Resourceful Healer. It's fine if you do a browse-through. Only stop at this point, please, and skip ahead to the next chapter.

When you're doing the slower kind of read, do the technique that follows. Afterwards check out our Q&As for fine-tuning.

1. Sit comfortably. Close your eyes.

2. Stretch your whole body, still keeping eyes closed. Afterwards resume your comfy position.

3. Stretch in a completely different direction, still keeping eyes closed. Resume your comfy position.

4. Stretch in a third different direction, still keeping eyes closed. Then back to comfy again.

5. Take three Vibe-Raising Breaths and return to normal breathing.

6. Pay attention to your physical body. What do you notice? Open your eyes long enough to write something down. Close your eyes again.

7. Send your body some feelings of gratitude. Then think, "This technique is complete now." And open your eyes.

What happened?

That wacky "Body Meet-Up"! So much could have happened to you just now. Let's bring on the questions.

Q. **You expected me to use the term "gentle" in connection with my body? Are you kidding? It felt like a zoo in there.**

A. Yes, sometimes there will be a whole lot to notice. Other times, the various parts of your body will feel peaceful, tranquil, etc. There's no predicting, really.

Gentleness has to do with the way you already used your Consciousness (Cleaning Supply #1) plus Breathing (Cleaning Supply #2). Gentleness will also be important for how you use the rest of your cleaning supplies, including Physical Self-Awareness (Cleaning Supply #3).

Doing our "Body Meet-Up" technique, did you notice your physical self in an easy, sloppy way? That's all I mean by "gentle."

What if you acted more like a member of the Spanish Inquisition, over-zealous or pushy or downright torturing? Go back and do the technique again. Only this time, please, be nice.

Q. **What if I couldn't feel anything at all about my body?**

A. Oh, do I ever understand that one. You could be describing me for the first 45 years of my life. Before I share what to do about it, are you ready for a laugh?

In 1990, my husband took me to an art gallery opening. I got all dressed up. We drove quite a distance to get there. Immediately I went to The Ladies to freshen up. While washing my hands at the sink, I noticed something unusual. A coat hanger dangling inside my fancy outfit — it was "dangling" upwards, in back of my neck.

You see, while getting dressed for our big night out on the town, I pulled my so-fancy dress from the closet. But I never removed that coat hanger. Not even when I put my coat on top of the dress. For the entire past hour, a coat hanger had been poking me in the neck.

Think I might have found that annoying? Sadly, no.

Unless I had seen that black curve of wire in the bathroom mirror, nudging my neck, I might not have noticed a thing all night. Such was the extreme state of my physical un-awareness at this time.

And yet hope springs eternal — for me, back in the day and possibly for you now, if you have similar stories.

Not noticing your own personal physical body can be mostly a habit. Another cause (as it was for me then) can be **STUFF**. That means stored-up emotional or spiritual garbage at the level of auras.

Depending on which STUFF is stuck, it can seem hard, or even scary, to notice your body.

In that case, for long-term improvement of body awareness, it's smart to find someone with professional skills for healing STUFF within your aura. You might need only a couple of sessions to heal lifelong blockage. However many sessions it takes, your entire quality of life will improve enormously with each chunk of STUFF removal. Plus, it will become effortless to use your natural Physical Self-Awareness.

Back in the day, I paid for a lot of help to heal old STUFF. How many sessions? I'll just say "Plenty." What matters now is that I have learned to feel comfortable in my own skin, to experience that I even *have* skin, to distinguish my skin from a wire coat hanger, and other proud achievements.

Before you schedule that first healing appointment, however, keep reading. Because you may have a very different reason for finding it tricky at first, using Physical Self-Awareness:

Q. **What if nobody ever taught me how to pay attention to my body?**

A. Annoying but true, that has been the case for many of us. Sure, growing up we received specialized lessons that included the physical body, like:

- How to eat with knife, fork, and spoon.
- Potty training.
- Tennis.
- How to dress cute.
- Sex.

Otherwise, we were taught zilch. Some people don't need training this way, but many of us do. Lack of training can be the only "big reason" why we have habitually felt disconnected from our physical selves.

So where to get that training? Right here. "Body Awareness Made Simple" is adapted from the physically astute work of Suzanne Scurlock-Durana, author of *Full Body Presence*. That book makes a fabulous follow-up, should you like the results from our next technique.

BODY AWARENESS MADE SIMPLE

Move into a comfortable seated position. Check that each foot makes contact with the floor. If needed, prop up each foot with something nice and firm, like copies of my other books.

Read through these instructions first. Then do them, taking peeks as needed.

For a fancy version of this technique, record the following steps, allowing appropriate time between them. Then play back the sound recording and follow your own instructions.

No peeking ahead, Resourceful Healer. It's fine if you do a browse-through. Only stop at this point, please, and skip ahead to the next chapter. When you're doing the slower kind of read, explore the technique that follows.

1. Adopt a playful attitude. The place where you are doing this technique is not the City Morgue, right? So long as a body is alive, fun is possible. Besides, you are doing a technique, not a lab test.

2. Close your eyes.

3. Take three Vibe-Raising Breaths and then return to normal breathing.

4. Notice how your feet make contact with the floor. Wiggle your toes, then let them rest. Do your feet feel heavy or light, big or small? How far away do those feet feel, anyway? Are they tingly, numb, or what? Write something down.

5. Move awareness up your right leg all the way to the hip. Then do the same with your left leg. Note any spots with a different texture or temperature.

(Please do not take the grim attitude of a medical diagnostician. And don't bother to interpret whatever you notice — which would be way too complicated for such an easy technique. Simply notice). Also, yes, write something down.

6. Start moving up your torso, noticing whatever interests you. Are there areas that seem extra big or small, strong or weak? How does the right side compare to the left side? How does the back

compare to the front? Whatever you notice, let your motto be, "How interesting!" Then write something down.

7. Arms come next. Wiggle your fingers. Stop and notice whatevers about your arms, hands, and fingers. Perhaps you will become interested in a part that gets a lot of use, like your thumb. Alternatively you might favor a normally overlooked part, like your left armpit. Play around, noticing yourself without judging or fixing. Then, of course, write something down.

8. My personal favorite, in honor of coat hanger wearers everywhere: Check out your head. Does it feel connected to the rest of your body? Notice anything else about your face, your neck? Write something down.

9. Stretch a little. Keeping your eyes closed, move in whatever way would feel good to your body.

10. Thank your body. (Surely you can find at least one nice thing to tell your hardworking body right now.)

11. Open your eyes and read your notes.

Every time you do this exercise, your experiences will be different. After a while, you will make up your own exercises. If you do some such exercise daily for a few minutes, you can upgrade your Physical Self-Awareness for life.

Sweet!

A personal note from the former hanger wearer.

Even a Resourceful Healer can do the silliest thing: Try loads of workshops and techniques to improve life, yet remain oblivious to one's own physical body.

You've seen the classic movie plot. A main character searches the world, only to discover that life's great answers have been there all along, buried in the back yard. Like a corpse, only pleasant.

That grateful seeker isn't just Dorothy in "The Wizard of Oz." It could be you. Hey, you don't even need a back yard or a cinematographer, only your dear, precious body.

Physical Self-Awareness just might become your favorite cleaning supply.

6. What Is an Emotion, Anyway?

Do you ever have emotions? Only always. Only every waking minute. Every waking minute of your life you have at least one human emotion.

Now comes the strange part. Despite being quite self-aware in general, some folks make an exception for their emotions. Especially at risk for doing this are... avid students of spirituality, psychic development, seekers who explore any of life's great mysteries.

Surprised? Sure surprised me, bumping into this discovery. During sessions with my clients, I would often ask, "What emotion(s) do you feel right now?" You might be amazed at the answers, including:

- The energy is stuck.
- I feel tightness.
- My life is wonderful, so I have every reason to be happy.
- I think I am having feelings about trust.
- I see a gorgeous, sparkling waterfall crashing onto big rocks.

How sad it is to hear such answers. Sad, incidentally, is an emotion. Human emotions have names like *happy, sad, scared, angry*.

Some of you Resourceful Healers are already experienced at using Emotional Self-Awareness. This involves paying attention to your feelings in a spontaneous, sloppy manner. You notice emotions like confusion, worry, sorrow, peace.

Doing techniques of Spiritual Cleansing and Protection, emotions that you feel may be quite subtle. They still count.

Cleaning Supply #4, Emotional Self-Awareness, can help you to notice more clearly what happens energetically in yourself and your environment.

Some of you Resourceful Healers won't need any encouragement to explore this. Emotional Self-Awareness will be your favorite and easiest-to-use among all five cleaning supplies. It's even possible that your life seems to be all emotions, all the time.

Meanwhile, some of you Resourceful Healers will feel just the opposite. The main emotion you notice is worrying whether you have any emotions at all. While many of you healers are right in the middle.

Regardless, I'm going to help you to use Emotional Self-Awareness effectively as Cleaning Supply #4 for Spiritual Cleansing and Protection. Let's play with the technique below.

COLOR-TRIGGERED EMOTIONS

Read through these instructions first. Then do them, taking a peek as needed.

For a fancy version of this technique, record the following steps, allowing appropriate time between them. Then play back the sound recording and follow your own instructions.

No peeking ahead, Resourceful Healer. It's fine if you prefer to do a browse-through. Only stop at this point, please, and skip ahead to the next chapter.

What, you're going to actually *do* the technique that follows? Excellent.

Do the following steps in a well-lit room. Proceed spontaneously, with zero expectations, free to be exactly who you are right now.

1. Sit comfortably with your hands in your lap. Close your eyes. Take three Vibe-Raising Breaths; then return to normal breathing.

2. Open your eyes. Look around and choose one color that catches your eye right now. It might be furniture, part of a painting, a desk object, etc.

Say out loud that you see that color on that object, e.g., "I see that blue part of my painting." (Don't worry about making an elegant sentence or giving a precise name for the exact shade, unless that readily comes to mind. It's fine to use a simple handle-type color name like *blue, brown, green,* etc..)

3. Close your eyes. Take one Vibe-Raising Breath and return to normal breathing.

How does the color that you have just seen make you feel?

Name the emotion(s) out loud, e.g., "That blue color makes me feel restless and annoyed."

Emotions have names like *restless, annoyed, happy, sad, scared, angry*. (If a feeling isn't obvious, make up a name to match that color. Do this in a quick, sloppy manner.)

4. Repeat Steps 2 and 3, only choose a different color this second time.

5. Repeat Steps 2 and 3, only choose a different color this third time.

6. Open your eyes. Look at your hands. Immediately close your eyes. Take three Vibe-Raising Breaths; then return to normal breathing.

Find the name for one or more feelings about yourself, here and now. Say the name(s) out loud, e.g. "Disgusted with myself. Weirdly hopeful."

7. Well done, Resourceful Healer. You have just completed one more useful exploration. Open your eyes.

What happened?

Those "Color-Triggered Emotions" can be quite surprising. So let's do some Q&A.

Q. Big deal. I named some emotions in Steps 3, 4, and 5. How is that going to help me get rid of ghosts?

A. Wait and see. For now, congratulations!

Q. What if my emotions felt vague, not colorful at all?

A. Name that vague thing. Be approximate.

Q. But I hate lying. I must be certain of things. Otherwise I'm being inauthentic, right?

A. Hardly. You're being "sloppy," which is exactly the right approach to take with all our techniques and exercises for Spiritual Cleansing and Protection (this one included).

Deeper perception within yourself is needed to use all five of our cleaning supplies. *Deeper, subtle, more abstract* — all these names apply.

Or you could call this direction for inquiry "Moving into a Non-Drama Zone." It's the opposite of *"Obvious. Surface. Hit me over the head with a large salami."*

Get used to this inner direction, rather than blaming yourself or insulting yourself with terms like "vague" or "inauthentic."

Q. **I noticed my usual lack of confidence. So what else is new?**

A. Ouchers, listen to what you just said! Could be, your usual habit is being an Emotional Theorizer rather than Someone Who Actually Uses Emotional Self-Awareness.

Sometimes folks take their emotions oh-so-reverently, as if observing statues at Mt. Rushmore. Such as saying "my usual" x, y, or z. (You know, like what you just did.)

Emotional Self-Awareness is more like noticing the weather in Hawaii, where the skies are ever changing, with a high possibility of rainbows, not only rain.

Determined to be psychologically honest, many a truth seeker makes up a compelling narrative to tie together my Emotion #1, my Emotions #2-5, plus Painful Events That Ruined My Childhood. Perhaps the whole collection has been titled "A Life Doomed to Misery."

Have you been doing that, Mr. Usual Lack of Confidence? Then cut it out, at least while using techniques of Spiritual Cleansing and Protection. Because grand emotional themes need not be mistaken for the spontaneous experience of your cute little emotions in the here and now.

Stories about emotions; psychological theories; your biggest generalizations or even teensy ones, will not be useful for the skill set of Spiritual Cleansing and Protection. Go splash some water over your face, sit down again, and revisit our earlier technique.

Q. **I didn't notice any emotion at all. So what?**

A. You're human, I notice. So you do have emotions. Therefore, the problem here involves learning how to notice your emotions.

Any time I ask you to name whatever emotion(s) you have here and now, guess what? There are two valid ways of receiving that data:

- You might have *an emotional experience*, a direct feeling like happy, sad, scared, angry. That counts.
- Or you might simply *receive information*. You might hear or see or just plain know the name of an emotion. This need not be a mushy gushy kind of experience. Not at all. You're simply receiving information. Well, that still counts.

Go back and repeat our technique for "Color-Triggered Emotions." Many people who receive information in the non-mushy-gushy-way are apt to discount it... until they have a sweet little Aha! It whispers, from deep inside, something like this:

"Biff. Calm down. You're doing better than you thought. Also, what you just experienced *does* count."

Q. Sorry, but you still haven't convinced me that I need to notice emotions. They're messy, if not disgusting. Why bother?

A. Unless you're prepared to be in touch with your human emotions, you're at risk for way too much drama in life. Why? You will miss life's subtler signals about problems until they reach the point of calamity.

Avoiding emotions also limits relationships. Think about your love life so far. Doesn't intimacy hinge on making contact with your own emotions? Perceptiveness about yourself is the basis for reading other people's emotions accurately.

Resourceful Healer, Emotional Self-Awareness is really useful for Spiritual Cleansing and Protection. Although not absolutely required, it is your Cleaning Supply #4. All your other supplies can help you, so this one isn't absolutely necessary; however, it's best to use the full set.

Q. Isn't it possible that I am just too evolved to have emotions any more?

A. Many idealists who meditate or practice psychic development have difficulty locating their own human emotions.

Either they notice nothing else or else they have purposely been ignoring their boring old human feelings, waiting to develop supposedly more high-class or psychically flashy emotions like perpetual equanimity.

Unfortunately, this mistaken ideal will keep those seekers stuck for a very long time. Paying attention at the human level is a pre-requisite for noticing angels and the like, then integrating the knowledge in a way that makes human life better.

Hence these final pointers for Emotional Self-Awareness. If you didn't get much from the technique for "Color-Triggered Emotions," I'm going to ask you to go back and experiment all over again. Only this time note the following points:

If you notice something about your energy, such as "stuck," you are paying attention to your *energy*, doing a kind of aura reading. You are not, however, in touch with your emotions.

If you feel sensations like "tightness," in your heart or elsewhere, you are paying attention to your *physical body*. Obviously, I must congratulate you! As you know, I'm a big fan of using Physical Self-Awareness for Spiritual Cleansing and Protection.

However, sensations in your physical body do not count as "emotions," so even extreme "tightness" does not qualify as an emotion.

Beliefs about life can be tremendously uplifting. Who but a grumpus would complain about "My life is wonderful, and I have every reason to be happy"?

Well, I would. Because emotions in the here-and-now are different from *wishes*. When invited to notice what you feel emotionally, that's a separate exercise from hammering yourself with a bunch of shoulds.

How about "I *think* I am having feelings about trust (or anything else)"? All I can say is, "Nice try." Take a deep breath. Return to Closed Eye Land and find out what really is happening there right now.

Should your quest for emotion bring up an *image* of any kind, wet or dry, smooth or slimy, that image symbolizes a feeling. Excellent! You're close, very close. Just ask inside how that image makes you feel emotionally. This answer will count as Emotional Self-Awareness.

Resourceful Healer, enjoy your Cleaning Supply #4 for Spiritual Cleansing and Protection. Or have horror or excitement or whatever else you authentically have.

I won't command you to do this, however. Because, as you'll see in our next chapter, only one person can use Your Power of Command to make your life better.

7. Awaken Your Power of Command

"I didn't know you had a voice," my Aunt Carol said. Her reaction to my taking voice lessons was understandable. Back in the day, before Autotune and American Idol, people actually used the term "Having a voice."

Supposedly some people were born with a lifelong, big, brawny way to sing, perhaps like having a bugle implant lodged between your jaws. Otherwise you had zilch. That's how many people understood vocal talent back in the day.

Today, what would happen if you asked a voice teacher, "Do I have a voice?" You would probably hear "Yes."

Any singer would benefit from learning skills for singing. Unless you take a few voice lessons, it's unlikely that you will even know the full range of your voice.

Cecilia Bartoli is a world renowned opera singer. Many glorious CDs ago, the stunning contralto didn't believe she even had "a voice." No, she aimed to become a Flamenco dancer. Good thing that Cecilia's mother was a voice teacher!

Don't worry. I'm not going to insist that you start singing, "Batti, Batti, O Bel Masetto" or even "The Hills Are Alive With The Sound Of Music." Singing was just an analogy. I want you to understand that you were born with a Power of Command that could fill an opera hall like La Scala. Or, at least, you could use that Power of Command to energetically clean the place up.

Your natural Cleaning Supply #5 is, arguably, your greatest asset of all for Spiritual Cleansing and Protection. Having a Power of Command means that you can heal through your voice. Specifically, you can ask for the type of healing you want. Assuming that you've also got skills, you will get results every time.

I'm assuming that you will ask within reason, of course. Don't bring Your Power of Command to the nearest bank and demand to "heal your finances" by scooping up all the cash in the place. (Not unless you carry a gun.) (Actually, not under any conditions.)

Your Power of Command is best used for skills of Spiritual Cleansing and Protection. As you follow the steps for each skill provided, Your Power of Command will activate. Consequently you can heal astral-level debris without breaking a sweat.

Activate Your Power of Command

In which situations, exactly, will Your Power of Command bring results? All five of the following conditions must be met.

Your words are *aimed* precisely where a problem is.

Often a newbie at healing will try to "fix everything." And guess what? Maybe there will be a wee bit of improvement as a result. With a newbie's standards, even a tiny result could seem perfectly satisfactory.

You, however, are not a newbie... or at least you won't be by the time you have completed the training offered here.

Besides, when reading these words you might think, "Hey, I placed out of the newbie leagues years ago. I'm already pretty darned sophisticated." Perhaps you're a professional healer or psychic. You could be adding this skill set to supplement an already awesome expertise.

Either way, you are in the process of developing a powerful new skill set. Spiritual Cleansing and Protection requires that you learn more than one technique for healing. Plus you will need to discern the need for one type of healing over another, depending on circumstances.

You know *what* to request.

Healing with Energy Spirituality takes more than faith. It takes skill. (Faith is optional, actually.) You really do need to know what to ask for.

"Help!" Now that's a good thing to shout loudly at a busy street corner when someone is trying to steal your wallet.

For a healer, screaming "Help" doesn't quite do the job. Not in a sophisticated way.

Learning what to request with Your Power of Command will make it work much more efficiently than a sincere, trusting, ultra-loud scream to the entire Universe.

You understand *intellectually* what you are requesting.

A full knowledge base, in the form of "Nuts and Bolts," will be offered with each new healing technique. Why bother?

In certain life situations, parroting words that are not understood may sometimes work just fine. Not so for Spiritual Cleansing and Protection.

Unless you own the concepts behind the words in a healing technique, you won't achieve full results. Not for Spiritual Cleansing and Protection, anyway. Parrots do not possess Your Power of Command.

You are in the *presence* of the Divine, actively engaged.

That part doesn't need to be difficult, not for this skill set. You'll see.

You have earned the *standing* to make your request.

Using Your Power of Command is a privilege. Learning any of the techniques in this skill set is, likewise, a privilege.

Activate, Don't Sabotage

Here come three examples of behavior that might seem okay in today's information overload culture. Yet they would compromise effectiveness for Your Power of Command when doing any of the healings in our skill set.

1. Instead of reading through each chapter, learning step-by-step, Rudy skips to the summary at the end. "To save time" perhaps?
2. Rhonda decides it would be way more interesting to get high on weed before doing our techniques because, supposedly, "Things go better with pot."
3. Roy thinks he is far too advanced to simply do any technique as offered. It's as though he's perpetually making a mashup CD.

    So Roy skips steps that seem dull, adds a touch of Reiki in the middle of one healing; next time he sprinkles in a bit of

Emotional Freedom Technique. Also, Roy considers it a plus to constantly ask his spirit guide to supply readings as a kind of running commentary.

I think I speak for all teachers of spiritual development everywhere when I say this: *"Worship is not required. But if you want to study with us, simple respect will make all the difference in the world."*

What constitutes "respect" (as defined by this teacher, anyway)?

- Learn a teaching thoroughly before you start playing around with it.
- Get official credentials from your instructor before you presume to teach others.

The day you disrespect your teacher is the day you compromise your spiritual standing to use a technique. When ethics are neglected, one of the very first things to go is your sacred Power of Command.

What if mistakes were made in the past? Maybe nobody had ever explained ideas like this to you. No repining. Now can be a new start.

Your Power of Command is a renewable resource. As you evolve spiritually, and act accordingly, that sacred power will develop along with the rest of you.

All this is a lot to consider, I know. Let's bring on some Q&A.

Q. **How do you know where to aim Your Power of Command?**

A. Learning skills of Spiritual Cleansing and Protection, we will go through one healing situation after another. (That's why we have Parts Two and Three of this program.)

Reading in detail about each type of healing, you will learn where to direct Your Power of Command. Certain words of truth will dislodge certain kinds of STUFF, bringing results automatically.

Q. **What if I get scared because I'm dealing with a horrible ghost or something? Couldn't I forget what to say due to panic?**

A. Education about ghosts and other astral-level debris really does make a difference. Even the bravest people can feel scared when they misunderstand the nature of an astral-level problem. Or what to do about it.

Hang with me, one healing skill at a time, and awaken that knowledge. Then your voice won't shake, nor will the rest of you.

Q. Glad you agree with me that it's important to know what to ask. I happen to be very, very picky about ideas. Why do I generate so many questions? Let me tell you.

With all due modesty, I'm exceptionally intelligent. Ironically, perhaps, I don't feel as though I have any Power of Command whatsoever. In fact, once I start asking my very smart questions, most people generally wander away.

Do you think that maybe I'll only be able to develop a Power of Command when talking with other people who are geniuses like me? Any thoughts?

A. Allow me to introduce you to relevant ways to request one healing at a time. Stick to that and Your Power of Command will work fine.

You know, there is such a thing as asking questions about what really matters to you. Then there is something separate. Which could be called "Showing off."

Here you are encouraged to do the former, not the latter. Manage that and Your Power of Command will work just fine.

Q. Knowing what to ask for sounds hard to me. What if I'm indecisive?

A. Can you wash your hands in a sink? Flush a toilet? That's how complicated your decisions will be for skills of Spiritual Cleansing and Protection.

Soon I'll take you through one particular skill at a time, explaining which simple technique to use. Then you can use it. No worries.

Q. Like these last two guys, I don't feel as though I have much Power of Command at all. Must I believe in myself?

A. As a Resourceful Healer, you might be ambivalent and sorta believe in yourself. Alternatively, you might not believe in yourself at all. Or you might believe in yourself fully, unless proven wrong.

Regardless, you can learn to use Your Power of Command.

Use as much Power of Command as you have available, neither more nor less. Combined with the rest of the skill set for Spiritual Cleansing and Protection, I think you're going to produce very real results.

This can build your confidence further about Your Power of Command and other aspects of your life as well. Imagine, one success building on another! This could be like constructing a new Wal-Mart as your own personal profit center!

Q. It's no minor point to me, your saying, "When you are in the presence of the Divine, actively engaged." Will I ever really be able to move there on purpose? Me? Into the presence of the Divine?

A. You already are There. To refine your experience of That, turn to our next chapter.

Q. What on earth must I do to develop what you call "The standing" to use my Power of Command? How good a person must I be?

A. Perfect in every way? No, that won't be needed. But yes, there is one definite requirement for using Your Power of Command effectively.

Become a Habitual Truth Teller

Ever hear the expression "Habitual liar"? Allow me to introduce you to an opposite term: Becoming a "Habitual truth teller."

There are really two types of people in the world, those who habitually tell the truth and those who don't.

Decide which you want to be and live that way. It's your choice. That simple.

Admittedly, some circumstances can force a person to lie, like a boss who mouths the words, "Tell her I'm out of the office."

The occasional prevarication will not turn you into a liar. But if your boss habitually asks you to lie, you might want to find a new boss and new job.

Offhand, I can't think of any honorable line of work that routinely requires fibbing. Lying is bad for the aura and stifling to the soul.

Bet you knew the part about the soul. How about "bad for the aura"?

I happen to be in a line of work where I teach **energetic literacy**. That means using deeper perception to examine reality in the here-and-now.

Over the years, I have developed three different lie detector tests. Each test involves reading **chakra databanks**, different parts of an aura which have specialties. Each major chakra contains 50 of these energy tubes, each with a different specialty.

For lie detection, an aura reader chooses chakra databanks related
to honesty.

- Verbal Integrity shows as a Throat Chakra Databank.
- Power Integrity is viewable as the Solar Plexus Chakra
  Databank.
- Spiritual Integrity is a databank that anybody with full
  energetic literacy can read at a person's Third Eye Chakra.

Based on reading thousands of auras, what have I learned about integrity? One little lie will not show, not in any of these three places.

Patterns of lying are different. They become obvious aurically,
whether lying through words (verbal integrity) or actions (power integrity) or lying as a motivating principle in life (spiritual integrity).

All patterns of lying can change. Until then, problems will be
evident to any aura reader who pays attention. Which eventually could
mean all people on earth.

In this third millennium, I believe, energetic literacy is going to
become nearly universal, just like Gutenberg literacy in the second millennium. If you can read this page, using the Gutenberg type of literacy
(reading printed words), you are fully capable of learning how to read
auras in depth and detail, and do this whenever you like.

Meanwhile, everybody reads auras to some degree, even if only
subconsciously.

This happens througha process I call **auric modeling**. This
means that, way down at the part of the aura corresponding to what
psychologists call the subconscious mind... your aura is busy reading
everyone else's aura.

Yes, you're busily gathering that data whenever you're in the room
with somebody else. Aurically each person's presence rings loud and
clear. Every nuance of talent, mixed messages, and amount of STUFF —
all that data registers subconsciously.

Yet one more reason to become a habitual truth teller!

Who notices whether you speak the truth?

Your current degree of authenticity sticks out all over your aura.
Clairaudient people can hear it right in your voice. Clairvoyant people
can see it. Same goes for every one of your innate gifts for energetic
literacy. (Most people have many such gifts. And everybody has at least
one valuable gift for developing full energetic literacy.)

Therefore, it will definitely show subconsciously to everyone if you are a habitual truth teller. Santa Claus knows, too. (Or he would if he were real.)

Does God listen to every word that you utter? Maybe not. But whenever you ask God to help with a healing for Spiritual Cleansing and Protection, guess what? Your standing to make such requests will become very relevant.

Imagine yourself in the *lively* presence of God (something which you're going to learn how to do at will several chapters from now — admittedly something that you will be doing in a non-flashy manner).

Hello! What shows? Auric modeling reveals your habitual level of veracity. Truthfulness or its lack are revealed quite plainly, no way to disguise it.

So what will happen with you when you stand before God, using your best skills of Spiritual Cleansing and Protection? Will your circuits shriek "Liar! Liar! Aura's on fire!"?

Not if you're a habitual truth teller.

Hey, if you aren't one yet, I have great news for you. Changing isn't necessarily difficult. Whatever happened in the past, that was a lesser stage of development. You can definitely become a habitual truth teller, starting now. All you need do is use your words to tell the truth. (If that's what you already do, acknowledge yourself for having one very useful habit.)

Truth telling status need not be absolutely perfect before you start using Your Power of Command:

Elaborate legalese isn't needed to equivocate, situationally define context, or otherwise provide, via long escape clauses, whether or not, to whatever degree, and despite any mitigating circumstances, mendacities have issued, directly or indirectly, from the facial area colloquially known as "Your big fat mouth."

Nope, you can be pretty sloppy. Just tell the truth. Do your reasonable best as a human being.

That's plenty. Automatically you will become the kind of person who can be called a "habitual truth teller."

Truthfulness can make a person's life simpler, beyond adding that yummy deliciousness of honesty. Simplicity comes because you don't need to over-analyze, hide, or prevaricate. Neither must you repent in retrospect, or flail yourself until you bleed, or pay some kind of cosmic Fibbing Forgiveness Fee.

Simply tell a reasonable amount of truth in every situation. Who decides which part of the truth to tell, how much detail to divulge? You. Probably you already are doing this. Such an easy, comfortable way of life! Habitual truth telling doesn't even have to get you into trouble.

"Tell me, Joe. Do I look fat in this outfit?"

"Gladys, that's a ridiculous question. I'm not going to answer."

Score yourself a truth point, Joe. That greasy, slippery old fibbing dynamic can disappear from your aura forever.

Why else truthfulness matters.

So far, we've established that Your Power of Command only works properly when you have integrity as a person. Consider that one more motivation to live and speak with honesty. Then guess. Who else notices?

Who notices, that is, besides you and God and Santa Claus sort-of and definitely every human being you ever meet? Who else in this crazy complicated world can find out whether or not you have the auric modeling of a habitual truth teller?

Ghosts know. They know instantly. That's because every astral being reads auras like crazy.

Did you ever think about the inner language of perception for an astral being? All of them speak "Aura" fluently.

Never does a ghost speak "Human" particularly well. Whereas we humans naturally speak a perception-based language, being all wired up with physical senses, five at least for most of us.

Long as the physical body works, each of us can speak "Human" just great. After death, however, the ability to speak "Human" drops away, along with the physical body.

So picture yourself, in that well-working body of yours, speaking "Human" just great. You're starting to use Your Power of Command to heal ghosts. How will they respond?

Sure, you have the right to move any ghost out of your own auric field or your bedroom or your pendulum or your favorite tree house. Except if you're a habitual liar, forget it. When auric modeling reveals patterns of lying, any self-respecting ghost can tell.

Why trust a liar to heal you? No matter how solid your technique, your natural Power of Command would be compromised if the equivalent of nose boogers were hanging down from your throat chakra.

Therefore Cleaning Supply #5, Your Power of Command, is not considered optional for this skill set. To succeed with it you will need to be — or become — a habitual truth teller.

EXPERIMENT WITH TRUTH SPEAK

Read through the following instructions first. Then do them, taking a peek as needed.

For a fancy version of this technique, record the following steps, allowing appropriate time between them. Then play back the sound recording and follow your own instructions.

No peeking ahead at the steps of this technique, please, if you're browsing. It's fine if you do a browse-through. Only stop at this point, and skip ahead to the next chapter.

When you *are* pursuing the slower kind of read, only then do the steps that follow.

1. Sit comfortably. Close your eyes.
2. Take three Vibe-Raising Breaths and then return to normal breathing.
3. Notice something about your emotions. Then notice something about how your body feels to you. Write something down.
4. Use Your Power of Command to say out loud, three times, "My name is Spiderman."
5. Repeat Step 3.
6. Say your real name out loud, three times, e.g., "My name is Rose Rosetree."
7. Repeat Step 3.
8. Open your eyes.

Speaking the truth strengthens the whole mind-body-spirit system. No wonder it also will strengthen Your Power of Command.

8. Resourceful Healing

Five cheers for you, Resourceful Healer! That would be one cheer each for:

- Cleaning Supply #1: Consciousness
- Cleaning Supply #2: Breathing
- Cleaning Supply #3: Physical Self-Awareness
- Cleaning Supply #4: Emotional Self-Awareness
- Cleaning Supply #5: Your Power of Command

Not only are these cleaning supplies indispensable for Spiritual Cleansing and Protection. Using these supplies on a regular basis, as part of a balanced life, will help you to live your full potential.

Once I led a workshop where students were introduced to their cleaning supplies. After a depth exercise, we did the kind of Q&A in this book. Janice raised her hand.

"Something strange is happening to my body. It feels weird and heavy. What's wrong?"

Discussion turned up another complaint about Janice's body: *"For no good reason, there are all these feelings in it."*

Further discussion followed. It became clear that Janice had just "moved into" her physical body for the first time in living memory. Sure, Janice had done mind-body-spirit techniques for years. Based on what? A chronic out-of-body experience.

After her introduction to basic Physical Self-Awareness, Janice spontaneously healed a physical problem that had bothered her for years. Let's do our own depth exercise with all Five Cleaning Supplies right now!

COMBINE ALL FIVE CLEANING TOOLS

Keep pen and paper handy for jotting down notes, or use your favorite electronic recording device. Read through these instructions first. Then do them, taking a peek as needed.

For a fancy version of this technique, record the following steps, allowing appropriate time between them. Then play back the sound recording and follow your own instructions.

No peeking ahead, Resourceful Healer. It's fine if you do a browse-through up to here. Only stop at this point, please, and skip ahead to the next chapter. Otherwise, here goes!

1. Sit comfortably. Close your eyes. (Your Cleaning Supply #1, Consciousness, switches on automatically.)
2. Take three Vibe-Raising Breaths and then return to normal breathing. (Using Breathing, your Cleaning Supply #2, is easy now, right?)
3. Notice how it feels to be you. This could be anything. Write something down.
4. Take three more Vibe-Raising Breaths and return to normal breathing. Pay attention to your *physical body*. What do you notice? Write something down. (Yes, that's using Cleaning Supply #3, Physical Self-Awareness)
5. Take three more Vibe-Raising Breaths and return to normal breathing. Pay attention to your *emotions*. What do you notice? Write something down. (Hooray, you have just used Cleaning Supply #4, Emotional Self-Awareness.)
6. Use Your Power of Command to say your name three times out loud. You have just realigned your sense of self. (Also you have just used Cleaning Supply #5, Your Power of Command.)
7. Repeat Steps #4 and #5.
8. Inside, say some words of closure, like "Well done!" or "Great, courageous job, Resourceful Healer!"
9. Open your eyes and look over the notes you wrote down. What changed? Notice.

Using your Cleaning Supplies in this sequence is a fine preparation for all the mighty skills to come.

9. Your
Date with the Divine

Well, Resourceful Healer, now that you're using all Five Cleaning Supplies, let's consider the rest of your healing team. Spiritual Cleansing and Protection is easy to do, provided that you team up with appropriate help.

Why date the Divine? Asking God to team up with you is especially helpful because:

- God is always available. Maybe you have heard the rumors about God being omnipresent, omniscient, all loving, etc. Well, those rumors are true.
- God has both personal and impersonal forms, so you're sure to find a form of God that suits you best for each type of cleaning job. (More on this later.)
- God will gladly help you for free.
- If the name "God" makes you feel weird, you can call it a different name. Including "It."
- Getting help from "God" or "It" is easier than you may think.

Before we go into the specifics of summoning that help, let's answer the question "Why bother God?"

Maybe your first reaction is to ask for help from an ancestor you're really fond of, Uncle Snuffy's late mom Muffy, perphaps. Or maybe your very best friend happens to be your guardian angel, Bernadette. You might relate to either of them far more comfortably than to an Almighty Divine Being.

For heaven's sake, maybe you're not a religious sort AT ALL. If you're not a believer, why ask God for help?

Remember, our goal isn't to test religiosity but to efficiently move out astral-level garbage. Three levels of life are available to people like you and me. Success with your skill set for Spiritual Cleansing and Protection depends on where you position yourself within these three levels. So let's consider what is special about each one of them.

Divine-Level Beings

Beings at the **Divine level** have bodies made of etheric energy, very fast moving frequencies. Think of a hummingbird. Think sweet!

You may, of course, add attributes like ultimate wisdom, the biggest love imaginable, and the most humongous creativity in all the known universe.

The impersonal aspect of God has that great paradox of a body so big it could be called "nothing."

The personal aspect of God means your choice of Archangels and Ascended Masters. All of these Divine Beings are available to help you, showing up in their very individual etheric-level bodies.

Teaming up with the personal or impersonal level of God — this is an indispensable requirement for your effectiveness with Spiritual Cleansing and Protection. More on Divine Beings soon.

Psychic-Level Beings

Beings at the **psychic level** have bodies made of astral energy, moving faster and lighter than our human vibe. Think of a robin. Think interesting!

Although astral beings don't move at the very highest frequencies, their vibes still rank higher — and flashier — than is normal for humans.

Astral beings come in many fascinating varieties. More on that later, too.

Human-Level Beings

Yes, that's you and me. **Human level** means earth-frequency energy. Basically, it's variations on the theme of mud. Vibe patterns for humans are slow but don't knock it until you've tried it. Wait, you *are* trying it. Right now.

Energy here moves really slowly (on purpose) since Earth School is designed for spiritual evolution rather than ease or comfort.

Being in human body has loads of benefits, like sex and emotions. Vibrationally we're low and slow, however. Think funky!

Who's Where

Perhaps all this theory about three levels sounds nice in a faraway sort of way. Maybe it seems like a geography lesson about some exotic part of the world, about as practical as collecting feather dusters.

Well, hello! If you want to develop effective skills at Spiritual Cleansing and Protection, you really need to pay close attention to this vital bit of theory. Soon you can make it come alive... in a way that brings powerful healing.

So let's explore all three levels more deeply.

Spiritual-level resources.

For practical purposes, there is only one Divine frequency. It makes the highest sound imaginable. For an analogy, think about the highest note on a piano — gorgeous because that Cosmic Piano is always perfectly in tune.

The Divine frequency is the highest! The holiest! The most compactly, completely perfect in every way!

Who, exactly would be living here?

- **Almighty God.** This version of Spiritual Source is omnipresent, omniscient, omnipotent, omni-loving.
- I've heard there are 10,000 names for God. That's probably an understatement.
- **Divine Beings**, individualized aspects of God, also live at the etheric level as Ascended Masters and Archangels. These are perfected beings, free and clear. Each one has a distinctive vibration.
- **Ascended Masters** have lived on earth but are available now as volunteers to help the likes of you and me.
  An Ascended Master may have founded a major religion or served as an extraordinary spiritual teacher or been immortalized through mythology. Examples are Jesus, Buddha, Isis, Kwan Yin, Athena, Merlin.

- **Archangels** are high-frequency angels, especially willing to be of service to humanity and way powerful. Examples are Archangel Michael, Archangel Raphael, Archangel Gabriel.

Psychic-level resources.

Of all three levels, the psychic frequency contains the biggest range of notes. For perspective, let's return to our piano analogy — useful since a piano has plenty of keys — 88 for a full concert grand. Let's say:

1. The very highest note symbolizes the spiritual level.
2. Moving down the piano keyboard, the next 75 keys correspond to the psychic level. (This is an analogy, of course. I don't mean to suggest that the psychic level literally contains 75 descending black keys and white keys that must be tuned regularly by your neighborhood piano tuner.)
3. That leaves one bottom octave at the human level — which amounts to a pretty big range of vibe, too, doesn't it? Seven white keys, with five black keys thrown in for extra nuance.

Why must the psychic level be so complex in this analogy about all the piano keys? Psychic (a.k.a. astral or celestial) beings support every world in the universe where somebody is evolving. (What, you thought Earth was the only cool spiritual growth academy?)

Astral help galore is needed in order for worlds like ours to function. Behind the scenes, astral beings handle innumerable tiny details, like where to put all those dewdrops each morning and how to make them all stick.

Which astral beings are we earthlings most likely to notice?

- The **Guardian Angel** who helps you each day is alive and well at the psychic level.
- All those gorgeous and helpful beings in your **Personal Angel Committee**, like spirit guides, live here too. These beings stay with you at the choice of your soul, even if you haven't summoned them consciously.
- Vibrationally they come from the highest level of consciousess available to you at the time they signed on to help you.
- **Nature spirits**, like devas and fairies, are mid-level sweeties.
- **Ancestors** can live at any part of the psychic level, whether high or low or in-between. But no matter how wise they may

be, none of these contactable relatives has gained spiritual Enlightenment.

(Why not? An Enlightened ancestor would no longer be hanging around at the astral level but, instead, would have moved up to the Divine level.)

- **Astral entities**, also known as "ghosts" or "stuck spirits," also can attract attention. Are you into contacting wise spirits through channeling? Guess where those entities live? Divine Beings don't take people over for trance channeling. So trance channeling always involves astral beings.

Sure, some of these entities might call themselves "Archangel Gabriel," "Jesus," or "Buddha."

If you lived as an astral being, planning to introduce yourself to a human-level channeler, wouldn't you choose an appealing name? Why go for something like "Osama bin Laden"?

Even at the human level, you can find plenty of people named "Archangel Gabriel," "Jesus," or "Buddha" — especially in mental hospitals. Why wouldn't beings at the psychic level give themselves similar names when seeking to influence, or temporarily take over, a trusting human channeler?

All spirits contacted through channeling live in psychic-level bodies, no matter what they call themselves. Some are remarkably helpful, like Lazaris and Hilarion; others maybe aren't so great.

If you want to evaluate such a spirit, it isn't especially difficult. Develop Stage 3 Energetic Literacy skills, where you can read auras in detail.

Find two photographs, one showing the channeler while being just a regular person; your second picture would show the channeler while being taken over by the entity.

Then research one photograph at a time, one chakra databank at a time.

For an example of this method, you might enjoy the comparison aura readings of Esther Hicks and Esther channeling Abraham in the how-to book *Magnetize Money with Energetic Literacy.*

Some astral realms contain relatively low-vibe angels who are still working out old fascinations with sex, alcohol, drugs, and/or violence.

Also, ta da! The psychic level includes every single form of STUFF that you will learn to release through our skill set of Spiritual Cleansing and Protection.

Human-level resources.

Resourceful Healer, we are not alone. People live among us. As you may have noticed, we earthlings come in various shapes, sizes, smells, and levels of spiritual development.

- Some of us are highly evolved, creative, loving, powerful, and intuitive.
- Others possess about as much yearning for spiritual wisdom as a rusty, bent nail.
- All of us share a common vibration, called "Human."

How very useful it is to be positioned at the human level. Give yourself credit, Resourceful Healer. You've got your five superb cleaning supplies. Plus, everything about your life is a resource for spiritual evolution: Relationships, sex, work, money, community.

Don't try our skills for Spiritual Cleansing and Protection unless you have a human-type body. You'll come to appreciate technical reasons for this as you develop this skill set.

Meanwhile you might want to take a moment to gloat. Human body, all taken care of — how convenient that you don't need to go shopping or settle for the best model you can afford. So glad that consumer aspect has already been handled!

Wait, there's more.

As they say on TV infomercials, "And if you act now, there's more."

To effectively use the skill set of Spiritual Cleansing and Protection, you need to know just a bit more about these three distinct levels of life.

Might you, as a human, already have contact with those other two levels? I mean even when you are not busy doing techniques of Spiritual Cleansing and Protection.

Abso-giddy-lutely! If you were *only* human, why would you even care about the other two levels? That business of Spiritual Cleansing and Protection — why would it even be necessary?

So let's take a more personal view of those three levels of life. How are they part of your everyday life?

Being yourself at the Divine level.

Your **soul** exists at the Divine level. That spiritual core within you is permanent and indestructible, made of etheric substance. It is also quirky, deeply human, astoundingly individual.

Also, your **Higher Self** dwells here. This version of your individual nature has never accepted the illusions of Earth School. Instead, this wise eternal portion of yourself stays mostly in the background. (Master hypnotist Marilyn Gordon calls it your "Wise Mind.")

From birth to death, also in-between lifetimes, your Higher Self serves as a silent witness.

You might imagine it as a giant-sized body surrounding your physical body. Or you might picture it as many of my regression therapy clients report it.

Let's use Gladys as an example. If her regression session includes re-experiencing what happens at death, at one point Gladys notices her that her physical body dies. (Aargh!) But then somehow the person inside of Gladys isn't "dead" at all.

Quickly she recognizes that familiar version of herself. It was there all along, only deep within her human identity. After death, that eternal version of Gladys starts moving upward, flying around in a different kind of body. It is made entirely of spiritual light.

Gladys' light body doesn't suffer from fear or pain or any of the illusions of earth. She learns what was accomplished soul-wise in that latest human lifetime. She sees more clearly than before.

Mostly astral-level now, and no longer human, Gladys' "dead" body contains a Divine portion, too, a glorious dollop of Higher Self. She is complete, just without human-type smelly feet, bags under eyes, etc.

Sure, go ahead and picture your Higher Self that way, if you like. Unless that makes you feel dizzy.

In which case, don't bother. Your Higher Self will stick around regardless. Do you normally have to repeat words like "lung" or "heartbeat" to keep your physical body parts working? Same (effortless) deal with your "Higher Self"! Whether or not you bother to think the name, It will be with you every day of your life... and beyond.

When people read auras, if they do a really good job, they are able to make contact with this Divine-level part of your aura. With full energetic literacy, it is called "Reading chakra databanks."

Since there are 50 per major chakra, plus additional chakra databanks in sub-chakras, you have hundreds. Without your trying one bit! And every one of your chakra databanks contain a **gift of your soul**, indelible as a fingerprint.

Being yourself at the psychic level..

Mostly your aura exists at the psychic level. Auras include multiple layers around your physical body, layers within layers, all made of electro-magnetic energy.

Yes, your auric field is mostly astral... except for that small, quick-silver, very fine part that is etheric (previously discussed).

In the language of psychology, the psychic level equals your **subconscious** mind. Sigmund Freud's genius discoveries, the Ego and Id and Superego, all reside here.

Freud was amazingly effective at helping practically-oriented people to start becoming aware at the psychic level, even if he never called it that.

Carl Jung added the super-important concept of The Collective Unconscious. Another of Jung's discoveries is Archetypes. Both Collective Unconscious and Archetypes support your life at the psychic level, where they live as astral components of your human identity.

Now comes the bad news about the psychic level within a human being. Neuroses are here. Post-traumatic stress can take up lodging, too. Any kind of stored-up emotional or energetic debris can get stuck at the psychic-level within a human body. As you know, my technical term for all this astral-level goop is "STUFF."

What an understatement, to say that astral-level STUFF causes problems in human life!

Fortunately, this STUFF can always, always, always be healed. To remove it, all you need do is bring healing with the appropriate skill set for healing that particular type of STUFF. Skill sets for doing this fall into three categories, named below in no particular order.

For **Energy Spirituality** the point of entry for healing STUFF is your *aura*. Skill sets include:

- Removing cords of attachment.
- Workarounds to minimize STUFF, like Thrill Your Soul Research.
- Aligning your name with what thrills your soul.
- And using skills of Spiritual Cleansing and Protection. (So here is your official context for this shiny new skill set. Aha!)

For **Energy Medicine** the point of entry for healing is your *body*. Healers move out blockage to energy meridians and acupuncture points. Some parts of you in the astral are sedated. Others are stimulated. Improving the health of your body aurically will automatically improve your physical health.

Then, because mind, body, and spirit are interconnected, everything about quality of life can be improved.

For **Energy Psychology** the point of entry for healing is your *mind*. Ever hear of Emotional Freedom Technique? Healers get your fingers a' tapping to change the astral-level patterning.

Many other holistic healing modalities promote change at the subconscious, or psychic, level, doing forms of Energy Psychology.

Hypnotists activate the vast healing resources available deep within the human mind. So do Shamanic healers, experts at EMDR, Pranic Healing, past-life regression therapists, etc.

What do all three mighty modalities have in common? Energy Spirituality, Energy Medicine, and Energy Psychology all aim to heal the aura first. Once that succeeds, human-type benefits follow automatically.

Being yourself at the human level.

Problems at the human level include disease, lack of money, pimples, frustrating relationships. What, you've already heard about this sort of thing?

Often problems at the human level are consequences of astral-level problems. At least, that's what I believe, and you are free to agree or not, especially after you have explored the results of Spiritual Cleansing and Protection. This huge learning planet has room for multiple belief systems and healing methods.

Many psychotherapists aim to fix problems at the human level. So do social workers, life coaches, and expert problem solvers who use plenty of other human-based skill sets.

Often there is some attempt to access the subconscious level or Higher Self. But it's done indirectly, through human memories, writing with your non-dominant hand, dream journaling, etc.

At best, this kind of healing work is slow. How could it not be? Human vibrations are slow. However, many people believe exclusively in human life, so they won't accept any other kind of healing. Consequently it's psychological healing, medical healing, or nothing.

In all fairness, let's note that sometimes a problem can't be resolved without these very human kinds of healing.

Neither psychic-level nor Divine-level methods can succeed in situations that demand exclusively human-level solutions. Twenty years of prayer or E.F.T. will not wash and wax your car, not even once.

Energy Sandwiches.

So isn't it great that you have the ability to develop and use a variety of skill sets? Resourceful Healer, you can develop skills that work at different levels, skills that can help you solve one type of problem at a time. In your tool box, are you allowed to keep both a wrench and a hammer?

Definitely!

Skills of Spiritual Cleansing and Protection will not solve every problem, be it human, celestial, or soulful. However, this particular skill set *will* move out several different types of astral-level debris.

You, the human, can use Your Power of Command to team up with Divine help, moving out problems at the in-between level. I call that making an **"energy sandwich."**

Now you have a working perspective on how you will be healing. Spiritual Cleansing and Protection will not be the only skill set you ever need. So keep making those regular appointments for dental checkups. Meanwhile, you can also experience how your human life glows up, due to moving out astral-level STUFF.

Part Two.
CLEAN UP
EVERYTHING
YOU OWN

10. Get Skills

Resourceful Healer, it's a big deal that you have been awakening (or upgrading) Your Power of Command plus four other great cleaning supplies. Energetically this has won you a certain kind of cosmic street cred.

Soon you will team up with God to do healing at the psychic level. Developing one effective new skill at a time, you can vanquish astral debris quickly and effortlessly. You can remove problems you've heard of (like ghosts) and even more common problems you haven't heard of yet (like psychic coercion).

Perfectly prepared now, you can make an important choice about how to proceed. Two options are available for developing skills at Spiritual Cleansing and Protection. They're equally powerful. So consider your choice to be simply a matter of taste.

Sampling.

For sampling, start with a quick, fast reading. Skip the techniques. Take this first read-through in the light-and-breezy spirit of social networking — like browsing a friend's wall at Facebook. After that fun read, move toward a different phase, "Skills Thoroughly."

Skills Thoroughly.

Read each chapter from start to end. Be sure to include the "Let's Explore" section. Take your time, Resourceful Healer, until you feel truly comfortable with each new type of healing. Then go on to the next chapter. Sure, you can begin immediately with this more advanced version. The choice is yours.

Work Those Skills

Whenever you get around to that Skills Thoroughly approach, the following tips may help:

Explore each technique in the order given. Benefit from my experience with decades of teaching Spiritual Cleansing and Protection. I've developed an orderly learning sequence that builds on success.

And lucky you! Those previous students had to work a whole lot harder than you, travel farther, make a bigger financial commitment, to learn the exact same healings you will be able to pick up right here.

I hope you will read the following pages as if I wrote each word just for you. To bring you a depth experience, I'll use the following sequence to teach you one skill at a time.

What It Is. You wouldn't think much of a dentist who couldn't tell the difference between a front tooth and a molar. Well, you are becoming an expert kind of healer yourself. Some of our technical definitions may be needed so you don't diagnose the woo-woo equivalent of mixed-up teeth.

Nuts and Bolts. For each kind of healing, what is involved technically? Let's delve deeply into the *whys* behind the *what*.

Explore the Results. Each new skill is set up like an experiment. Go for an up-close-and-personal experience of this particular form of healing.

Helpful Uses. Spiritual Cleansing and Protection techniques are extraordinarily useful. Any one of the healings could be a book in itself. Because we're all so busy these days, I will simply summarize the wide range of practical applications.

Resourceful Healer, you can use these ideas to fast-track your way through years of experience that I have had with a wide variety of clients. I worked hard so that you wouldn't have to.

True Tales. Just for fun, I have some cool stories to share with you.

Take This Healing Further. This is my very favorite part, Resourceful Healer. Extra ways to use this skill set give you the equivalent of free cars, higher class hotel rooms, new clout for relationships, and more. They're like free apps for your Cosmic Me-Phone.

Summary Box. For quick reference, each chapter that teaches a healing technique will end with a summary box. Once you have completed that chapter, you "own" that technique for practical purposes. Turn to that summary box and follow those instructions whenever you like. You can heal like a pro.

Very Important, Resourceful Healer

When I ask you to do any technique, whether that be "Let's Explore" or instructions in the Summary Box, please do *only* what is asked. You'll get better results.

Compared to what? Don't volunteer for harder work than is needed.

In the past, some of my students shocked me with well-meant but counter-productive volunteer efforts. I discovered these hardworking students were making techniques way more complicated than necessary. Which didn't help one bit.

So let's be clear. To do any technique from Rose Rosetree, you never have to make yourself into a different kind of person from who you are right now. No need to think differently, develop different feelings, or lose 40 pounds. No need to read energy constantly or behold lights twirling around the room.

Be yourself, Resourceful Healer. Without trying hard, you're naturally set for success with the complete skill set for Spiritual Cleansing and Protection.

Still not sure what I mean by "way more complicated than necessary"? Here are some very specific ways that less could be more.

Bring your normal mind.

Personally, I am not coordinated enough to do any technique from this skill set while chewing gum. You might be, but let's not risk it. Park the gum.

Similarly, set aside cigarettes, snacks, and any drink more complicated than water. Paying "full attention" need not be energetically expensive. It's easiest to be yourself if that's all you're doing.

Silence any background music.

Hey, I love music as much as anyone. It's really great for hypnosis, for instance, and I do have the skill set of being a professional hypnotist. Were I planning to hypnotize you, I would insist on playing music. What we'll be doing together, however, is not hypnosis. So please turn off the TV(s), remove earbuds, etc.

Astral-level debris makes its own kind of background noise. By learning these healing techniques where it is relatively quiet, you will be in a better position to tell when psychic-level noise has stilled.

No need to scrunch up your forehead.

Relax, Resourceful Healer. You can notice great results from these healings by simply being awake. Awake, not hyper-vigilant or terrified in advance, as if preparing for electroshock therapy.

Can you learn with a friend or a group?

Absolutely! Your experience might be better than otherwise. These friends would have to be physically present with you, in the room. (And also not chewing gum.)

Friends through technology won't help, however. Turn off your cell. No texting or tweeting, please. Let those emails pile up. Later you will have so much more to tell your friends.

Dare to be simple.

While you are learning these skills, never, ever mix them up with other skills you have learned. Otherwise you may never find out what a particular skill set can do for you. Want to get creative later, mix-and-matching your skill sets? First give yourself a few months to master each skill. Every technique for Spiritual Cleansing and Protection can bring you more clarity on your chosen path.

Systematic study won't slow you down in the long run. Learn one chunk of wisdom at a time and then you can get creative in a really productive manner.

Unless you know what any skill set can do all by itself, how can you decide which technique to use when? Avoid creating one big enthusiastic mush of "Everything I have ever learned or could improvise."

Whatever your aspirations as a Resourceful Healer, try this bold simplicity of learning. It will bring you the quickest mastery.

11. Cut Astral Ties and Win the Lottery

Ever feel spread in too many directions? There you are, a moist, golden pat of YOU. It's being spread on the bread of your day. Imagine how, every day, you begin as that one shiny new pat of butter, perfect for spreading as needed.

Well, what might explain the feeling that somehow your daily bread has expanded while you personally have shrunk?

Seen any toddlers lately? No lack of butteriness there. Kids spread joyfully in every possible direction.

Once you were that kind of toddler. How can you feel like such a dry lump now? Sure, you could explain this problem in many ways, such as:

- Adult responsibilities.
- Health problems.
- The economy.
- Parental unit's fault.
- Life must always involve a cruel lack of butter.

Now, consider another possible cause of feeling spread so thin, something you can fix right now. Astral ties — oh, you guessed that's where I was going? Once you learn how to remove astral ties, your quality of life can go up, up, up. (Or, if you insist on using that butter idea, sideways, sideways, sideways.)

My favorite image for removing astral ties is "Win the lottery." Imagine what you would do if given such a huge amount of cash.

Alas, I'm not authorized to hand you that money. But if you substitute the word "energy" for "money" and then do this healing…. Well, yes!

Greater physical energy, emotional energy, even sexual energy, can be yours. And wouldn't that be worth a million dollars to you?

So many ways you can win at life, just by removing the sadly common problem of astral ties!

Astral Tie Healing: WHAT IT IS

People are sticky. Whenever you talk to one or text one, scratch one or sniff one, some of Person A rubs off energetically onto Person B.

This energy flow happens in both directions through one teensy thread of psychic-level energy called an **astral tie**.

What if you, Person A, have higher vibrations than Person B? You'll lose more energy than you gain. Same thing if you have more energy invested in the interaction, compared to silly Person B.

Let's assume that Person B has annoyed you, demanded something unreasonable, offended your nose greatly with her smell, etc. That astral tie will drain you more than otherwise.

True, a few of your astral ties may bring you energy. But surely you have better ways to receive energy, no string attached.

Astral-level strings aren't a great way to exchange energy with others. They're more like getting a white elephant gift that's totally incompatible with your personal taste. In short, astral ties are pathetic, if small, energy drains. And how long do they last, physically, at the astral level? Maybe years. Maybe longer than a couple of years.

How thick are they? Only as thick as the filament that a spider spins for its web. Incidentally, how lovely a look is that? Unwittingly carrying loads of spider-web-like filaments attached to your aura? Especially since even one tiny astral tie can drain your life force energy!

Annoying though one astral tie would be, what if you carried a whole bunch? Well, Resourceful Healer, you do.

That bunch of spider-web-like filaments can create a whole bunch of problems, which is why our first official skill of Spiritual Cleansing and Protection will be to remove them.

Astral Tie Healing: NUTS AND BOLTS

To master any skill of Spiritual Cleansing and Protection, you must first understand it. Let's take the language of this healing apart piece by piece. Italicized words are followed by explanation.

I ask Jesus to please do this healing with me. (Or substitute the name of another Divine Being of your choice.)

For this healing, you will need the help of a Divine Being, someone embodied rather than the universal aspect of God. Most of us find it hard to think about Universe reaching into its pocket to pull out cosmic scissors and then snip away astral ties.

So begin this healing by choosing a god or goddess, either an Ascended Master or an Archangel, for the purpose of helping you heal. (Some of you Resourceful Healers will be prepared to wing this. However, you may prefer to skip ahead to the more detailed explanation in Chapter 14, "Deepen Your Power of Command.")

As you prepare to cut astral ties, know this: You always have the right to co-create healing along with a Divine Being.

Do you already have an ongoing relationship with a Divine Being because you practice a religion like Christianity or Buddhism? Great.

If not, Divine Beings don't care as much as you might assume. Religion is a human thing, not required by these higher-vibrational embodiments of omniscience.

They will love you and work with you regardless of religious affiliation. Simply use your natural Power of Command to assemble a powerful healing team, you the human along with your choice at the etheric level. By using Your Power of Command to speak the first words of this healing, what happens instantly? You effectively summon your choice of Divine Being. Right where you are! Superb!

Sure, clairvoyants may see Her or Him, resplendent in a shining body of etheric light. But seeing clairvoyantly is not the least bit necessary. Results are the point of a healing, right?

Resourceful Healer, you can experience results in a personal way. (In fact, you will get to do that very soon — in our next section, "Explore the Results.")

Meanwhile, why must *you* be the one to choose the Divine Being? Well, you are the one doing the healing. People at the other end of each astral tie don't get to choose, which is certainly convenient. Otherwise, you might be waiting a while to get back all 500 RSVPs.

Incidentally, there are no bad side effects to this healing at the other end of each astral tie. The Divine Being will do the work and skedaddle, no hanging around for a tip.

Never fear that, for instance, your choice of Divine Being might take over the will of Jonathan Livingston Seagull III (the person at the other end of one particular astral tie). If you choose Jesus, Jonathan will not be converted to Christianity. If you choose Athena, Jonathan will not be drafted, kicking and screaming, into worship of random goddesses from Greek Mythology.

Feel confident, Resourceful Healer. You have every right to request your choice of Divine Being to co-create this healing. Now, what comes next?

Jesus, locate all the astral ties between me and xyz.

How useful is that? The Divine Being with whom you co-create this healing possesses something that, for a human, would qualify as a superpower. Any Divine Being has **Cosmic GPS**, able to instantly locate every single one of your pesky astral ties.

Remember, Divine Beings live at the spiritual level. Vibrationally this is higher than the psychic level, home of astral ties. Also, both these levels are way higher than your view from the human level.

Therefore, a Divine Being like Jesus can put a human GPS to shame, locating all of your astral ties instantly.

To turn on this Cosmic GPS, all you need do is request that the Divine Being pay attention to whichever astral ties you just named.

Rather than pay attention where else? Oh, first noticing all the other random interesting things in the entire Universe. Then, eventually, getting around to your various astral tie locations.

To direct Divine attention, just use Your Power of Command and include that useful verb *"locate."* Right in the middle of your energy sandwich, you get the healing requested.

Now, how about the *"xyz"* part of this healing. How will you fill in the blank?

Name all possible suspects. If you want, you could go so far as to say, *"All the astral ties between me and everyone else in the world."* (Actually, I use that bit of language fairly often.)

But sometimes you may prefer to name specific people. Which you can do even if you don't literally know the person's name. For example:

- My upstairs neighbor in the apartment building.
- Everyone who lives in this silly apartment building.
- Also the landlord.
- Everybody at the party last night in the apartment upstairs, that loud drunken shindig that would have gone on until

4:00 a.m. if I hadn't called the police.

• Plus all those grumpy policemen who arrived on the scene.

You see, it isn't required that you supply any full legal names. Cosmic GPS can locate all these folks for you just fine.

What if you're only guessing which people to name in an Astral Tie Healing? That's okay, too.

You are hereby given official permission to be on the grabby side whenever you do an Astral Tie Healing.

What's the worst that can happen if you name several possibilities where, it turns out, no astral ties exist?

No results. When nothing needs to be cut, there are no results... but no penalty either.

So splurge on that "xyz" part of your sentence. Feel free to name anyone at all, anybody you suspect of being connected to you through an astral tie, no matter how far-fetched the possibility.

What, you feel guilty doing this expanded version of xyz? Afraid this might make you some kind of astral tattletale?

Well, get human already. Nobody needs astral ties, no more than you need to wear mud in your hair. You cannot possibly name too many xyz's.

When you clean a mud spot on your kitchen floor, do you feel sorry for all the disappearing little muds?

Cut and dissolve all of them now.

How delicious, what happens next with this healing. Your Divine Being cuts every one of the astral ties simultaneously. It's like going to the quickest beauty salon or barber shop imaginable.

But you don't want to stop your healing there, no no! Otherwise your aura might temporarily look like a wilted porcupine, with loads of snipped astral ties flopping around for the next few days until they dissolve randomly on their own.

Better to have the whole mess cleaned up now. So remember to request that the astral ties also be *dissolved.*

For complete and instant dissolving, it helps that you're collaborating with someone at a higher frequency than the psychic level where the mess exists. Jesus, like all Divine Beings, has access to light that moves faster than any astral tie.

Therefore, dissolving the tie will be way easier for Him than it would be for you. Although I sure would enjoy seeing the TV commercial for an astral tie vacuum cleaner. Wouldn't you? Of course, such a contraption wouldn't work. Far as I know, even our cleverest human-level machines don't work at the psychic level.

Okay, what if so far you have been naughty? What if you ignored my request to use Your Power of Command to team up with a Divine Being? What if, instead, you called on a psychic-level being, like your good friend Mambo, your Guardian Angel?

Mambo already has plenty to do, protecting and guiding you, day and night. He isn't at a higher vibrational frequency than the astral ties and, therefore, would find it much harder to dissolve them.

What if you have been really, really naughty? Suppose that you didn't use Your Power of Command to include any Divine Being at all. You figured that you could handle this healing completely on your own, so you changed the words to this: "I notice all the astral ties between me and xyz. I cut and dissolve all of them now."

Plenty of folks do affirmations on their own. "Every day in every way, I am getting better and better." Who could object to that positive kind of speech?

Well, me. Techniques of Spiritual Cleansing and Protection are different from affirmations. Here you are using Your Power of Command to co-create with a Divine Being.

Experimenting with affirmations won't bring results for psychic-level trash removal. *Your being human* is the deal breaker.

It's as if you were shopping in a department store with 10 floors. There you are, browsing on Floor #2 (being a very advanced person but still human). Astral ties are like merchandise located on Floor #5. Good luck at finding that merchandise or doing anything with it.

You can affirm all you like, "I find great deals in the Fifth Floor Home Electronics Department." Nonetheless, you won't be able to buy so much as a AA battery.

Okay, this analogy isn't perfect. The purpose of Astral Tie Healing isn't to take merchandise home but the opposite.

Still, humor me for now and do the healings in this skill set just the way they're presented. Whether you facilitate an Astral Tie Healing or use the more advanced healings that follow, results are known to be excellent only if you do these techniques exactly as taught.

Find out if, in a subtle way, you gain that peace of mind that people associate with winning the lottery. Experiment afterwards.

Then fill everyone (who desires it) with love and light, power and peace.

How important is it to speak this last part of the healing? It's only the most important part of all! Technically you are requesting a **fill-up**.

What if you don't fill up after removing astral ties? New astral ties will creep back minutes later, so you will have totally wasted your time.

Allow the Divine Being who assists you to plump you up again, plus help everybody else named in the healing. It's easy, since all you need do is use Your Power of Command.

Maybe you also noticed my tiny escape clause: Everyone *"who desires it."* Not everyone gets the love goodies. Amazing how I could write all this in a three-word clause! That's because I am not a lawyer.

Amazing but true, not everyone appreciates your generosity. Not everyone wants to bathe, either. Would any of this be your business?

Only how do you figure out in advance which of your xyz's want to receive the love goodies?

Conveniently you won't need to interview the soul of each individual named in your healing. That's the Divine Being's job. Yet one more reason to have a Divine Being do that cleanup along with you!

In the twinkling of a human eye, Jesus (or any other Divine Being) will take the survey, note all responses, and deliver blessings appropriately.

You, of course, want all the love goodies, right? Since you are co-creating this healing, your goodies will appear automatically. While you're at it, why not help these not necessarily "significant" others? Such an easy good deed — it will take no effort beyond making the simple request.

I love the last sentence of our Astral Tie Healing, escape clause and all. It provides the perfect happy ending. You can walk away from this healing with a good feeling — in part, because you have indirectly helped others as well as yourself.

Astral Tie Healing: EXPLORE THE RESULTS

Now let's shift into your first-time experience of the healing. *Read* this four-part exercise only when you are prepared to actually *do* it. (Sampling? No worries. Skip ahead to our next section.)

Okay, Resourceful Healer. Move into a comfortable seated position. Check that your legs and arms aren't crossed. That way life force energy can move through you most freely, which will help you to effectively use all your Cleaning Supplies.

Keep pen and paper handy for jotting down whatever you experience. When I ask you to write something down, open your eyes just long enough to grab the paper. Write fast and sloppy. Immediately afterwards, close your eyes again.

Feeling ambitious? Then make a recording of your voice going through the full sequence for the healing. Be sure to leave pauses inbetween so that you can follow your own instructions.

Do all four of the following parts, one step at a time. (Unless you have made that recording for yourself, open your eyes as needed to take a quick peek.)

Part One. BEFORE PICTURE

1. Close your eyes. Take three Vibe-Raising Breaths and then return to normal breathing.
2. Notice how it feels *in your body* right now. Ask inside for some words to describe this. Open your eyes long enough to write those words quickly.
3. Immediately close your eyes. Take three Vibe-Raising Breaths and then return to normal breathing.
4. Notice how it feels to be you *emotionally* right now. Ask inside for some words to describe this. Open your eyes long enough to write those words quickly.
5. Close your eyes and tell yourself, "This Before Picture is complete. Fine job!"
6. Open your eyes.

Part Two. DO THE HEALING

Words for the Astral Tie Healing are summarized in a box at the end of this chapter.

Use Your Power of Command to speak these words aloud.

Note: Paper clips and Post-It Notes are excellent ways to flag these end-of-chapter boxes.

Each healing in our skill set for Spiritual Cleansing and Protection will be in a stately box at the end of a chapter. You will want to turn to these instructions again and again.

Part Three. AFTER PICTURE

Now let's find out what has changed for you.

1. Close your eyes. Take three Vibe-Raising Breaths and then return to normal breathing.
2. Notice how it feels *in your body*. Ask inside for some words to describe this. Open your eyes long enough to write those words quickly.
3. Close your eyes again. Take three Vibe-Raising Breaths and then return to normal breathing.
4. Notice how it feels to be you *emotionally* right now.
5. Ask inside for some words to describe this. Open your eyes long enough to write those words quickly.
6. Close your eyes and use Your Power of Command to say out loud something like this, "I just did a great job at Spiritual Cleansing and Protection. Now this After Picture is over."
7. Open your eyes.

Part Four. ASSESS RESULTS

Read what you wrote before and after the healing. How do they compare?

Noticing results from a healing is like giving yourself a tip after excellent services rendered to the planet.

Removing astral ties frees you up energetically, so get used to how it feels... this comfortable way of feeling more like yourself.

Astral Tie Healing: HELPFUL USES

What is the point of learning to do a healing like Astral Tie Healing, the first one in our skill set? Okay, in addition to the brag factor. You're free to annoy your friends by saying, "I know how to x-out our astral ties. And you don't. Nyah-nyah."

Then, if you really want to rub it in, you could do the Hokey Pokey.

Personally, though, I'm more interested in the practical benefits of mastering this Astral Tie Healing. For me, that's what it's all about.

Finally, you can leave work.

What, you thought it was enough to commute for an hour or, perhaps, punch a time clock? My friend, you have been taking bits of people home with you.

Not just your boss or employees, either. Even the commute back and forth can put you in touch with plenty of people who then link to you via astral ties.

What if your official job description involves dealing with the public? Even worse! You're really at risk for even more burnout due to astral ties... unless you know how to move them out.

Hey, you know how to do that now. Just include "Everyone else in the world" in the "xyz" part of your Astral Tie Healing.

Stop telling that story.

Gus really annoyed you at the bowling alley.

It wasn't anything, really, what happened with the team bowling in the lane right next to yours. And, in the grand scheme of things, really, it didn't matter at all how this jerk, Gus, picked up your favorite bowling ball and started using it. Then, after you complained, he said you couldn't prove it was yours and, besides, that ball belonged to the Big Boys Bowling Alley.

But you liked that bowling ball. Of course, you know what happened didn't matter. Not really.

Grrrr, ever since you got home from bowling, you have been telling that story to anyone who would listen. Your best friend has heard it three times already. Actually you've been restraining yourself. Grrrr for sure.

And how you wish random people didn't annoy you that way.

Well, the cause of that sticky story might be your astral tie to that sticky person Gus.

Often the problem is simply an astral tie. We tell ourselves "Don't sweat the small stuff." Meanwhile that small stuff is tug, tug, tugging on us anyway.

To stop feeling that small stuff is big stuff, we need more than a new attitude. We need clean.

Next time you catch yourself telling a Gus-type story, excuse yourself and apply first aid in the form of the Astral Tie Healing. If you don't know Gus' name, or even if you do, you could make your "xyz" really inclusive:

"All the people I have ever bowled with, plus everyone who has ever bowled at the Big Boys Bowling Alley."

Enjoy driving more.

Are you a Highly Sensitive Person? Are you simply someone who dislikes driving in a car? Either way, you know how draining those trips can be. Hours after a routine commute, you might still remember certain tailgaters.

Congratulations, in a weird way. What you're really remembering are the astral ties formed every time another driver gets on your nerves. And soon you will be such a pro at moving out astral ties!

Your prompt to use the healing can be quite simple. Any time when you are NOT driving and you start feeling bad due to remembering some rude, crude drivers, Aha! Do the healing. Take the two minutes.

You can even speak out the healing words while stuck in traffic.

Admittedly other STUFF in your energy field could cause problems, such as an outright driving phobia that might require professional help to remove.

Still, you may find that your whole problem with carryover driver's annoyance is solved by the *occasional* healing of astral ties to other drivers. For many of you Resourceful Healers, that's all the healing you will need.

Spiritual Cleansing and Protection doesn't fix everything. None of our techniques is meant to be done all day, every day. If problems persist, that's your invitation to seek expert help from a mental health professional or a skilled practitioner of Energy Spirituality, Energy Medicine, or Energy Psychology.

Less guilt and worrying.

Worrying, guilt, oy vey! Has it occurred to you yet? Worry and guilt can be ways that people explain to themselves how bad they feel due to astral-level debris, including invisible astral ties.

Say that something gets under your skin. You keep scratching it, mentally and emotionally. Only you don't call it "scratching" but "worrying."

Since the energy drain from an astral tie is subconscious, your conscious mind may deal with that hidden problem by blaming something you *do* know about consciously.

Blaming something or someone familiar. Like your friend Vonda, who happens to be having a lot of problems right now.

There you are, at the end of the day, chewing over Vonda's problems along with your broccoli. Right at the dinner table, unbeknownst to your conscious mind, guess who is sitting right there along with your physical body? It's your aura.

Included in your aura, if you were counting, you might find 412 astral ties sticking right out of you, itching away.

In this example, only one astral tie is to Vonda; the rest are to other people. But the conscious mind emphasizes what you've been thinking of recently. So a thought bubbles up, "Vonda. Worry. Worry. Worry."

Get the picture? So there you are, feeling so drained. You figure it just has to be about Vonda and how much you care about her.

As if.

Astrally you're wound tighter than a maypole, only less colorful. None of those astral ties amounts to much. It's just a tiny thread, a mosquito-bite kind of drain. How those teeny ties do add up, though! (Or subtract up.)

Now you can cut that out. At least cut all your astral ties. Find out how you feel then.

Social networking without strings attached.

Do you spend a few minutes each day at Facebook or some other social networking website? Okay, many happy hours? Social connections are good for us... mostly.

But every time you click-and-read somebody else's story, photos, etc., you are forming an astral tie. New way to think of the worldwide web, right?

Not everyone hanging out at those websites is totally lovely. Or even is the person *claimed* to be there.

However, one thing is for sure. Every single online creature does have a someone behind that online identity. That is the person with whom you will form an astral tie.

Nearly as fast as the click of a mouse, you can cut astral ties to everybody at Facebook. Why not keep all your positive connections but lose the energy drains? Having online friends should be a good thing, right?

Avoid Healer's Burnout.

Are you a healer? Wonderful that you do all that good work! You might heal clients as a professional therapist or physician; alternatively, it could be volunteer work with cutting cords of attachment, Reiki, E.F.T., etc. Perhaps you're the go-to person for friends seeking to dump their latest love troubles.

Or maybe you are really smart with computers. Lucky you! Everybody at work treats you like a walking Help Desk.

All that service counts in the grand scheme of things. Healing is wonderful work, generating superb karma. Every healer deserves to have a great life. Except oops....

Whenever the relationship between you and Client Charlie involves healing, an astral tie will drain you afterwards. Sure, helping people is lovely. But honestly, did you purposely sign up to volunteer energetically 24/7, losing energy in random ways?

Healer's Burnout is a very real problem. One way to avoid it is quite simple. After every healing session, please cut astral ties. Do it secretly if you're worried about seeming weird (or weirder than usual).

Personally, I officially include an Astral Tie Healing when working with most of my clients. First session, I explain the concept, request and receive permission from my client; then I'll take a minute at the end of our time together to do the healing properly.

That way I don't merely free up my client. I model good energetic hygiene. It's educational for my client, facilitating the healing while we are still together. (If there isn't time during the session, I will cut the astral ties afterwards.)

Resourceful Healer, however you work out your own ethical stand on this, use the Astral Tie Healing to avoid Healer's Burnout.

Fatigue relief for psychics, channelers, and mediums.

Psychics, channelers, and mediums have a little-known occupational hazard, too. Unless they know how to remove astral ties effectively, every human client clings on with an astral tie. So does everybody contacted from the Other Side. Such a pile-on!

You sweet woo-woo practitioners, think of other psychics, channelers, and mediums whom you have known. How many grow physically heavier by the year? How many can't stop smoking? How many live with chronic fatigue?

All the skills of Spiritual Cleansing and Protection could help. Clearly the place to start is an Astral Tie Healing.

Doesn't instruction in mediumship, etc., typically come with techniques for self-protection? Sure, and sometimes this is rigorous.

Meaning no disrespect, however, often there is no clear knowledge about Spiritual Cleansing and Protection. Which is, after all, a completely separate skill set. A skill set where removal of astral ties is just the beginning!

Astral ties can connect you to every single person you meet, in any dimension — everyone whose body is energetically sticky.

By definition, that excludes Divine Beings. But it sure does include each and every psychic-level being you made contact with as a psychic, channeler, or medium. (Also, of course, every time you are the client of such a practitioner.)

Whenever people purposely make contact with psychic-level energies, or do depth readings of any kind, astral ties are formed. Remove them after work with each client.

Astral Tie Healing: HYPOTHETICAL TALES

Next chapter, you will learn how to move out stuck spirits, a.k.a. ghosts. They are disembodied astral entities, people who have physically died but not yet moved off the earth plane.

One chapter from now, I predict, you will become very effective at doing this kind of healing. Which will be great for you and also help every stuck spirit involved in the healing.

Resourceful Healer, astral ties can be involved in this, too. Imagine this scenario — hypothetical but important in a very practical way.

Roamin' Ralph Waldo and 300 other stuck spirits move out the very first time you do the Stuck Spirits Healing. Isn't that great?

And nobody is more pleased than Roamin' Ralph Waldo. Hanging out in his psychic-level body for a couple hundred years, stuck as could be, the poor guy felt terrible. Finally — thanks to you — he's free.

Fast forward a few years, earth time. Now Ralph Waldo lives at the appropriate heaven for him. Say he's sitting around the campfire, getting high with John Denver and other new buddies. Everyone's swapping stories about the nicest people they've ever known.

Well, Ralph Waldo starts to tear up. He tells everyone about you, the person who saved his life, as it were.

"Woo-hoo" shrieks the throng. "Let's go meet this great and mighty energy healer."

An astral tie makes it easy. Think of a fireman sliding down a fire pole. Think of Hansel and Gretel, scattering breadcrumbs to help them backtrack through the woods, a crumby path that anybody is able to take. Think of any homing signal between yourself and another person.

Resourceful Healer, unless you remove astral ties at the end of a Stuck Spirits Healing, you could attract thousands of stuck spirits for each one that you personally free up from earth.

Such a complement, courtesy of Roamin' Ralph Waldo. Reminds me of something my son said, back at age eight: "I annoy because I love."

Not to worry, I'll be sure to include the Astral Tie Healing as a required part of the Stuck Spirits Healing.

By contrast with this habit of automatically cutting astral ties, consider all the optional everyday uses described earlier, like leaving work without taking astral ties home with you.

For uses like this, you're the one who will decide, "Gee, why don't I take one minute to clear out all my astral ties?" After you master this part of our skill set, a minute or two is all it will take.

Astral Tie Healing:
TAKE THIS HEALING FURTHER

Could an astral tie be the *only* reason you always feel drained after visiting your weird Cousin Buddie? No, but astral ties are a *likely* reason. Even if there were some other reason for your feeling like recycled Styrofoam, it can't hurt to cut your astral tie.

Now that you know how to do this healing technique, let's consider other ways that your sweet but strange Cousin Buddie could drain you... and what to do about it.

Hurtful behavior.

What if Buddie behaves in a hurtful, obnoxious manner?

In that case, objective action is needed, not simply tweaking the energy between the two of you. Use your words. Or perhaps get support from a counselor.

Either way, don't expect any technique of Spiritual Cleansing and Protection to substitute for appropriate action in objective reality. Communicate out loud, clearly and authentically.

Woes of an unskilled empath.

Can a certain kind of pain wreck your life, simply because you're an empath?

Ouch, yes!

By definition, an **empath** is born with at least one lifelong gift for directly experiencing what it is like to be other people. No empath is born with skill, although any empath can develop it. Unfortunately, an **unskilled empath** constantly picks up STUFF from other people.

If this is a problem for you, use the Astral Tie Healing but also make it your business to become a skilled empath. Knowing how to remove astral ties will make it easier for you to develop the completely different skill set that all born empaths need.

Mind-body imbalances.

Say that you just loathe your cousins Dasher, Dancer, Comet, and Blitzen. Other people bother you, too. It feels as though all their energies stick to you constantly. Every day you struggle.

If you feel like you have more energy holes than a lawn sprinkler, go immediately to a mental health professional, get a physical checkup, or consult a professional practitioner of Energy Spirituality, Energy Psychology, or Energy Medicine.

What if the problem is smaller, and just a few relationships upset you? Then most likely your problem is cords of attachment, for which the most appropriate practitioner would be trained in Energy Spirituality.

Astral ties vs. cords of attachment.

Sooner or later, you can remove any cord of attachment. Your first step is to understand what on earth these cords are. Many people today are confused about the difference between cords of attachment versus astral ties.

Here is the lowdown on cords. What happens when you become interested in your very good-looking friend Pat, or anybody else, for whatever reason? Two important energy structures are created automatically, connecting your energy field to Pat's.

One structure is called a **spiritual tie**. This is a good thing, made of energy from the Divine level.

Your spiritual tie stores imprints from everything good that ever happens between yourself and Pat: All the love and learning, the sharing and caring and personal growth.

Even if eventually you wind up disliking Pat, so you never speak to each other again, you still would get to keep the engagement ring. I mean, the spiritual tie.

The second energy structure between you and Pat is formed on the psychic level. This is a **cord of attachment**. By definition, this isn't nearly so lovely.

Yet you have no choice, being human. Once you become interested in Pat, you will be given a cord of attachment along with your spiritual tie. Not negotiable, any more than having to deal with the Law of Gravity!

Incidentally, it's likely that Pat developed a spiritual tie and cord of attachment to you around the same time that you got yours. Consider that none of your business. Pairs, pairs, pairs! Yours separate from Pat's!

By contrast, astral ties — unlike cords of attachment and spiritual ties — involve one energy structure shared between two people.

While an astral tie is a skinny little filament that draws about as much energy as a nightlight, each cord of attachment can carry a huge energetic charge between you and the "cordee."

You could consider this a kind of energetic brainwashing. Regardless of psychotherapy or "working through your issues with Pat" or anything other than effective aura-level healing, that cord of attachment STUFF will persist until the last minutes of your life.

When a cord of attachment is properly cut, the healing is permanent. Will you develop another cord later on?

- No, you get only one cord of attachment per person per lifetime.
- Also only one spiritual tie per person per lifetime.
- Also only one human head, since there are limits to everything on earth.

Many an aspiring healer tries to cut cords of attachment at the astral level, using only a wish and a prayer. You, however, believe in getting results.

Resourceful Healer, you are not someone who would settle for just imagining that you take out the garbage. You're the kind of person who will firmly grab that bag o' stink, take it out of your kitchen, and make sure it lands in the dumpster. That's why you are learning this complete skill set for Spiritual Cleansing and Protection.

Discomfort that people blame on cords of attachment can sometimes be due to various types of astral-level debris, exactly the kinds you are learning to heal now.

Furthermore, developing *this* skill set is easier. Which makes it a better place to start your training in Energy Spirituality. Learn the skill set for cutting cords of attachment *second*, if possible.

Speaking of this first Resourceful Healer's skill set, I have already mentioned healing stuck spirits. Ready to learn? It's our very next chapter. Such a coincidence!

Astral Tie Healing

I ask Jesus to please do this healing with me. Jesus, locate all the astral ties between me and xyz.

Cut and dissolve all of them now.

Then fill everyone (who desires it) with love and light, power and peace.

12. Quickly Heal Stuck Spirits (Ghosts) To Free Both Them And Yourself

That ugly term "ghosts".... Euuuw, it sounds so harsh. "Astral entities" sounds wrong to me in a different way, far too clinical. As for "disembodied spirits," that might be confused with vodka or some other drink that leaves you "breathless."

Look, we might as well start off with a comfortable name for these astral-level guys and gals. Learning to heal them need not be unpleasant for anyone concerned. Therefore, I have come up with the term "Stuck Spirits." Unintimidating, I hope. Also definitely true.

In order to master this healing, you will need to feel un-intimidated. For one thing, chances are that you're carrying dozens of stuck spirits in your aura, right here and now.

Our latest skill will free you up fast, simultaneously doing the entities a big favor as well. Prevention would be a plus, so I'll include tips to help you avoid picking up stuck spirits in the first place. Let's hear it once again for Spiritual Cleansing and Protection!

Healing Stuck Spirits: WHAT IT IS

What are stuck spirits, anyway?

Maybe the rumors have reached you. Death happens.

The bad news is that after death the physical body stops working, regardless of how many preservatives have been in your food.

The good news is that death hardly counts as the end of a person's existence. In the words of the great regression therapist Coletta Long, Ph.D., "You will always be in some body, somewhere."

How can a person be "dead" yet remain very much alive?

Resourceful Healer, if you're familiar with auras, you know part of the answer. **Auras** are sets of bodies made of electro-magnetic energy. During life, this set of bodies supports the physical body. At death, a person's entire set of spiritual bodies lifts right up from that useless old physical wreck (not that I mean to be insulting). Then this spiritual set o' bodies, "spirit" for short, goes on to that soul's next place of development.

At least that's what happens usually. Mediums and other psychics who specialize in afterlife research can tell you a lot more about this. Alternatively you might prefer the view of your neighborhood pastor, the guy who preaches sermons about heaven vs. fire and brimstone in The Bad Place.

Long before you picked up this book, I have a hunch that you had heard about death and formed a set of beliefs about where people go. The purpose of this book is not to argue with whatever you already believe.

Our main concern is with the living — especially you. Our secondary concern is those who live neither-here-nor-there — stuck spirits.

You see, certain people don't take the usual quick 'n easy route to heaven or wherever. Which people, exactly?

- Alcoholics, potheads, drug addicts, and anyone who happened to be "high" right before death.
- Anybody who dies suddenly and/or violently.
- Atheists adamant in their belief that there is no place to go.
- True believers terrified that they will go straight to Hell... and therefore refuse to budge forward an inch.
- People with a really strong attachment to their home, their pile of money, their revenge, etc.
- People motivated to deliver some final message or complete other unfinished business. This makes for great movies like "Ghost Town" or "Sixth Sense" but isn't much fun when that stuck spirit attaches to YOU.

So what happens to all those stuck spirits, after they lose hold of that familiar, warm physical body? Here's an analogy.

Say that you see a film at an old-fashioned movie theater. The person who sat there before you parked some used chewing gum. You sit right on it. Afterwards that gum goes home with you.

Gum stuck to your pants is not personal, right? That's the point of this analogy about having stuck spirits attach to your aura. When healing them, you're not dealing with some sinister, hateful force out to get you, merely a kind of leftover at the psychic level.

Incidentally, "**astral attachments**" is a popular term for these discarnate entities or stuck spirits. Doesn't that sound scary? Well, how scary is chewing gum?

Fact is, most stuck spirits happen to feel more comfortable when attached to a live, human body. Since theirs is no longer available, someone else's will have to do.

Stuck spirits will attach to just about anyone else's body, if possible. Since billions of live, warm, human bodies populate earth, ghosts can choose quite freely. Who wins their favor?

Remember, from a live person's perspective, "Winning their favor" means installing yet one more lodger in the "boarding house" of your aura — a rent-free facility that your conscious mind never knew existed, let alone realized that you had been running for years.

Which criteria could make a person so attractive in that way, subconsciously turning your aura into a happy home for folks like Roamin' Ralph Waldo?

- That person's aura is nice and big, holding a great deal of light.
- The person is a born empath, not yet skilled, with an aura to match.
- The person's aura (as well as the rest of the person) happens to be drunk on alcohol, stoned on weed, or otherwise under the influence of a recreational substance.
- Untreated mental illness can cause a person to shift energetically out of balance, blowing bits of that aura wide open.
- Even if there isn't a true mental health problem, when somebody lives with large amounts of accumulated STUFF, that person's aura can contain gaps that are attractive to stuck spirits.

- Everyday lifestyle has included channeling, mediumship, or constantly seeking feedback from spirit guides — where instruction has not addressed potential problems related to entity attachments.
- A well-meaning person has experimented with a meditation technique to simply "Open to the light" or "Ask for guidance from whoever is out there from the other side."
- Spiritual addiction can cause a person to become aurically out of balance.
- Habitually, for any reason, a person's aura may not be as structurally sound as it could be, which would make it extra-attractive to stuck spirits.

After you learn to do the Stuck Spirits Healing, I'll explain how to avoid being so gosh darned desirable to stuck spirits. (See "Helpful Uses.") However, any time you suspect that stuck spirits have become part of you, heal first. Ask questions later.

Why? You may think better. Also you could feel more like yourself, emotionally and physically. Furthermore, having stuck spirits in your aura creates a certain psychic-level fragrance. To use a technical term, it's a "Yecch Factor." Not so great for a living person's quality of life....

Ever walk by a stranger and feel that Yecch Factor? "Something is terribly wrong with Zelda. Not dangerous exactly. Maybe crazy? Hopefully not, but something about her sure feels like vomit."

Faster than you can think "Whatever," your feet have started to cross the street. Why? Your subconscious mind has alerted you to the Yecch Factor, and self-actualizing folks generally avoid this whenever possible. Conscious assessment doesn't even have to become involved.

Sadly, it's not unusual for a perfectly normal person to be carrying around a couple dozen stuck spirits. Smoking a few joints at that party or trying some free-form experiments with mediumship may cause some "freeloader boarders" to move in for decades, upping the quantity of auric yecch.

That Yecch Factor can really kick in when the number of stuck spirits increases past 300-400, which is more common than you might think. Zelda could unknowingly be hosting 5,000 or more stuck spirits.

I have helped plenty of clients in Zelda's position. And I do mean "helped." Because there are so many benefits from receiving this particular healing.

Healing Stuck Spirits: NUTS AND BOLTS

As usual, I'll introduce the healing in italics with commentary added. At the end of this chapter, you will find the same healing summarized in a box. Go for it! Not only will you feel better. The Roamin' Ralph Waldos of your neighborhood will feel better too.

Stuck Spirits Healing – Always include all three parts

Part One. EDUCATE AND RELEASE THE SPIRITS

With this healing you aren't just ridding yourself of a nuisance. You're actually helping stuck spirits to become unstuck. Finally, a chance to feel like a philanthropist without having to first become rich!

Kwan Yin, please do this healing with me.

Co-create with any Divine Being you choose. Just be sure to ask for a Divine Being. And one in a distinct body, rather than some impersonal form of God. Here I'll invite compassionate but feisty Kwan Yin, a goddess from Buddhism.

Why bother to choose a personal aspect of the Divine? Why not simply ask for "God"?

For this healing to work effectively, stuck spirits prefer to interact with a distinct Divine Being in a body of light, someone they can see and hear. The universal, twinkling, joyful presence of God won't satisfy this need. (Nor will an astral-level being like your guardian angel.)

All you Dear Ones, I am speaking to each of you personally, along with Kwan Yin.

Notice? Indirectly you are saying, "Yo! Participation in this ceremony is not optional."

Also your words clarify that two different speakers are involved with facilitating this healing. You represent the human level. Plus your choice of Divine Being is chiming in from the spiritual level, doing a kind of simultaneous translation. A stuck spirit may prefer listening to either one of you or both. No worries.

Hello and congratulations. This is a healing ceremony just for you. I am so happy to be able to help you.

Note the friendly, even affectionate, tone. Remember, if you must, that stuck spirits aren't terribly secure. Automatically they magnify all negative emotions like fear or anger — yet one more reason for you to speak calmly when facilitating this healing.

Relax and receive this healing. The past is over. You are safe now and filled with the presence of God. (Repeat this paragraph as needed.)

Prior to this healing, stuck spirits have existed in a sleepy, confused state. As you wake them up, naturally they need words of reassurance.

Imagine that you have fallen asleep on a train. Some kindly passenger wakes you up. If that happened to me, I'll tell you what my first reaction would be, huge embarrassment.

"Everyone could see me sleeping. Uh-oh. Could my skirt have slipped up to my shoulders? Was my underwear clean? Tell me I wasn't snoring or picking my nose!" Life offers so many possibilities for embarrassment. Alas, they don't end with physical death.

Anyone woken up on a train might wish for the kindly passenger to say things like, "There, there. That's okay, Dear. You didn't do anything horrible. Far as I can tell, you're still wearing all of your clothing."

Resourceful Healer, you're doing something equivalent in this part of the healing. "You are safe now," etc. gives each stuck spirit a kind of calm-down talk, like a kindly pat on the shoulder.

If you are sensitive to the spirits' reactions — which is NOT a requirement to do this healing successfully — soon you will feel a kind of collective sigh. The whole group of stuck spirits relaxes. Same thing if you were the kindly passenger waking up Rose on that train. Eventually you would notice that I had calmed down.

Then, mercifully, you would stop patting my shoulder and repeating, "There, there."

Similarly, when the stuck spirits move into that calmed-down feeling, you can stop what I have called "Repeat this paragraph as needed."

What if you don't feel a blessed thing? No worries. Simply repeat the words for 30 seconds. This will satisfy the "as needed" requirement.

You are being completely filled with Divine love. God loves you, no matter what. You deserve that because of who you are deep down.

Love brings healing. Being reminded of God's love can bring a great deal of healing.

Sometimes a person doesn't feel worthy of receiving all that love. Normally, that's okay. God won't force anyone to accept love. Being eternal, God has plenty of patience for waiting around until that individual feels ready. It's a cute game of acceptance that is sure to have a happy ending, sooner or later.

But "sooner or later" gets a little old in the case of stuck spirits. For weeks or months or hundreds of years, a stuck spirit has felt completely cut off from God's love. Enough already!

There you are, along with the Divine Being, speaking in stereo to that stuck spirit. It always works. Message received!

You are being completely filled with Divine truth. So you can recognize who you are and where you are. Everything is okay. Before you were stuck. Now things are going to change for you in a wonderful way.

Ah, having felt The Love, it becomes so much easier to handle The Truth. "Dead" people don't feel dead inside. So it can be hard for them to accept their current position. Roamin' Ralph Waldo's inner conversation might go like this:

"Oh, the physical body that I no longer have, that is the part that died. Me and my body of light — the real me — that isn't dead at all. Except heeeeeyyyyyy, I have been kind of stuck, haven't I?"

And now you are being completely filled with Divine light. It is all around you.

Notice! Although you are here on earth, no longer do you have a physical body of your own. Instead, you are in a body of light. You are still you. You will always be you. And if you need healing or forgiveness, God will give it to you right now.

Oh, I just love this part of the Stuck Spirits Healing. This is where the Divine Being turns on big lights to illuminate the whole room.

Back at the start of the Stuck Spirits Healing, it's as though you and the Divine Being meet in the dark with all those stuck spirits. Most have no clue who they are, where they are, what they are.

With your first words of the healing, it's as though a tiny lamp is lit, quite a contrast to the darkness but still a pretty dim bulb. Why? That wee bit of light parallels the self-awareness of the typical stuck spirit.

Now that you have coaxed each stuck spirit into a state of greater self-awareness, this gentle use of Your Power of Command does the equivalent of flicking on a cosmic light switch. A huge illumination fills the room, bright and clear.

If you're a visual person, you can appreciate how much better the spirits can see their reality now. If you're more an auditory person, like Rose Rosetree, imagine the voice of Charlton Heston (or some other deep god-like voice) saying "Hellloooo!"

Notice this, too. You are free from fear and pain and everything else about the earth's vibrations.

Trust me. That's a message you would definitely want to hear if you had been stuck in a physically-dead semi-snooze, waiting for something better to happen.

What is going to happen, anyway? Having no more physical body means no more spiritual evolution is available to that stuck spirit regardless of how long it sticks around at Earth School.

No physical body? Game over. Until Roamin' Ralph Waldo goes to his next place of development, he's simply stuck. No matter what story he tells himself while biding his time. Once stuck spirits realize they're spirits, many illusions of Earth School can instantly lose their hold.

Goodbye, fears that your body can be hurt or destroyed! Goodbye, dread of mosquito bites and hangnails! Farewell, hassles over gravity, lack of money, pimples!!!! Stuck spirits, all your struggles are over.

Now Kwan Yin is going to escort you personally to your next place of development, the place that is right for you. Go now, with joy and peace.

If you're clairvoyant, you will see this happen. If you have developed different gifts of deeper perception (through studying either energetic literacy or psychic development) you will have some other way to register the exit of all the stuck spirits. It's delightful.

Part Two. PUT IN SOMETHING GOOD

Never, ever just do Part One of this healing. Unless you include Part Two, what will happen? Very likely, the same number and type of stuck spirits will show up immediately, taking up residence right in your aura.

Whenever you merely remove something from the psychic level and don't put in something good, you will instantly attract more of the same. In a later chapter, we'll discuss this concept in detail. For now, just do the full healing; include all the parts.

I call on Kwan Yin to fill this place and me with Divine love, Divine truth, and Divine light.

How sublime is that! You want that quick, yummy infusion of Divine goodies? Well, ask.

Immediately, you will receive it. Some of the best things in life really are free.

Also, your request for this particular lovely freebie helps keep you safe energetically, given Part One of the healing. Consider it the psychic-level equivalent of putting on insect repellent.

Even if it weren't so nice being plumped-up with self-aware consciousness, the Divine goodies would be a must for completing a Stuck Spirits Healing. Remember, Resourceful Healer, this skill set is called "Spiritual Cleansing and *Protection*."

I close off my aura to all but my own Higher Self and those beings of the highest vibration who are with me at the choice of my soul.

This part of the Stuck Spirits Healing is such a big deal, let's save a fuller discussion until the section that follows, "Healing the Five Vulnerabilities." For now, just say the words aloud. Your well-aimed Power of Command, in conjunction with etheric-level intelligence, will help you do something rather important. Trust that.

Part Three. REMOVE ALL ASTRAL TIES

Remember astral ties? You definitely do not want to keep around astral ties to any stuck spirits whom you have just helped.

I call on Kwan Yin to cut and dissolve all astral ties between every stuck spirit who has been involved in this healing and me.

Could anything be simpler or more elegant? Except for an engraved dinner invitation from The White House. Wait, Divine Beings don't offer those.

Fill us all with love and light, power and peace — as much as each one of us is willing to receive. Now this healing is done, and I'm grateful.

Resourceful Healer., if you don't feel grateful, you don't have to say that last part. Only remember that gratitude is a powerful emotion for spiritual evolution. Any random crumb of gratitude that you manage to feel will return to you in the future. It will return bigger, perhaps the equivalent of a complete, shiny new birthday cake. At The White House.

Anyway, your healing of stuck spirits is now complete.

Healing Stuck Spirits:
EXPLORE THE RESULTS

Whew, that was a lot of theory to move through. Still, all of it was common sense, right? Now let's shift into your first-time experience of the healing.

Move into a comfortable seated position. Check that your legs and arms aren't crossed. That way, life force energy can move through you most freely, which will automatically improve your results with all Five Cleaning Supplies.

Keep pen and paper handy for jotting down whatever you experience. When I ask you to write something down, open your eyes just long enough to grab the paper and do some quick, sloppy writing. Afterwards, close your eyes.

Are you very ambitious? Then make a recording of your voice. Go through the sequence of parts and steps for the Stuck Spirits Healing. Be sure to leave pauses between steps.

Either way, here we go. Do the following steps, one at a time. (Open your eyes as needed to take a quick peek.)

Part One. BEFORE PICTURE

1. Close your eyes. Take three Vibe-Raising Breaths and then return to normal breathing.
2. Notice how it feels *in your body* right now. Ask inside for some words to describe this. Open your eyes long enough to write those words quickly.
3. Immediately close your eyes. Take three Vibe-Raising Breaths and then return to normal breathing.
4. Notice how it feels to be you *emotionally* right now. Ask inside for some words to describe this.
5. Open your eyes long enough to write those words quickly.

Part Two. DO THE HEALING

Speak out the words of the Stuck Spirits Healing. (Find this in a box at the end of this chapter.)

Part Three. AFTER PICTURE

1. Close your eyes. Take three Vibe-Raising Breaths and then return to normal breathing.
2. Notice how it feels *in your body* right now. Ask inside for some words to describe this.. Open your eyes long enough to write those words quickly.
3. Immediately close your eyes. Take three Vibe-Raising Breaths and then return to normal breathing. Notice how it feels to be you *emotionally* right now. Ask inside for some words to describe this. Open your eyes long enough to write those words quickly.
4. Close your eyes. Inwardly say something to signify conclusion, e.g., "Excellent exploring! I did great! Now this After Picture is done." Open your eyes.

Part Four. ASSESS RESULTS

Compare what you wrote before and after the healing.
What were you supposed to feel by the end? Nothing specific was required. But you just might have noticed some relief, lightness, feeling more like yourself, etc.
Soon I'm going to teach you how to prevent having stuck spirits move into your aura in the first place. Beyond that, once every six months you might want to use Your Power of Command for this healing, just for good energy hygiene.
Consider that a minimum for keeping yourself clear.

Healing Stuck Spirits: HELPFUL USES

Have I ever discovered a lot of uses for this healing over the years!

Popularity.

Once you know how to keep yourself clear of stuck spirits, expect your popularity to improve. Your popularity with other humans, that is.

Think of it like this. There is a kind of inverse ratio. The more popular your aura is with stuck spirits, the less likely that you will be popular with live human specimens.

Yes, without knowing it, you may be suffering from the Yecch Factor. In retrospect, I'm sure I once had it. Once upon a time, before learning how to do the Stuck Spirits Healing, I smelled quite ripe in that rank, astral kind of way.

What if you, too, used to have this kind of psychic-level body odor? Even your best friend wouldn't tell you.

Fortunately, this healing is very quick. After you're used to doing it, the whole process can be faster than a quick shower.

Mental clarity.

What other benefits can result from this healing? It's a big deal, releasing all those stuck spirits attached to your aura.

Probably you will become clearer inwardly, less likely to say, "I don't know." Compared to what?

- *Can you name three terrific things about yourself as a person?* "I don't know."
- *On a scale from 1-10, how confident do you feel?* "I don't know."
- *How are you feeling today? Right now? Anything about you at all!* "I don't know."
- *At your job, do you feel motivated to accomplish great things?* "I don't know."
- *Okay, after you get out of work today, what is one thing you would like to do?* "I don't know."

Well, consider this. The cause of inner fuzziness may be as simple as saying, "Slowed down self-esteem and miscellaneous spiritual sleepiness intensified by slews of stuck spirits." (Try repeating that one fast.)

Did you ever turn a radio dial and hear static between the stations? Stuck spirits in your aura or home create a kind of low-level static. Although you may be very used to living with static like that, you have a simple way to tell if this problem has crept up on you, Do the Stuck Spirits Healing.

Afterwards notice the contrast in how you feel. For some folks, astral static mainly affects how you feel about your physical body.

Static from stuck spirits in your aura can make it hard to feel some rather personal parts of you, such as your ribs, thighs, back of head, where the coat hanger is supposed to lodge, etc.

Just kidding about that coat hanger, of course.

Static, that's all it is. Does astral static contain a unique quality that you will notice in itself? Will you wake up in the morning and think, "Gee, it's really crowded in my mind-body-spirit + extra spirits system"?

Probably not. Instead you will seem **spaced out**. Or else you might become **accident prone**. (Falling over your feet is easy if you can't feel them.)

Fear not. Even if you have begun to routinely bang into furniture, our simple healing can help.

It's not that stuck spirits have permanently removed parts of your body, any more than static obliterates a brick-and-mortar radio station.

With a radio dial, you would just need to find the radio station more accurately. For Gladys, a person who wants to tune into her physical body, she just needs to get the stuck spirits out of her aura. Then, yum! There's only Gladys in Gladys.

Consequently, the Stuck Spirit Healing can help most people to develop a stronger mind-body-spirit coordination.

Emotional stability.

Don't fear that stuck spirits are wicked. Seldom do they mean a person harm. However, a stuck spirit's astral-level body is not supported by a personal, God-given, flesh-type body. Consequently these entities aren't emotionally stable. Automatically stuck spirits magnify negative emotions, such as:

- Fear
- Anger
- Despair

This emotional instability can be similar to what happens when a big drinker turns mean under the influence.

For an example of the tipsy-type problem, consider your bar-hopping friend, Margarita. Drinking alcohol moves her, aura and all, into a state of connection with energy frequencies at the psychic level.

This may be a pretty low-vibe part of the psychic level, actually. Yet compared to the human level, that's enough to feels "high."

After a couple of drinks, Margarita enjoys a pleasantly plastered feeling, like having one foot in the human world and her other foot in the astral.

Unfortunately, other astral entities exist at this particular place where Margarita visits, via the liquor. These entities aren't stuck spirits on earth but inhabitants of that particular astral realm.

So long as she's "under the influence," Margarita's aura is, well, under *their* influence. Should she start feeling slightly annoyed about anything, those nearby entities will start magnifying her anger with a rousing "Rah, rah." Before she knows it, Margarita will, most likely, begin yelling, too.

A person need not drink alcohol for moods to be distorted by stuck spirits, the kind you have just learned to heal. Move them out and some of those black moods that Margarita suffers from when sober... may seem merely brownish.

Energetic security.

Roam freely, when you own this healing. No longer will you have the **hitch-hiking problem**.

We've already considered that stuck spirits are in a slightly woozy, confused state. However, they keep one major ability to focus after death. Shopping!

Yes, the loss of a physical body causes just about everything else to go: Mental clarity, emotional joy, spiritual security, tasting a good pizza, even enjoying sex. But every stuck spirit retains the ability to shop.

In its vague way, each stuck spirit is constantly shopping. "Whose body-mind-spirit would make a more comfortable home?"

As you already know, entities prefer people with really big auras, provided that those auras also happen to be nice and open. In addition, as you have probably figured out without my telling you, stuck spirits can live in anybody's aura *rent free*.

Honestly, if you lived in a Motel 6 but then learned you could trade up to a Hilton in that same neighborhood, wouldn't you move?

Well, stuck spirits are physically dead, not stupid.

Okay, let's shift perspective over to regular everyday human life. Say that you go to the supermarket — you, the owner of a juicy, big, wide-open aura.

Ha, you thought you were just grabbing a head of lettuce.

Remember? That supermarket happens to be full of people. Also their stuck spirits.

Perhaps that includes Roamin' Ralph Waldo, who has been comfortably dwelling with the gal right behind you in line. Faster than you can say "Bag those chips and cookies," Ralph Waldo scoots onto your aura. Moving mission accomplished!

By the time you have finished this chapter, and followed the step-by-step instructions to keep your aura comfortably closed, this hitch-hiking habit will stop happening to you. So fear not.

However, if you want to pause right now and have a good cry over how much you have suffered already from picking up riders like Roamin' Ralph Waldo and his kind, I'll sympathize.

Often, when I teach workshops, students will tell me how hard it has been for them, dealing with all those stuck spirits.

- Joe used to find it hard to leave home.
- Gladys thought she was asocial for life.
- Fabiola had convinced herself she was crazy.

So many interpretations are possible for one same, simple, very fix-able problem.

Healing Stuck Spirits: TRUE TALES

Has this ever happened to you? To accelerate personal growth, you decide to take a seminar. Eagerly you spend both your precious weekend and your hard-earned cash, all for the sake of more success or better relationships or whatever else is the goal of the seminar.

Despite enjoying the material, somehow you feel worse with each passing hour. By the time you go home, you definitely feel worse than you did in the first place.

Well, of course you feel worse. You have returned home with 4,322 new stuck spirits. Originally, they had been stuck to the other course participants, but then they saw you and yum! They hitch-hiked.

Before I knew how to protect myself from stuck spirits, this kind of thing happened to me whenever I took a seminar. No matter how much I enjoyed the material, it could take me months to recover from one short workshop.

Fast forward to my life at seminars now, as someone who owns the skill set for Spiritual Cleansing and Protection. Golly, now I am usually the one *giving* those seminars. Sometimes, at the first meeting, I'll ask for a show of hands, "How many of you typically hate going to seminars?"

Often it's the majority. But not something that happens when people take mine. Ha ha!

Even when the topic of the seminar isn't Spiritual Cleansing and Protection, I use my skill set during the breaks to make sure that my darling students never leave a seminar of mine with new stuck spirits attached.

Now, you can do the same for yourself. Let the healing begin!

Healing Stuck Spirits:
TAKE THIS HEALING FURTHER

Resourceful Healer, knowing how to heal stuck spirits can change your life. And you have just learned the quickest and most effective method I know.

Still, an ounce of prevention is worth a pound of cure. So let's revisit the question of avoidance. How can you keep from taking on astral beings in the first place?

For clues, let's return to our earlier list about attractiveness.

Pay special attention if your aura is big, holding a great deal of light.

What makes an aura big? You have a lot of life force energy running through you. That energy can be used for anything in life that you wish to accomplish, give, or learn.

Having a big aura is a celestial form of leadership. For protection from stuck spirits, you only need to change one thing: Learn how to close off that huge aura.

An easy method will be explained later in this chapter. But the problems listed below are especially likely to affect you if your aura is large to begin with. Let's consider those possible contributing factors right now.

Having the aura of an unskilled empath.

Empaths are born, not made. Unfortunately, every empath is born unskilled, too.

Unskilled that empath will remain… until learning an effective skill set for waking up inside. You have read a bit about this earlier in our discussions of the Astral Tie Healing and the Stuck Spirit Healing.

To deepen the concept, I think it's important to understand that becoming a skilled empath requires awakening humanly. This protects the empath from spontaneously taking on STUFF at the level of auras.

Why bother mentioning something that sounds as weird as the term "empath"? Like it or not, empaths are born rather often.

You may know about the lifelong gift for mind-body sensitivity called being a "**Highly Sensitive Person**" or HSP. Altogether HSPs amount to 20% of the population worldwide. Only 1 in 4 HSPs is an empath, but that still means millions of people — and, quite possibly, you.

Sure, you. Because empaths are the most sensitive people in the world. And, really, which kind of person do you think would be most apt to notice problems with stuck spirits or other forms of astral garbage?

How would I define being an empath? Right from birth, you have at least one significant gift for directly experiencing What It Is Like To Be Other People.

As a born empath, your gift(s) might be physical, emotional, intellectual, spiritual, environmental, or animal, etc.

Being an unskilled empath means that your waking hours are filled with super-quick, **unskilled empath merges** with other people.

This happens regularly, a kind of aura-level habit of opening up, connecting, and then taking on some of the other people's STUFF (astral-level chunks of fear, pain, etc.). Well, sometimes this includes taking on their stuck spirits, too.

Unskilled empath merges happen hundreds of times every day, with the action taking place on the level of auras and the subconscious mind. To prevent this from happening, the talented but unskilled empath simply needs to develop a different kind of skills, empath skills.

Of course, becoming a skilled empath requires a dedicated skill set. More books and teachers appear every year to help empaths. It's exciting how many talented healers today are busily developing ways to help empaths. Unfortunately, success doesn't necessarily occur just because someone aims to help HSPs and empaths to "cope with their sensitivity." Beware methods that sound good on the surface but do not work deeply enough to transform your energy field. Here is a short list of techniques that *will not* help an empath at the level of auras:

- Attempting to strengthen boundaries.
- Avoiding draining people and psychic vampires.
- Trying to figure out which feelings (and STUFF already lodged in your aura) belong to you versus belonging to another person.

- Visualizations of any kind.
- Putting up an energy shield or wall.

Effective techniques to become a skilled empath *will* help you to wake up from inside as a vibrant, effective human being. Doing this brings many benefits, including automatically turning your empath gift(s) OFF.

Once basic skill is developed, an empath can safely experiment with the bonus set of techniques designed to help empaths safely turn their gift(s) ON. This is amazing fun, but optional.

How hard is it, learning this complete skill set? Not hard! Compare it to learning how to ride a bicycle. Likewise, this is a skill set you will never forget.

What about protecting yourself until you become skilled as an empath? Use the technique to close off your aura supplied later in this chapter. In addition, routinely do the Stuck Spirits Healing once a week. (For non-empaths and skilled empaths, it's generally enough to do that same healing technique just once every six months.)

The aura (and rest of the person) is drunk or stoned.

Unfortunately, drinking alcohol has the side effect of opening up one's aura to stuck spirits. This happens long before falling-down drunk. It happens when even slightly sloshed.

Depending on your sensitivity to alcohol, even one micro-glass of micro-brewed beer, even one teensy goblet of exquisite wine, might do it. Temporarily the happy drinker becomes a kind of babe magnet and boy magnet... for disembodied entities.

Similar consequences (and allover worse consequences for anyone's aura) result from smoking weed, taking LSD, sniffing cocaine, hobbling the aura with heroin, etc.

After you are sober again, do the Stuck Spirits Healing. You'll feel a bit more like yourself.

Long-term you might note that all your Five Cleaning Supplies work better without any exposure to recreational substances. Living substance-free brings a natural high with cumulative benefits for your sense of identity.

Chronic chemical imbalances.

Certain kinds of chemical imbalance require help from a mental health professional. Otherwise life is a constant struggle against anxiety, depression, etc.

In contrast to recreational chemicals like marijuana, prescription meds. are designed to re-balance the system. When psychiatric medication is a really good fit, the benefits include normalizing life all the way down to the level of the auric field.

Admittedly, it may feel beyond humbling, having to adjust to the need for shrink-prescribed medicine. There's incentive, though. Such medication can make a continent of difference for quality of life, maybe even a whole world of difference.

Have you ever wrestled with the idea of taking psychiatric medication? Then please remember, millions upon millions of people share a similar secret. Thanks to these balancing pills — which are nobody else's business — there can be such improvement, it's miraculous.

I do look forward to the day when mental health problems are no longer stigmatized in society. Meanwhile, don't stigmatize yourself. And do take your meds if needed. Now you have an extra motivation: Helping yourself to stay free of stuck spirits.

Accumulated STUFF apart from stuck spirits.

Auric imbalance, even when severe, is not necessarily a mental health issue. The cause of trouble might be having the mind-body-spirit system stuck with huge quantities of the astral-level debris that I call "STUFF."

Let's consider the example of Draco. Causes of his imbalance could be one or more of the following:

- Problems related to Draco's mixed-up patterns involve energy meridians ("Quick," I'd tell Draco. "Find yourself an expert at Energy Medicine, acupuncture, or other holistic healing at the physical level.")
- Dysfunctional patterns from cords of attachment flow through Draco's subconscious mind 24/7. (For help, I'd recommend healing by means of Energy Spirituality.)
- Frozen blocks of energy at the cellular level are still active from Draco's past. All those troubling incidents at Hogwarts! (I would recommend healing with Energy Psychology.)
- Problems related to the *full* skill set of Spiritual Cleansing and Protection, not just stuck spirits. (Resourceful Healer, you are learning, you're learning. Soon Draco might become one of your clients.)

STUFF has many varieties, you see. Yet STUFF can always, always, always be healed. Stuck spirits attached to your aura, for instance, would definitely count as STUFF. Each different healing you learn for Spiritual Cleansing and Protection can remove a different type of STUFF. Additional types of STUFF can require other specialized skill sets for removal. To further improve your quality of life, you might wish to bring in a professional healer. Researching different STUFF-removal specialties, you might want to Google terms like Energy Spirituality, Energy Medicine, Energy Release Regression Therapy, Energy Psychology. Or ask friends for their best referrals.

Woo-woo occupational hazards.

What if your lifestyle has included channeling, mediumship, or constantly seeking feedback from spirit guides? Guess who can stow away afterwards?

Along with spirits whose advice has been requested, along come Roamin' Ralph Waldo and his buddies. After the séance, the entity party won't necessarily be over... not until stuck spirits are healed.

That's what I'd call an *obvious* occupational hazard for participating in these woo-woo activities. An *indirect* occupational hazard involves a serious, though very healable, aura-level imbalance. Too much dependence on guides or spirits can cause **spiritual addiction.**

Millions of spiritual seekers today suffer from this problem. Do they have a clue? Of course not. (For details, see my blog, Deeper Perception Made Practical, www.rose-rosetree.com/blog.)

Meanwhile be aware that channeling, mediumship, and the like can have the side effect of attracting stuck spirits. By the time a major spiritual addiction develops, it's a bit like the **Flypaper Effect.** Loads of flies, buzzing on the sticky trap, attract yet more flies.

Of course, woo-woo approaches can bring great comfort when a person feels stuck in life. Just keep in mind that the daily need to find Big Answers can be a major sign, all right. A whopping show-stopping sign that major STUFF needs to be healed!

No psychic reading, no matter how good, creates permanent healing of STUFF. Resourceful Healer, you can appreciate. From the perspective of energetic literacy, a reading is not a healing.

A reading is a reading. By contrast, you have just learned how to do a certain type of healing.

So consider yourself warned that, more c
ing in spirit-led sessions as a client will result
spirits. Conducting woo-woo session can place
What if such activities are a treasured par
ment? Just use your new healing skill to stay c
Beyond that, I think you will find it reall
plete skill set of Spiritual Cleansing and Protection. rsycmc coercion,
which you will learn to heal in Chapter 15, is another common side
effect of a spirit-guided lifestyle.

You can keep the good on your spiritual path, lose the rest.

Healing Stuck Spirits: TRUE TALES

There are two kinds of people. What, you've heard that before? I mean
two kinds of people as in:

- Those who naturally keep their auras closed, and
- Those who naturally keep their auras wide open.

For the first category, think of Jack Nicholson, John Wayne, your favorite sumo wrestler, Madonna, or Angelina Jolie. Some people naturally
keep their auras slammed shut. Fans may love them, partly, just for that
reason.

Do you, too, generally keep your aura closed? Congratulations.
That means you are unlikely to personally take on stuck spirits unless
you suffer from one of the problems we have discussed previously, such as
heavy drinking.

But what if you're like the majority of people? Then you naturally
keep your aura wide open. Which you can easily fix. Here's how.

HOW TO STRENGTHEN YOUR AURA

Your Power of Command makes it easy to train your aura to
strengthen its boundaries, thereby reducing how often you will
need to do a Stuck Spirits Healing. Use these words:

*"I close off my aura to all but my own Higher Self and those
beings of the highest vibration who are with me at the choice of
my soul."*

...rceful Healer, your entire mind-body-system works like a ...nt computer loaded with fabulous software. One of the programs installed by the manufacturer — just because you are human — is the program called "Close Off My Aura."

Use Your Power of Command to remind yourself of this truth. Automatically you will reboot that software program.

For this reboot to work well, I recommend that you say the above sentence aloud for specific amounts of time in the following sequence:

- 10 minutes a day for Week One
- 7 minutes a day for Week Two
- 5 minutes a day for Week Three
- And then as needed

Do you have time for this form of stuck spirit prevention? Sure. You can even multi-task with these words, saying them during a shower, when·driving your car, jazzing up your walk down the street, even while singing in the rain.

Worried about seeming weird in public? Open up your mobile phone and pretend to be talking to someone. (You are, actually. A rather important someone.)

So many ways to use Your Power of Command to train your aura! Pretty soon you will know the sentence by heart. Before then you can write it on some paper and carry this in your pocket.

Those 10 minutes or so need not be consecutive, either. The suggested daily minutes are a cumulative total for that particular day.

Should you exceed the recommended number of minutes, there will be no cosmic penalty.

What is the meaning of that "as needed" part at the end? After the first three weeks of rebooting, you will notice right away whenever you're near a place or person with a bunch o' stuck spirits. This sense of proximity will become a feeling or kind of intuitive reflex.

When you feel it, just use Your Power of Command to firmly close off your aura. Enjoy the effortless experience of having your aura nicely protected, posting the equivalent of a large "Keep out" sign. This will be visible to any stuck spirits in the vicinity.

Which locations are especially likely to have a bunch o' stuck spirits? They often congregate/shop in:

- Hospitals
- Liquor stores
- Bars
- Night clubs
- Gambling casinos
- Churches, mosques, spiritualist centers, etc.
- Your friendly neighborhood Department of Motor Vehicles
- Yet one more reason to stay out of jail!

So relax and appreciate that your life is about to become far less (astrally) overwhelming. You have officially completed a powerful skill set for Spiritual Cleansing and Protection.

Healing Stuck Spirits

Part One. EDUCATE AND RELEASE THE SPIRITS

Kwan Yin, please do this healing with me.

All you Dear Ones, along with Kwan Yin, I am speaking to each of you personally.

Hello and congratulations. This is a healing ceremony just for you. I am so happy to be able to help you.

Relax and receive this healing. The past is over. You are safe now and filled with the presence of God. (Repeat this paragraph as needed.)

You are being completely filled with Divine love. You deserve that because of who you are deep down.

You are being completely filled with Divine truth. So you can recognize who you are and where you are. Everything is okay. Before you were stuck. Now things are going to change for you in a wonderful way.

And now you are being completely filled with Divine light. It is all around you.

Notice! You are here on earth but no longer have a physical body of your own. Instead, you are in a body of light. You are still you. You will always be you. And if you need healing or forgiveness, God will give it to you right now.

Notice this, too. You are free from fear and pain and everything else about the earth's vibrations.

Now Kwan Yin is going to escort you personally to your next place of development, the place that is right for you. Go now, with joy and peace.

Part Two. PUT IN SOMETHING GOOD

I call on Kwan Yin to fill this place and me with Divine love, Divine truth, and Divine light.

I close off my aura to all but my own Higher Self and those beings of the highest vibration who are with me at the choice of my soul.

Part Three. REMOVE ALL ASTRAL TIES AND COMPLETE THE HEALING

I call on Kwan Yin to cut and dissolve all astral ties between every stuck spirit who has been involved in this healing and me.

Fill us all with love and light, power and peace — as much as each one of us is willing to receive.

Now this healing is done completely, and I'm grateful.

13. For a Free Vacation, Move out Thought Forms

What's the best part of winning an all-expense-paid trip to a fabulous resort in the Caribbean? Oh, do I have good news for you!

Sadly, the news is not that this book comes with free plane tickets and hotel vouchers. The good news concerns the best part of any vacation. By the time you have read this whole chapter, including "Explore the Results," you will receive that very same benefit. All without having to spend a nickel.

Ever notice? What is usually the deep down most refreshing part of any vacation? It's voluntarily exiting home, especially leaving behind all the toxic energies that you're so used to.

Yes, from an energy perspective, a vacation takes you away from most of your usual collection of negative thought forms.

Some are in you, of course. Limiting your speech and actions, thought forms crawl inside the most private parts of your brain.

However that's only the start. Plenty more thought forms are stuck at home: The people and pets, the clothing and furniture. Astral-level thought forms surround you, lodged inside everything you own.

Negative thought forms reside in the walls, deep as the foundation and electrical wires, surfacey as paint and wallpaper.

Can't thought forms be dumped out with the garbage? Some can. But most stay. For one thing, plenty of negative thought forms are stuck inside your trash can right now.

Not to alarm you, but negative thought forms are even planted firmly inside your favorite pair of blue jeans.

Don't get out your spray bottle of Woo-Woo Potion #909. But yes. Horrible thought forms could even be lurking underneath your bed.

Energetically the great thing with vacations is that you can leave all these thought forms behind. There's no place like home... with its distinctive assortment of chronic astral-level worries.

No wonder vacationing feels so good. It isn't just the gorgeous beach and the pina coladas.

Luckily, I'm about to teach you how to use Your Power of Command to remove negative thought forms at will, for which you will need neither spray bottles nor cocktails.

Negative Thought Form Healing: WHAT IT IS

Negative thought forms are astral debris created by repeated thoughts, words, or actions.

Back when you were a kid, maybe your mother said, "Stop making that face. It could freeze on you." Thought forms are the internal version, as in "Stop thinking that negative thought. It could turn into a nasty thought form."

Even if your motives for repeating that thought are quite lovely, energetic results of all that repeating could be simply awful. For instance, what if you keep blaming yourself for things that happen to others?

Sure, that could be done for noble reasons, e.g., You have a huge heart, plus you don't know yet about the perils of negative thought forms.

However noble your motivation, all that misplaced responsibility will create a big, ugly thought form that becomes your personal problem, e.g., "I'm sooooooo bad and guilty."

Alas, thought forms aren't only inflicted upon us by us. Friends and lovers can send them our way. Ex-spouses, for instance. For instance, "Pat is sooooooo bad and guilty."

Who else could have lodged nasty thought forms in you? Some of the culprits could be surprising.

Back in childhood, maybe you had someone in your life like Aunt Matilda. Supposedly, she was a sweet old thing. Really, she was a stealth nagger who could often be overheard complaining about you, saying, "The child is stupid and weak and never will amount to anything."

Psychologists know that insults from others, like negative self-talk, can lodge in your subconscious mind, harming self-esteem.

What most psychologists don't know yet is that the subconscious level more-or-less matches up with the psychic level. (Thank you, Dr. Freud, for making aura-talk acceptable to the scientific community!)

Repeated thoughts, whether positive or negative, take form on that psychic level, a.k.a. within your subconscious mind.

Exhibit A: Picture gigantic grey blobs called "Stupid," "Weak," and "I'll never amount to anything" (courtesy of Aunt Matilda). Well, that could be a picture of some of your negative thought forms right now.

Ouchers! What's a person to do?

For starters, from now on please avoid insulting yourself. Joking or not, any negative words you use repeatedly will create thought forms.

Second, Resourceful Healer, are you very bold? Then you might want to have a little talk with Aunt Matilda. Ask her to stop with the insults.

Third, conventional wisdom might tell you to start using affirmations to counter negative thought forms. But let's consider that last choice from the perspective of energetic literacy.

Have you ever tried **affirmations**? These are snippets of positive self-talk intended to clean up your subconscious mind. Ideally, they counteract all negative thought forms.

Perhaps you or someone you know routinely uses affirmations for this purpose. Maybe even Aunt Matilda, in her private moments, could be heard muttering, "I am kind to small children."

Nice! Maybe Matilda's well-meaning thought form looks as good as Harry Potter's silver stag patronus. (Although inwardly she lives at Azkaban.)

Affirmations do help to *counteract* negative thought forms. However, it's pretty tough to crank out enough affirmations to balance all the negative thought forms in your life, not unless you turn affirmation chanting into a full-time job.

Do you really want your life to be about "The battle of the affirmations"?

Will you ever create enough silver stag thought forms to outnumber all the stinky grey blobs?

Wait. Consider a different approach. Move out all your negative thought forms completely. Insert positive ones.

Quick, assemble your Five Cleaning Supplies and let's go!

Negative Thought Form Healing: NUTS AND BOLTS

Resourceful Healer, let's take the language of this healing apart piece by piece. As usual, words to speak aloud are italicized, followed by explanation.

I call on Omnipresent God to shine Your light of truth...

Enter someone new! So far our healings were co-created with a Divine Being in a body. For this healing, instead, I recommend teaming up with the impersonal aspect of God.

Whenever you use skills of Spiritual Cleansing and Protection, it is not required to visualize what is happening. All you need do is to use Your Power of Command plus your other four cleaning supplies. That will produce great results.

Visualizing might be helpful right now, however, for teaching purposes. So let's do some inner pretending in order to bring perspective on the difference between teaming up with Impersonal Everywhere God versus a Divine Being in a form like Jesus or Kwan Yin, any Ascended Master or Archangel. Because of the healings you have done so far, you have the perfect background to understand this.

So think about an astral tie, like a tiny string between you and Aunt Matilda. Lo and behold! As you speak the words of our Astral Tie Healing, here comes Archangel Gabriel.

Personally, I like to imagine Him with a large pair of scissors, golden, and having extremely sharp blades. If you prefer, you could think of Him as having extremely sharp fingers.

Whatever kind of cutting you visualize, isn't it easier having a Divine Being do the cleanup work for an astral tie? For contrast, imagine it happening with the impersonal aspect of God.

When I imagine that universal, omnipresent aspect of God, I think about the air, especially on a windy day, when air swirls in that cute mysterious way of the wind, halfway between visible and invisible.

Resourceful Healer, how do you imagine that God in everything?

Maybe names can help. There are wonderful names for the impersonal aspect of God, like The Universe or Divine Love or The Holy Spirit.

Whichever name you prefer, play with the thought of having That cut your astral ties. Okay. The scissors come out of where, exactly?

Not so easy to imagine, is it? Which is why I always invite an Ascended Master or Archangel to do an Astral Tie Healing.

Next, let's reminisce about doing the Stuck Spirits Healing. Imagine that you are convincing stuck spirits to go off somewhere new with Somebody New. Only that "Somebody" is too big to have a definable body. Such a hard sell!

So that's why you did that Stuck Spirits Healing along with a Divine Being, somebody with a definite, distinct body.

And not just any old body! For this healing to work effectively, you had to co-create with a someone having an etheric-level body. By definition, this is going to be impressive for a psychic-level spirit.

Still, it's not overwhelming when you start a Stuck Spirits Healing by bringing in a Divine Being. Just one person, after all. Just one pair of arms (unless, say, it's Saraswati). Not overwhelming.

Now how about a Negative Thought Form Healing? Here we have the opposite problem as healers. So many thought forms, spread so far apart, and nary a brain among them. More like dust, or old carpet stains, negative thought forms could be lodged in different strands of your hair, in your thumbs, in your cells.

Some of those thought forms could be located in parts of your kitchen stove that you've never thought about. And surely you shouldn't need to read the stove appliance manual before you can remove all those awful thought forms.

So complicated this cleanup job would be if you needed people in bodies, any kind of bodies, to do the work! Remember the part of "Fantasia" with The Sorcerer's Apprentice? Mickey Mouse keeps bringing in all the brooms with the buckets, yet the cleanup is never complete.

Enough imagining! I don't want you to get nauseated from the overwhelming nightmare of doing a Negative Thought Form Healing. It can be very pleasant. Really. Just use Your Power of Command to request the God In Everything to do the cleanup for you, nice and impersonal and totally efficient. Ah, relief!

Okay, let's finish the first sentence of our Negative Thought Form Healing, "*I call on Omnipresent God to shine Your light of truth...*

into all the negative thought forms in xyz.

All your xyz's can get so cluttered with thought forms. Seriously, this is like spiritual algebra, where you get to solve the equation. Which negative thought forms do you wish to heal?

- • All negative thought forms within me.
- • All negative thought forms in those mirrors on my bedroom ceiling.
- • My car, especially because I have never, ever had it detailed.
- • All the clothes I just bought dirt cheap.
- • Hey, how about every single thing that I own in this world?

Go ahead. Fill in the xyz blank with one of these or several or whatever else you prefer to name instead. (If only Algebra Class back in high school had options like these. Surely I would have scored a higher grade.)

Lift them out right now.

Remember, dissolving thousands of negative thought forms is a new kind of skill for Spiritual Cleansing and Protection. It's not like snipping an energy tie or coaxing a stuck spirit to leave. We need something sophisticated in a new way.

What's required is to separate the quick from the deadly, the saucepan from the burned bits of stew at the bottom.

After all, this healing aims to help you keep the good parts and move out the bad; to perform a non-wrecking kind of surgery within yourself and everything you own in this world; plus thoroughly scrub every place where you live and/or work.

If you're still into visualizing, just now, as an exercise for understanding how this healing works, here's an image: Imagine ugly little crumbs of stale energy popping right out of your head. You could even picture these negative thought forms like dandruff, except less alluring.

Also shine your light into the underlying concepts and patterns related to those thought forms. Move them all out, too.

What happens when you keep around a whole bunch o' negative thought forms? Over time, they produce grandchildren. Not literally. Don't be creeped out. I'm just using an analogy to approach this potentially revolting subject.

The principle is that, over time, pain produces deeper pain. Fear produces deeper fear. Remember how President FDR said, "The only thing we have to fear is fear itself"?

Such an understatement! Thought forms can produce fear about fear about fear about fear to the 10th power — horrid old thought forms, concepts, and patterns.

For a refreshing contrast, let's bring up our ridiculous, hypothetical example of Aunt Matilda calling you "Stupid." Once you got enough "Stupid" thought forms lodged into your subconscious mind, they could take on a life of their own.

Subconsciously, you could develop concepts like "Ways that life can become senselessly tragic for stupid mess-ups like me."

As those subconscious concepts proliferate, entire patterns can develop related to that original negative thought form. Like Rambo movie sequels, only more of them.

If negative thought forms were studied academically in universities, there could be entire departments and dissertations devoted to the grim spread of negative thought forms, concepts, and patterns. Only, please, let's not study them. Instead, let's simply ask God to remove them.

For all these thought forms, concepts, and patterns, move their vibrations faster and faster until they dissolve into pure light.

Just in case you were wondering, that is precisely how a Resourceful Healer scrubs away thought forms.

(Take three long, slow, deep breaths.)

The precise amount of extra breathing will be up to you, of course. Also, which nostril(s) to use.

Now, God, please create a complete new set of positive thought forms, concepts, and patterns to replace the ones that were moved away.

Resourceful Healer, remember our important Spiritual Fact of Life? "For every take-out in a healing, you must do a put-in."

Otherwise your healing won't last for long.

Why? Nature abhors a vacuum. Unless you purposely add something to fill the vacuum created, something similar to the old patterns will creep back in.

Good news for us healers, right? Now you have official permission to toss aside all modesty when doing the Negative Thought Form Healing. Do the think-big, luscious job of put-in. Choose wonderful thought forms to insert into your brain.

So many great possibilities! Use Your Power of Command to improvise at will, brilliantly naming whichever new thought forms you would like to install.

Would you prefer to keep things simple? Sure, you could just ask for "Whatever is equal and opposite and positive, compared to what just was dissolved." But if you have a hankering for any particular thought forms, now is a great time to name them.

- I'm smart.
- I'm powerful.
- I like myself.

Relax. You can't possibly ask for too many good things. God is helping, remember. And God is such a fan.

(Take three long, slow, deep breaths.)

As usual, the amount of celebratory breathing is totally up to you. It's respectful to take at least one deep breath, in honor of the dozens or hundreds of new thought forms being installed, plus all the new positive concepts and patterns.

It is done. It is done. It is done.

God doesn't need your help to figure out when something has been done. However you might.

Speak these words of closure for the benefit of your subconscious mind. In my experience, God has never expressed annoyance, not once, because I made this repetitious statement.

When using skills of Spiritual Cleansing and Protection, it does help us humans when we say things like "That's all, folks." Closure makes it easier for us to move on from a healing.

Which brings us to another vital Spiritual Fact of Life: For the best results after completing any spiritual or psychic technique, go back to being normal.

Normal is good for you. Much better than staying in the mentality of "I had better keep on healing and scrubbing and perfecting, world without end."

Fugeddaboutit. Much better to relax and resume being yourself in a normal way.

Thank you, God.

Resourceful Healer, as you become experienced at using the Negative Thought Form Healing, you will appreciate how much it can improve your life. So, yes, you might wish to express a little gratitude at the conclusion. No groveling is required, of course. Nor is it expected that you will offer God a tip.

Negative Thought Form Healing: EXPLORE THE RESULTS

Now let's go for experience with this Negative Thought Form Healing.

Move into a comfortable seated position. Check that your legs and arms aren't crossed. This will add to your clarity of experience.

Keep pen and paper handy for jotting down whatever you notice. When I ask you to write something down, open your eyes just long enough for some quick, sloppy writing. Afterwards, close your eyes.

Feeling ambitious? Record this exercise. Be sure to leave pauses between steps so that you can follow your own instructions.

Either way, here we go. Do the following steps, one at a time.

Part One. BEFORE PICTURE

1. Close your eyes. Take three Vibe-Raising Breaths and then return to normal breathing.
2. Notice how it feels *in your body* right now. Ask inside for some words to describe this. Open your eyes long enough to write those words quickly. Immediately close your eyes.
3. Take three Vibe-Raising Breaths and then return to normal breathing.
4. Notice how it feels to be you *emotionally* right now. Ask inside for some words to describe this. Open your eyes long enough to write those words quickly.
5. Close your eyes and tell yourself, "This technique is complete. Fine job!" Open your eyes.

Part Two. DO THE HEALING

Speak out the words of the Negative Thought Form Healing. (Find it in a summary box at the end of this chapter.) Use Your Power of Command to speak these words aloud.

Part Three. AFTER PICTURE

Now let's find out what has changed for you.

1. Close your eyes.. Take three Vibe-Raising Breaths and then return to normal breathing.
2. Notice how it feels *in your body*. Ask inside for some words to describe this. Open your eyes long enough to write those words quickly.
3. Close your eyes again. Take three Vibe-Raising Breaths and then return to normal breathing.
4. Notice how it feels to be you *emotionally* right now. Ask inside for some words to describe this. Open your eyes long enough to write those words quickly.
5. Close your eyes and say aloud something like this, "How convenient that I don't have to buy all new things. Yet I still have that free-as-air feeling. Excellent! And now this healing is done."
6. Open your eyes.

Part Four. ASSESS RESULTS

Read what you wrote before and after the Negative Thought Form Healing. How do they compare?

Give yourself credit, savoring this latest technique. Using Your Power of Command for a Negative Thought Form Healing is... positively... a big deal. Now you can vibrationally clean up everything that you own in this world. Make it all new.

Negative Thought Form Healing: HELPFUL USES

Negative thought forms reflect our deepest fears, our most painful experiences with the likes of Aunt Matilda. These bits of astral-level drek add up, too, like dust bunnies on a never-swept floor.

We've already discussed how our Negative Thought Form Healing can provide the equivalent of a free vacation. Beyond escaping from daily grunge, here are some uses I have come to adore.

Strengthen your free will.

It's tiring, dealing with negative thought forms. Sometimes you will take two Giant Steps forward, using free will. Afterwards old negative thought forms can drag you back several Baby Steps.

At which point many a spiritual seeker gives up. "It wasn't meant to be," we think.

Ridiculous! Next time you're tempted to give up on anything, stop and do a Negative Thought Form Healing. Then take a good, clear look at objective reality. Follow up with some regular old human-type problem solving. Keep moving forward, fuller speed ahead.

Look, I'm not going to claim that this type of astral debris is the *only* foe of free will. In fact, our skill set for Spiritual Cleansing and Protection contains future chapters that will add greatly to your effectiveness at accomplishing things in objective reality.

Resourceful Healer, it's a big deal that now you can explore do-it-yourself removal of negative thought forms. That empowers you to use your free will more vigorously than ever.

Why? You're refining your deep down sense of being YOU. The you who has free will.

After a fight.

Ever visit a friend and blech! It feels like you just missed a big fight. Something is hanging in the air, and it sure ain't used tissues on a clothesline.

Actually, I don't suggest that you heal your friend's negative thought forms. Also never, ever volunteer to energetically fix up bossy Aunt Matilda's apartment, much as the place could use it. Being your own healer is plenty; no need to start rescuing everybody on earth who suffers from blech-bad thought forms.

No, it's plenty to fix up your personal space. Speaking of which, what if the aforementioned fight happened in your home or your car?

Soon as you can, use Your Power of Command to execute the Negative Thought Form Healing. Afterwards folks who visit you won't have to tut-tut about all *your* fight vibes.

After a trauma of any kind.

It's a big deal when a date has stood you up or you just lost another job or Aunt Matilda just threatened to cut you out of her will (yet again).

Hey, your big trauma could be a pimple. You are the one who decides what qualifies as horrible.

The question isn't "Do you have the right to your pain?" but "What are you going to do about that trauma?" I recommend:

1. Begin with speech and action. Use your best skills for problem solving on the human level, so-called "reality."
2. Calm yourself down physically. Make yourself a nice cuppa iced tea — and then pour it over your head — or whatever else seems medically sound.
3. Reach out to friends for help.
4. Then be sure to do a Negative Thought Form Healing.

Otherwise, you will consciously get over the problem eventually. But horrid thought forms will remain in your clothing, cell phone, even that flat-screen TV and all your other prized possessions.

Energetically fumigate that healing salon.

Professional healers and volunteer healers, now hear this: Washing those sheets won't fix much. Any room where you do physical, emotional, or spiritual healing can become... a hotbed of psychic-level releasing.

Perhaps your professional training included some techniques to keep yourself clear between patients. Excellent! But what did you learn to do for your healing space, beyond basic hygiene and maybe some tips for cheerful décor? You know:

- Hide any cute but controversial ornaments like a pair of dice.
- Even if you think that shrunken head is inspiring, spare your more nervous clients.
- Don't leave overflowing recycle bins right next to the massage table.

Sure, all that is good so far as it goes. By now you can understand why healing spaces collect negative thought forms.

When you clean your office routinely, clients will like you more than ever. You will also like yourself more than ever, since less astral clutter means less confusion all around.

Professional healers — and here let's include all you Resourceful Healers who work in beauty salons — you are among the greatest heroes of this world. All that service to others ennobles your soul. Hey, it shouldn't also grime up your workplace.

Cleanse your wardrobe.

Let's talk wardrobe for a moment. Do you have any idea how energetically cluttered most clothing is?

For instance, what about your favorite pair of jeans? So what if you shopped hard to find them? And you launder those jeans so faithfully. Well, those jeans contain designer... thought forms.

Yes, these thought forms have been designed by every mood you have felt while wearing them, every single time you have worn that particular garment.

Thought forms also enter your clothing from all the conversations you have had in the room where your closet is. Closet doors won't keep out thought forms.

- Ever yell at the zipper when pulling on your jeans, freshly shrunk from the dryer? Uh-oh.
- Ever had sex in that bedroom? Ever have boring sex?
- Insomnia? (Not necessarily during the sex.)
- A loathsome flu where you felt so sure you were dying, you wrote a will?

Psychic-level energy travels quite nicely on its own, whether or not you have been paying attention.

And, not to be morbid — because you really can clean up all negative thought forms — consider where else your clothing has been.

How you love that nice, cheap dry cleaning franchise. Except, did you know? Crabby Crispin, an employee you will never meet, truly hates his job. Unintentionally he squirts in poison vibes while working the machines. (You know, like spot cleaner, only stickier.)

Oh, did you buy that new coat from a swanky boutique? How lovely! But unless you were the first one to try it on, negative thought forms may linger from plenty of previous shoppers. (Astrally we humans are oh-so-connected.)

Unbeknownst to you, could your nice warm winter coat have been made in a sweatshop? And maybe a high-class designer could have been involved in creating your garment, someone who hates all people of your gender and sexual persuasion. (Oops. What not to wear!)

Don't even begin to think about the provenance of clothes you bought used from that yard sale or thrift shop or eBay. (Great bargains all, except for the thought forms.)

Unless you live in Utopia, suffering humanity can junk up your clothing for sure. Every one of your prized possessions could become messed up quite thoroughly on the astral level.

Only don't worry. Just do the occasional Negative Thought Form Healing on "Everything I own."

Energetically detail your car.

Whatever you use for transportation, maybe it's time to clean that up, too.

Detailing cars is a fascinating art. If you've never had it done, I recommend it. Such a delightful illusion, having your car so thoroughly cleaned that even the dashboard smells like new. You can almost ignore the last 100,000 miles on your odometer.

How about the opposite extreme, cars that are brand new? Proud owners of the latest model can become so upset at the first ding or scratch. What don't they know?

Ha, you know. Or can guess. Cars absorb negative thought forms quite automatically. (Yes, you could think of this as an "automatic transmission.")

Have you ever suffered through the quaint experience of a traffic jam? How about that quickly forgotten — but very real — terror right after some crazy driver missed you by inches?

After a fender bender, your car will never be the same again energetically... Except, hold on. Brake lights on. Sure, you can pull over to the side of the road for three minutes and use Your Power of Command to do a Negative Thought Form Healing.

Go ahead, make Aunt Matilda wait those extra minutes before you go pick her up.

Negative Thought Form Healing: TRUE TALES

Skeptical that negative thought forms could really be a big deal? Consider what happened when I taught my first workshop at a lovely Buddhist center in Tokyo.

Soon as I entered, I could feel the devotion and caring with which this sacred place had been run for generations. The technical term is "lovely."

My sponsoring company, VOICE, had rented out a large room for the weekend so that I could teach an Aura Reading Workshop.

Before teaching anything, I routinely do a certain volunteer job. Can you guess what, Resourceful Healer? Even though this Meditation Center looked absolutely lovely, I immediately got to work healing stuck spirits and astral ties.

Frankly, I wouldn't even teach "Counting to Ten" in a room filled with stuck spirits. Harder than necessary!

Teaching the skill set of aura reading would definitely work easier when the room wasn't rife with astral debris. (As you may remember, any place where people do religious practices, like a big Buddhist Center, tends to attract stuck spirits.)

"Whew, glad I had time to do that!" I thought. It felt so much better in that room, having healed all the stuck spirits and astral ties. Soon I was sitting in front of about 40 Japanese students, all of us alert and eager. By my side was Yumi-san, a brilliant interpreter.

So why did I feel so bad?

You guessed it! But by the time that I figured out what was needed, the class had officially begun.

What to do? I announced an experiment:

"A certain kind of energy healing is needed to make this room more conducive to learning. To save time, I'll just say the words for that healing really fast in English, no translation. Still, the healing should work even if you don't understand the words.

"Students, please close your eyes and pay attention to how you feel. Maybe you will notice a change. Maybe you won't. I'd ask you later."

Quickly, I used My Power of Command to request a Negative Thought Form Healing. While I was at it, I facilitated removing all Negative Thought Forms from my students. But the real biggie was yanking out the most gigantic thought form I had ever encountered in my life. Associated with the Buddhist Center, the ginormous thought form went like this:

"You may study here all you wish. But never will you fully understand this teaching."

Hey, that's one way to keep students coming back for more! All it takes is one teacher with this attitude and, bam, there goes a whole Buddhist Center.

Maybe the regular students at the Center have learned somewhat more easily since that healing was accomplished. Maybe those expert

Dendo Center teachers have become more willing for old students to graduate and allow new students to eventually graduate too.

I wouldn't dream of taking such a survey. But I did ask the students in my class, "Did you notice a difference?"

Every hand went up. (And the workshop went great. Those students could fully understand *my* teaching, ha ha!)

Negative Thought Form Removal: TAKE THIS HEALING FURTHER

Name away. In other words, while God is dissolving the negative thought forms, you can name some of them.

Naming will add oomph to your personal experience. Or, if you're doing the healing for a client, you can impress that client.

How to find the biggies? Right after requesting that old thought forms be dissolved, close your eyes.

You're already going to be taking some deep breaths. Afterwards, ask inside, "What are some of the biggest negative thought forms being healed now?"

Open your eyes and say those names out loud. For example:

I call on Omnipresent God to shine Your light of truth into all the negative thought forms in me and my new apartment.

That includes feeling scared, suspicious, the idea that people are scary, only fools trust people, you never know when people will turn on you. Lift out those thought forms right now.

Then, when you get to the put-in part of the healing, do more naming. Depending on what you named before, say the opposite out loud.

When you do this, patterns or concepts may get mixed with the thought forms. That's okay. Your job is to blab away spontaneously, not to analyze.

Use words or complete sentences. Either way, Your Power of Command will work fine. Here are some examples.

REPLACING NEGATIVE THOUGHT FORMS

OLD VERSION	NEW VERSION
Scared.	Safe.
Suspicious.	Curious.
People are scary.	People are wonderful.
Only fools trust people. Begin any relationship with wariness. Test everyone.	It is smart to trust people unless given good reason to do otherwise.
You never know when people will turn on you.	My intuition helps me to do excellent reality checks on people, keeping me safe.
Other people have great intuition, not me.	My intuition about people is excellent.
I'm terrible at naming thought forms.	I'm talented at naming thought forms.

Negative Thought Form Healing

Part One: REMOVE THE NEGATIVE THOUGHT FORMS

I call on Omnipresent God to shine Your light of truth into all the negative thought forms in xyz. Lift them out right now.
(Optional: You can name a few of the most important thought forms being healed.)
Also shine your light into the underlying concepts and patterns related to those thought forms. Move them all out, too.
For all these thought forms, concepts, and patterns, move their vibrations faster and faster until they dissolve into pure light.
(Take three long, slow, deep breaths.)

Part Two: FILL UP WITH POSITIVE THOUGHT FORMS

Now, God, please create a complete new set of positive thought forms, concepts, and patterns to replace the ones that were moved away.
Make them equal and opposite to whatever has been removed.
(Optional: Use Your Power of Command to improvise at will, naming new thought forms you would like to put in place.)
(Take three long, slow, deep breaths.)
It is done. It is done. It is done. Thank you, God.

Part Three.
FREE YOURSELF
FROM WITHIN

14. Deepen
Your Power of Command

The following discussion is not for the spiritually timid, nor the avowed atheist. What if you consider yourself an atheist yet somehow you have felt drawn to Spiritual Cleansing and Protection? Maybe you're not as staunch an atheist as you used to be.

In this chapter we'll deepen Your Power of Command by exploring one of my all-time favorite techniques, "Command a Connection to the Divine." Use it to join up your consciousness with your choice of Divine Being.

Doing this is a must for Spiritual Cleansing and Protection. To some degree, you have been doing it already, like the Astral Tie Healing that started, "I ask Jesus to please do this healing with me."

Why request help from a Divine Being or, simply, God? By now you're very familiar with the facts of life concerning the three worlds. Quick recap:

- *Human life* is more interactive than most people think. Energetic literacy reveals two higher-vibrational levels that interact incessantly with our earth reality.

- Problems you're learning to heal, a.k.a. "STUFF," are stuck at the *astral* level.
- The skill set for Spiritual Cleansing and Protection is effective because you use Your Power of Command to team up with help from the *spiritual* level.
- You can heal STUFF from both outside directions: Help from a higher vibration (thanks to your choice of Divine Being) and also your own presence at a lower vibration (your way powerful human self).
- Making this kind of energy sandwich allows you to heal astral-level debris most efficiently. One way or the other, STUFF can't resist being healed from both directions simultaneously.

Now I want to help you understand, and fully own, an invaluable asset for spiritual healing, Command a Connection to the Divine.

Command a Connection to the Divine: WHAT IT IS

Command a Connection to the Divine is a deceptively simple technique. Using Your Power of Command in this way will intensify a quiet ongoing connection that already exists in a less vibrant form.

Basically, you will purposefully name one favorite choice of spiritual-level being. Bam! You're connected... in consciousness.

While the technique couldn't be easier, making your choice of Divine Being could seem a bit complicated initially. Although Command a Connection to the Divine isn't exactly what I would call "difficult," more is involved than simply saying "Hey, you" to some random term for Higher Power.

So let's explore further.

Being human, you carry a distinctive kind of vibrational energy. There is one — exactly one — physical form that out-pictures your essence as a soul (at any given time while you are enrolled here at Earth School).

Gaining or losing some weight might get you a big reaction from some folks you know. Spiritually, however, weight isn't as big a deal as it seems. Fat or thin, old or young, how many physical bodies do you get at any given time? One.

By contrast, God has many forms, going far beyond the need for a fat wardrobe plus a skinny wardrobe.

Each of God's forms intensifies a particular kind of vibrational energy at the spiritual level. The first step for sorting this out is to make a distinction between *impersonal* forms of God versus the forms that are *personal*.

Impersonal forms of God.

These formless forms of the Divine are in you, everyone, and everything. You might think of This as waves or particles.

Either way, It transmits a shining and sparkling energy, the ultimate sweetness and light, plus love and power. God's presence lives inside and outside everything on this planet, be it made of earth, air, fire, water, or ether.

Will you need a visual or emotional image in order to make contact with this impersonal aspect of God? Must you scrunch up your eyes and sing, "From sea to shining sea"?

Of course not. Impersonal God is here and everywhere now... whether or not you break a sweat trying to visualize It.

When using our technique for Command a Connection to the Divine, sometimes your purpose will be to connect with an impersonal form of God. Then you will just choose any appropriate name.

Having a simple intent to connect adds plenty of oomph, nothing fancier needed.

Plain vanilla "God" would work fine. Or you can choose something fancier, including:

- Almighty God
- Omnipresent God
- Holy Spirit
- The Universe
- Highest Power
- Spiritual Source
- The Lord of All
- Lord of Mercy
- The Source of Life, even
- The Energy Field Supporting All Life.

Names like these count as "impersonal" because they are synonyms for God as an abstract presence.

Personal forms of God.

By contrast, personal forms of God are beings in a body of etheric-quality light, with a particular uniqueness encoded in that name. Think "Physical form made of super-duper great light" or "Distinctive Identity."

Unless you have been living in a cave for all your last 10,000 lifetimes, you're already familiar with many of these vibrational forms. Only they have not necessarily been referred to as "A personal, not-worship-requiring, totally talk-to-able, form of God."

Instead you may have been informed of certain (questionable) worship requirements. Authority figures like priests and witch doctors may, supposedly, have been necessary to introduce you to God and instruct you in the oh-so-proper manners.

Meaning no disrespect to religion professionals, their services are optional. With Command a Connection to the Divine, you can easily summon help directly. Make your own toll-free call to the Divine Being of your choice.

I have yet to encounter a personal form of God who requires that people fall on their knees. That's merely human custom, obligatory only if it pleases the humans directly involved.

Dare I put this even more bluntly? In some cases, the rules and rites of religion mostly serve as very human attempts to control other humans. Such rules aren't necessary for connecting your consciousness to the Divine.

Human, Divine, Celestial...
What's the Big Deal?

Why do I call these personal aspects of God "Divine Beings"? That's my attempt to distinguish them from *celestial* beings, who exist at the psychic level.

Also, as you've probably noticed, Divine Beings are way different from *human* beings. The Ascended Masters may have had a human incarnation with the famous name, Archangels definitely not. Ever hear of these Guys and Gals?

- St. Francis
- Jesus
- Krishna
- Kwan Yin

- Buddha
- Isis
- Archangel Raphael
- Archangel Michael
- Archangel Gabriel

Who *doesn't* count as a Divine Being? You may have a hero or teacher or even guru who is tremendously important in your spiritual support system. You might consider that person to be absolutely enlightened, perfected in every way, like the words to that traditional American hymn:

Here she is, Miss America. Here she is, your ideal.

Only perhaps wearing more dignified clothing than is customary for the swimsuit competition.

Such a person might seem like the perfect choice when you Command a Connection to the Divine.

But nooooooo. Your amazing hero isn't dead. (Which is a good thing, right?) Therefore, consider that person your Inspiration, your Ideal, your Ultimate Human Being, your Cosmic Beauty Contest Winner. Just not an Ascended Master.

Don't bother trying to convince me otherwise. You would also have to persuade all beings on the entire astral realm. Because they sure can tell the difference.

Over 25 years of experience with Spiritual Cleansing and Protection have convinced me that psychic-level beings don't respond as strongly to an *Enlightened Human* as they do to a *no-longer human* (and, thus, 100% etheric) Ascended Master.

No disrespect is meant to your favorite teacher. Keep that sacred relationship. Lucky you to have it! If it's any consolation, you don't need much of a relationship with any Divine Beings to qualify for co-creator status. Simply use the technique in this chapter to request maximum help. Command a Connection to the Divine or use any technique you prefer to get you there. Just do it... with the following exception.

About celestial beings.

Why not Command a Connection to the Celestial instead?

Many of you Resourceful Healers are used to seeking guidance from your favorite psychic-level being. That could mean your Guardian Angel, your favorite Spirit Guide, or spirits of your ancestors.

Do this as much as you like, in general. Only please don't substitute "celestial" for "Divine" with our shiny new technique... or any other skill of Spiritual Cleansing and Protection. By definition, Command a Connection to the Divine requires that you connect at the spiritual level.

Why? Remember where all the goop is? The psychic level, of course. And when psychic-level STUFF is stuck within human auras, that level corresponds to a person's subconscious mind.

Well, how smart is it to team up with help at the psychic level when your goal is to *remove* something from the psychic level?

With all respect to those exquisite celestial beings, in some cases, they might live at a lower level than the junk you're attempting to hoist up and out.

No wonder some techniques for moving out a stuck spirit take weeks. Or longer. Or, possibly, forever. (Which is a polite way of saying, "However earnest, an astral-based attempt at healing may not produce any significant results at all.")

Whenever a healer needs a really long time to release routine astral debris, that's probably someone whose healing method relies on celestial beings rather than Divine Beings.

Admittedly certain jobs can be done better by celestial beings than Divine Beings, such as predicting your future. Besides psychics, some marvelously talented physical healers depend on help from psychic-level beings.

For instance, if you read carefully, toward the back pages of books like *Hands of Light* by Barbara Brennan or *Wheels of Light* by Rosalyn Bruyere, you will find discreet mention of receiving help from an astral-level guide. (Reminds me of the back pages of the menu at great Chinese restaurants, where one encounters the true native delicacies like "phoenix talons," a.k.a. chicken feet).

Some healers even operate what I call an "Astral-Level Ponzi Scheme." Not nearly such a good thing. But a topic for another day. (Feel free to research that topic at my blog, www.rose-rosetree.com/blog.) Meanwhile we've got big healing plans here, an upgrade to Your Power of Command. Up next, a rather personal question.

Do You Need a Calling?

How much of a calling must you feel before you can succeed at the technique for Command a Connection to the Divine?

Zero. Which is why this technique is called "Command" rather than "Beg."

Now it's true that some people have a special relationship with one particular Divine Being. Sometimes this happens after being very involved in a religion. Other times there is no obvious reason (in the context of this lifetime, anyway). The person just happens to feel a certain connection throughout life.

This was the case for Sarah, one of my clients who had The Virgin Mary living right in her heart chakra, abiding with her 24/7. During an aura reading, I noticed Mary's wonderful presence. So, of course, I mentioned it to my client.

Sarah burst into tears… of relief. Then she said, "I was born on Lady's Day in the Philippines. That's a day sacred to The Virgin Mary, and I always did feel connected to her. When I was still a girl, my family moved to America. We became Baptists. I wasn't supposed to have a relationship with Mary any more. But I did. It has been my secret joy."

Sure, one particular Divine Being can sometimes dwell within a person's aura. Most of us don't have this extra bit of good karma. We have other bits. No, I can't put on this page exactly which special bits you have. Sorry.

But I can tell you this. Regardless of whichever spiritual gifts and graces you have been given for this lifetime, your list can definitely grow to include an ability to Command a Connection to the Divine.

In addition, if you like, starting right now, you can start to develop a special relationship to Kwan Yin or Archangel Michael or some other Divine Being of your choice. For that, be consistent in choosing that particular Divine Being whenever you Command a Connection to the Divine.

Even special relationships of this nature can change, however. You might work closely with one Divine Being for decades. Then, somehow, your inner allegiance might shift. That isn't called "being fickle" but "exploring." Frankly, exploring, evolving, and learning are the universal purpose for all humans at Earth School.

Far as I know, Divine Beings don't mind this a bit, so why should you?

When facilitating sessions of Energy Spirituality, I will ask my client, "Who is your choice of Divine Being for your session today?"

Depending on that client's choice, I will Command a Connection to the Divine in that particular way.

This has given me a direct experience of every Divine Being on our list, plus many more.

Never, ever, has a Divine Being refused to come and help, full force. Quicker than you can say "Cocoa Puffs," that Divine Being arrives, beautifully dressed in His or Her body of quick-moving light.

If you ask for two by name, both will come. And...

- Will they ask for your membership card?
- Will they complain, "I haven't seen you in church lately"?
- Will they demand that you swear undying allegiance?
- Will they produce temple garments, such as Mormons wear?
- Will they whine, "I don't know. Last time you called on Buddha. I'm too jealous. Before I do any work for you, do you promise to buy me flowers?"

Of course not. Problems like these are human. Problems like these are refreshingly absent from the Divine Level, which is one of many reasons why Command a Connection to the Divine could easily become one of your favorite techniques, just as it has become a favorite for me.

Conflicts.

What if you have been doing the naughty thing of comparing yourself to others? Around now you might be feeling some pretty bad conflict over Command a Connection to the Divine.

For instance, you could be giving yourself a hard time over Mr. Cutie, a friend who is soooooo connected to Archangel Michael and brags about it constantly.

Well, how do you think he got such a close relationship? Mr. Cutie doesn't merely brag about Archangel Michael. He talks *about* "Mikey" to others, talks *to* Him when alone, pesters Him much of the day, salutes Him first thing in the morning, and signs off before falling asleep.

Anyone who communes this much with another person for an extended period of time will, eventually, develop some sort of relationship. Sure, that could include getting cozy with one's choice of Divine Being.

Some people evolve faster that way, devoted and faithful. Many of us evolve faster by playing the field. If you were to spend less time comparing yourself to the Mr. Cuties of the world, you could learn faster how *you* most enjoy Command a Connection to the Divine.

But maybe you're still worrying. Another possible conflict over Command a Connection to the Divine involves psychic coercion, a problem that you will learn how to heal in our next chapter.

Meanwhile, let's turn to a practical app. Perhaps someone you know is acting a bit pushy about which Divine Being should matter most to you. Say that your neighbor Mindie-Belle has only one favorite topic of conversation, "My relationship with Jesus."

While she putters around the garage doing weekend chores, Mindie-Belle wears tee shirts with slogans like "Jesus is my savior." Okay, whatever helps Mindie-Belle mow that lawn, right?

Unfortunately, Mindie-Belle also checks on you regularly, as in, "Hi, how are you today? If you don't mind my asking, what is your opinion of Jesus Christ?"

How I wish I were making up the example of neighbor Mindie-Belle. At least I changed her name here.

Regardless of what your neighbors or family members may think, you are the one who gets to choose how you will request help from Divine Beings.

Nothing is more personal than your choice ... whether for prayer now or at 3 a.m. after you wake up from a scary dream.

Fully owning the skill set of Spiritual Cleansing and Protection, you can unflinchingly Command a Connection to the Divine with your choice of Divine Being.

Fortunately you cannot really choose wrong.

Belly up to that bar.

Just in case you are still feeling squeamish about choosing a Divine Being in order to Command a Connection to the Divine, here is my favorite analogy. Imagine that it is Saturday night and you're in the mood for love. So you take yourself over to a really excellent night spot, The Lucky Bar.

Soon as you walk in, you see loads of great prospects. This crowd is friendly, kind, smart, well dressed.

Have you ever hit the jackpot! All the folks here are good looking. All happen to be your choice of gender and sexual orientation. And, hooray! Everyone seems to find you extremely attractive.

Guess how it works in The Lucky Bar? Choose any date you like. You can spend a fabulous night, being loved. You will never get pregnant, never get a disease. Only one catch: You must make the first move.

Beyond my analogy, that's how spiritual life works. The co-creating with the Divine part of life, anyway.

Every single Ascended Master and Archangel will come when called by name. Every single one will be delighted to work with you.

Why would that be? Imagine for a moment that you are a Divine Being. Only let's use a human example. Say that you have a really big talent, like being super smart at geometry.

Some cute kid down the block, smart little Sal, finds out about you. Sal asks if you would spend just a few minutes to help him. You do.

Afterwards, this tiny favor makes all the difference for whether or not Sal passes his mid-term and eventually goes on to college and has a fabulous life.

Wouldn't helping Sal for those 10 minutes make you feel great?

I think Divine Beings feel something comparable. Except they are not in limited human-level bodies with only a fixed amount of energy and time available. Besides having infinite resources (due to living at the Divine Level), Archangels and Ascended Masters really enjoy helping people who ask to co-create with them.

It wouldn't work nearly so well if the Divine Beings barged in, unasked, to teach us all that they thought we needed to learn.

Imagine that version! Poor Little Sal has no clue that he needs help. There he is, spacing out over his geometry homework. Suddenly You, a Divine Being, march into his room. You slam the geometry book closed and announce, "I am an archangel, sent by God. Now I will teach you how to use a protractor, young Sal, whether you like it or not."

The kid might start whimpering. I sure would. At 63, I consider myself pretty much a grownup. But if some random Divine Being arrived unannounced, and armed with a protractor no less, I just might start whimpering.

For this reason, or others best known to themselves, Divine Beings respond to invitations. No, they don't generally pop in like an overzealous neighbor, demanding to solve your math problems. Instead Divine Beings respond very lovingly whenever a human being Commands a Connection to the Divine.

This technique works equally well with God's impersonal forms. The Holy Spirit, for instance, responds beautifully. Every single time.

Could anything in all the Universe be more adorable than how Almighty God manages to stay in the background? It's as if the very air had pockets for hiding. Somehow the All in All plays in this manner until a person decides, "Enough already. I'm ready to win life's great game of Hide and Seek."

Want to start winning that game? For a small amount of time each day, use the technique to Command a Connection to the Divine.

Command a Connection to the Divine: NUTS AND BOLTS

As usual, we'll analyze each chunk of the healing piece by piece.

St. Germain,

Decide which Divine Being you choose to team up with so that, on this particular occasion, you can create healing.

Choose either an Ascended Master, an Archangel, or else just plain God.

For the "just plain God" option, use any of the impersonal names for God mentioned earlier in this chapter. Or choose some other name that you find more appealing. One of my clients, severely allergic to religion, always used the name "Lia."

In today's example, as you have probably guessed, I will use the name "St. Germain." This Ascended Master's claim to fame is a leadership role during the Age of Aquarius.

St. Germain, be here with me now in your body of light.

Every Ascended Master or Archangel has a distinctive physical form. Remember Princess Leia in her hologram in the Star Wars movie? Picture that, only made of light, more gorgeous, different hairstyle, maybe taller. Also, as it happens, real.

Alternatively, if you are doing this technique with the impersonal aspect of the Divine, speak out this variation for the first line of the technique:

Holy Spirit, be here with me now as a super-charged presence.

Divine presence can be very abstract — like water, which might appear in the form of a shapeless puddle or an even more shapeless wad of steam.

You might recognize that water more easily if it took a more solid form, like an ice cube, so why not ask for that? *Super-charged presence"* means a vibrational form that would be relatively solid for you to perceive, given your current stage of development.

If asked, The Holy Spirit (being rather smart) will instantly compute what this abstract form would be for you and appear in that way.

It's still going to be very, very subtle. Don't expect it to look like frozen cubes that can pop out of an ice cube tray.

(Close your eyes. Take one slow breath in, hold, breathe out, hold. Then return to normal breathing and open your eyes.)

Basic breathing keeps us alive, yet breathing can do so much more. Fascinating variations are used for sports and many performing arts, for different stages of sex, for all sorts of enjoyment. Why, breathing is even our Cleaning Supply #2!

With Command a Connection to the Divine, *you* spontaneously set the pace for one gorgeous, complete round of breathing. This bit of improv is just the thing for intensifying your unique experience, here and now, as you activate the presence of the Divine.

However you pace it, and whatever you happen to feel inwardly, this one slow breath will shift your consciousness towards being more present to God. Simultaneously God will be pulled into you.

Isn't it perfect that *you* would set the rhythm for this call and response?

You are, after all, using a technique to *Command* a Connection to the Divine: First, naming your choice of Divine Being. Then trumpeting your summons through silence and breath. Next you will sum up what has happened so far and extend it:

I awaken my Power of Command...

This is not a begging technique, notice?

So many religious and spiritual practices supply us with sweet ways to beg, to implore, to supplicate, to humble ourselves as God's children.

Supplications can have great beauty. However, many of us have been there, done that. With the utmost respect, we feel ready to become God's grownups. We're ready to co-create.

Your co-creative Power of Command has been given to you by God. If you wanted to be fancy, you could call it "My Divinely-Given Power of Command."

Acknowledging this does not mean you're greedily demanding too much, no more than if you were to say, "I'm going to notice that I have Divinely-Given Skin All Over My Body."

Yet, if it is to be effective for healing, your Divinely-Given Power of Command must *awaken* within you. This happens automatically after you say out loud, "I awaken my Power of Command."

Resourceful Healer, you're making the situation crystal clear, not only to God but to your own subconscious mind and Higher Self, even to your unconscious relationship with Earth's collective consciousness.

I awaken my Power of Command to co-create with you now.

Sacred power is a mighty force that requires a direction in order to flow. You have just initiated this flow, bringing purpose to God's infinite potential to flow as creative energy.

Together, let us bring more Divine light, love, and power into Earth.

Back in school, did you ever study Shakespeare? King Henry V could give the ultimate rousing speech about going into battle. Reading it, you'd be thinking, "Good show! Now they're really gonna fight."

Only then the actor playing King Henry stops and launches into more speechifying. And then more speechifying.

Living today, your cosmic battle cry can be short and sweet. No dawdling required.

Make your list of requests as long as you like. Only you don't have to. Because the basics you need will be covered if you just ask for life's three indispensables. Most humans do need all three:

- Divine light for evolving spiritual awareness on the path to Enlightenment.
- Divine love to make all relationships worthwhile.
- Divine power because human beings deserve that, too.
  Without power we're more like doormats.

(Close your eyes. Take one slow breath in, hold, breathe out, hold. Then return to normal breathing and open your eyes.)

Well done! You, the human, are present with your consciousness gently acknowledged.

Now your choice of Divine Being is present in that same way, too.

Together you have become a super-charged, effective, love-based healing team. This is the perfect basis for your facilitating techniques of Spiritual Cleansing and Protection.

Command a Connection to the Divine:
EXPLORE THE RESULTS

Now let's shift into the experience of doing this technique, in contrast to reading about it. Check out the following instructions once to get an overview. Then begin Technique Time.

Move into a comfortable seated position. Check that your legs and arms aren't crossed. That way, life force energy can move through you most freely, which will result in the clearest inner experience possible at this time.

Get pen and paper for jotting down whatever you notice. When I ask you to write something down, open your eyes just long enough to grab the paper and do some quick, sloppy writing. Afterwards, close your eyes. Ambitious? Then make a recording of your voice. Go through the sequence of parts and steps. Be sure to leave pauses in-between so that you can follow your own instructions.

Either way, here we go. Do the following steps, one at a time. (Open your eyes as needed to take a quick peek.)

Part One. BEFORE PICTURE

What fun, to compare relatively lively connections to God. Because you have always got something Great going.

1. Choose which Divine Being you choose to connect with, doing the Command a Connection to the Divine technique on this particular occasion. Write the name down for now.
2. Close your eyes. Take three Vibe-Raising Breaths and then return to normal breathing.
3. Notice how it feels *in your body* right now. Ask inside for some words to describe this. Open your eyes long enough to write those words quickly. Immediately close eyes.
4. Take three Vibe-Raising Breaths and then return to normal breathing. Notice how it feels to be you *emotionally* right now. Ask inside for some words to describe this. Open your eyes long enough to write those words quickly.
5. Close your eyes and think some conclusion language, e.g., "This Before Picture is done. Fine job! Top of the morning to me!" Open your eyes.

Part Two. DO THE TECHNIQUE

Every time you do this technique, choose *one* Ascended Master, Archangel, or the impersonal aspect of God. Be consistent in using that name when you do that particular healing, just for that particular time. Other times doing the same technique you could substitute the name of a different choice, again being consistent. Go ahead and do the technique in the Summary Box at the end of this chapter, using the name you just wrote down in Part One.

Then let's add something extra (not in the standard technique) as a teaching exercise. Say this out loud:

"St. Germain, please turn up the intensity of what it feels like for me being in Your presence. I want to experience your unique qualities as a form of the Divine. Please, make the experience as vivid as I can comfortably handle."

Excellent! You and the Divine Being of your choice are strongly connected in consciousness.

However, results from this technique tend to be subtle. You're not stuck like Siamese twins or some other obvious physical connection. So now is a great time to bring out your Cleaning Supplies and do an After Picture, as follows.

Part Three. AFTER PICTURE

Let's find out what has changed for you.

1. Close your eyes. Take three Vibe-Raising Breaths and then return to normal breathing. Notice how it feels *in your body.* Ask inside for some words to describe this.

2. Open your eyes long enough to write those words quickly.

3. Close your eyes again. Take three Vibe-Raising Breaths and then return to normal breathing. Notice how it feels to be you *emotionally* right now. Ask inside for some words to describe this. Open your eyes long enough to write those words quickly.

4. Close your eyes and tell yourself something to express a sense of completion, e.g., "One more unique but subtle experience has been given to me, one more magnificent co-creation with the Divine. Thanks, God." Open your eyes.

Part Four. ASSESS RESULTS

Resourceful Healer, compare what you wrote before and after Command a Connection to the Divine.

Did you notice results? At the very least, you have learned a new skill.

Doing this technique 20 different times, each time with a different choice of Divine Being, you will receive 20 different (subtle) experiences. But even if you always Command a Connection to the Divine with the exact same form of God, your experience may feel different every time.

If that happens, don't blame God. Your human mind-body-spirit is constantly evolving, which gives rise to different experiences.

That's a good thing. You get what you need. The more practice you have with Command a Connection to the Divine, the more you will appreciate that God always does a superb job.

Command a Connection to the Divine: HELPFUL USES

God is everywhere, whether you lift a finger or speak a word. So why bother with this commanding technique?

Upgrade all your other skills.

Command a Connection to the Divine is indispensable for best results from every technique of Spiritual Cleansing and Protection, including those you have already learned.

Now would be a fine time to revisit every technique you have learned so far, even the exercises related to your Cleaning Supplies. (Of course, all have been typeset in boxes to make them easy to find.)

At the very start, add Command a Connection to the Divine. Then continue with the technique as described. Enjoy bigger, better results.

For the very best results, make this technique part of your Preparation Process whenever using your skills of Spiritual Cleansing and Protection. That will bring you greater effectiveness (and more interesting inner experiences) for the Astral Tie Healing, Healing Stuck Spirits, and Negative Thought Form Healing. Also, of course, command That connection before you learn the rest of the skills in Part Three.

Guidance.

When you must make an *important* decision, how can you access the clearest wisdom possible?

This technique is your ticket. Just don't get into the habit of using Command a Connection to the Divine for making the *minor decisions of everyday life*. Divine co-creation makes a poor substitute for good old-fashioned human use of free will.

For everyday choices you are fully equipped with a mind, a heart, and direct feedback from your body. Spiritually this helps you evolve. Now, it's very sweet when people seek constant superior guidance.

- What would Jesus do?
- Would it be okay with my spirit guide if I buy Cocoa Puffs from the supermarket?
- When I go to the toilet, should I only do #1 or this time could I be allowed to do a #2?

Asking Divine or celestial beings to make everyday choices for you — that can become ridiculous. Even a way to outsource your life.

Ironically, too much of this outsourcing, however well meant, can slow down a person's spiritual evolution. To evolve here on earth, we grownup humans are authorized to make choices all on our own.

There's even a technical term for doing that. **Self-authority** means making decisions for yourself, decisions based on what seems important to you,

This universal, sacred gift means that you can recognize your own truth. Internal validation, yum! It's far different from having other people tell you what you should feel, think, want, or believe.

The opposite would be depending upon "external validation," which slows down spiritual growth. All your Five Cleaning Supplies are forms of internal validation.

Protecting your precious self-authority is my big personal agenda for Spiritual Cleansing and Protection. The results you discover, the techniques you use, everything about this skill set is designed to bolster your spontaneous self-acceptance. Incidentally, self-authority is also a requirement for developing full energetic literacy.

What if you are wrestling with an especially tricky, important choice? That would be an exception to the rule of depending totally on your own self-authority.

When life becomes extra tricky, such as the need to make a really vital decision, why not seek advice from the wisest humans you know? It is also perfectly reasonable to seek higher wisdom, as with the following technique.

A SIMPLE TECHNIQUE FOR REQUESTING GUIDANCE

Here is one way to proceed that will honor your own spiritual self-authority. For best results doing this, begin with your technique to Command a Connection to the Divine. Follow it up with a specific request for guidance. For instance:

Within 24 hours, St. Germain, please help me to make a wise choice about whether to buy the new house on Mulberry Street.

That simple!

Your request will be noted. In 999 cases out of 1,000, your answer will come in very human ways. This does not make it less of a miracle.

What does "Human ways" mean? Not big flashy signs and synchronicities. Instead:

- You will have a productive, useful, human-type thought that decides you.
- Or maybe some new information will come your way. After doing a reality check on that information, you decide.
- Or a surge of emotions might help you to make up your mind. After all the facts you've accumulated, suddenly one choice feels much better than the other.

Note that such experiences would not feel as though you're being taken over by an all-knowing space alien.

The point of evolving during a human lifetime is, surely, not to swap your emotions (or any other part of your precious self) for a takeover by anyone else, however admired.

A Divinely-inspired answer to your request will, most likely, seem like your own idea. Inspiration can dawn while you do perfectly human things, such as:

- Make a written list of pro's and con's about your choice.
- Use skills of energetic literacy to do "Soul Thrill Research."
- Write down your personal goals for the next full year, which then provides a context for the choice you are making now.

Human activities like the following will let in more spiritual light than ever... when you Command a Connection to the Divine.

Facilitate bigger healing for yourself or others.

What if you do healing work, either professionally or as a volunteer? Healers need the separate skill set of Spiritual Cleansing and Protection. It isn't included in the study of Reiki, Quantum Healing, Energy Medicine, Healing Touch, acupuncture, etc.

Mostly you will need Spiritual Cleansing and Protection to help you to clean up after a session of healing, making sure that you don't carry forward astral ties, negative thought forms, or stuck spirits.

However, you can really sweeten up your healing practice by doing something in advance, our technique for Command a Connection to the Divine. That will make it a God-flavored healing session, bringing extra power.

For discretion, it's appropriate to Command a Connection to the Divine in private, before you begin speaking to your client.

When you do self-healing in private, how much easier you will find it to be discreet!

Remember, all you need do is one quick sequence, the technique exactly as taught here.

No, you do not have to constantly crane your neck during the entire healing session that follows, sneaking a peek at St. Germain's outfit that day... as if playing a perpetual game of "Where's Waldo?"

No need to try extra hard to feel or see Divine energy; no need to try hard in any way!

Resourceful Healer, your skills of Spiritual Cleansing and Protection are meant to make your life simpler, more rewarding. And easier, not more complicated.

For best results, simply Command a Connection to the Divine. Then move on. Pay attention to the healing work itself.

Extra oomph.

Might you be preparing yourself to slalom in the Olympics? Any special endeavor, really, can use the benefit of preparing in a way that adds spiritual oomph.

Well, just Command a Connection to the Divine. Then, whatever the task where you'd like extra oomph, know that you're co-creating. Do your best as a human, knowing that you are supported to the max from the Divine level.

Command a Connection to the Divine: TRUE TALES

Once I did a workshop where I taught Command a Connection to the Divine. Taylor, a strikingly handsome young man with big eyes, raised his hand. He said, "I'm scared to ask God to help. I might get The Devil instead."

We talked. Taylor's aura was horribly clogged with STUFF. Had he been a teddy bear, the guy might have split a seam. His aura included every kind of STUFF that you are learning to heal in our skill set for Spiritual Cleansing and Protection; no wonder he had felt drawn to that workshop.

Fidgeting in his seat, Taylor wasn't exactly optimistic. All his previous attempts at self-improvement had backfired. Now the poor kid was scared to request a connection to God. Just Taylor's luck, he would probably get some scary guy with bad breath and horns.

After I talked with Taylor a bit, he calmed down and settled on a choice for the moment, Archangel Michael. It reassured my student to understand that he didn't have to *believe* he could attract help from a Divine Being. All he needed to do was use the basic steps to Command a Connection to the Divine.

What happened? Taylor's first experiment didn't strike him dead. Afterwards he felt calmer, actually. Soon he found it easy to Command a Connection to the Divine. Results began flowing in.

Beyond that day's happy ending, Taylor's story of growth continued. After three weekend workshops in a row, we held a graduation ceremony. Taylor told the group that he used to fight with his daughter every day. Somehow, fights hadn't come up for.... how long had it been now, a week?

And maybe Taylor used to have a drinking problem. Only he hadn't been drunk for, how long? Maybe a couple of weeks?

Resourceful Healer, simply having less STUFF in your aura 24/7 can make a huge difference to a person's quality of life. When destructive patterns simply fall away, with no struggle, isn't that the best?

Taylor told the group that now he felt hopeful about healing his other problems. Already, I could tell, he had improved his resourcefulness by about a zillion percent. And no longer did he fear connecting powerfully to a Divine Being.

Command a Connection to the Divine: TAKE THIS HEALING FURTHER

Now that you know how to Command a Connection to the Divine at will, maybe you're wondering if it could really be that simple. Let me offer some historical perspective.

Here is a hypothetical version of what our Stone Age ancestor Fred Flintstone had to do if he wished to connect with God:

- Fred felt like part of a tribe, not so much a distinct individual whose thoughts and feelings mattered. In fact, Fred grunted more than you probably do.
- Fred had no idea about how to seek a Divine connection on his own. So he would go onto Facebook and ask others in the tribe to help him. Okay, really, he would approach the tribal leader.
- If approval was given, that leader would summon everyone else in the tribe.
- Together, the tribe would hunt down a large animal. Kill it. Roast it on a spit. Then offer it up for God to eat.
- Other rituals besides the burnt offering would be observed. Perhaps everyone in the tribe would fast all day. Or get drunk. Or dance until they fell down exhausted. Maybe an orgy by mutual consent?
- All this summoning would be beautiful in every way. I hope.
- After all this was over, Fred Flintstone could be present while the tribal leader officially connected everyone present to God.

Humankind has evolved a great deal since then. Today, we can still ask for the support of a group. Many people do this by belonging to an organized religion. Which can be beautiful in every way, definitely.

However, living today, people can also make the relationship a two-some, where one human being connects with one Divine Being. Where the human gets to choose which version of Divine Being.

The catch.

What's the catch with Command a Connection to the Divine? The vividness of your experience will depend upon the state of your mind-body-spirit system. So here are seven important choices to deepen that experience:

1. Is your priority to grow as a person, not just get an instant fix?
2. Is your sincere motivation to help someone — whether others or yourself? (Note that a "sincere motivation" is different from being just plain desperate.)
3. Does your typical day include some kind of spiritual practice? ("Spiritual practice" means something that produces results, a practice that works for you currently. That doesn't need to be time consuming. Currently my daily routine takes 15 minutes.)
4. Have you permanently released most major STUFF from your aura? One simple way to tell is this. During your waking hours, do you function mostly in present time? (Often replaying the past or worrying about the future indicates that large amounts of STUFF are still cluttering up one's aura.)
5. Do you refrain from smoking weed? (Marijuana dumps huge quantities of STUFF into a person's energy field.)
6. Do you eat food that agrees with your own personal body? (This might change over time. But please don't assume that being a vegan or raw foodie is the ideal for a spiritual seeker. The most important ideal, surely, is to give your physical body the kind of food it prefers.)
7. Do you get enough sleep? (If you manage this on a regular basis, you will definitely improve the clarity of all Five Cleaning Supplies for Spiritual Cleansing and Protection.)

All these choices can help you more easily hear the still, small voice within. In which case you know that a "vivid" experience of the Divine can also be subtle.

But no worries. Even if vivid and subtle don't make sense to you in the same sentence yet, even if your role model is Fred Flintstone at his silliest; even if your diet stinks, and basically you wouldn't recognize a subtle, spiritual experience if it hit you over the head, guess what?

Any Divine Being you request will connect with you anyway! Every single time you request it!

Therefore, you will always succeed whenever you do the technique for Command a Connection to the Divine. Whether or not your inward experience is crystal clear (yet), results will follow.

After you Command a Connection to the Divine and ask for help, technically that conversation could be called "Prayer" or even "Powerful prayer."

It's amazing how often people do routine prayer without stopping to make contact with God by using a technique like Command a Connection to the Divine.

This is like leaving your message on somebody's voice mail. Only, oops, you never dialed that call in the first place.

Or maybe you never even listened for a dial tone on your land line, never checked that your cell phone had juice...

Well, hello! You're empowered now. You could even consider yourself "initiated," if that word has meaning for you.

What else is needed for you to enjoy using Your Power of Command productively for the rest of your life?

While awake, keep your regular human wits about you. And once a day, or more, enjoy using the life skill called "Command a Connection to the Divine."

Command a Connection to the Divine

Every time you do this technique, choose one Ascended Master, Archangel, or name for the impersonal Aspect of God.

For a personal form of the Divine, say, " *St. Germain, be here with me now in your body of light.*"

For the impersonal form of the Divine, say, "*Holy Spirit, be here with me now as a super-charged presence.*"

(Close your eyes. Take one slow breath in, hold, breathe out, hold. Then return to normal breathing and open your eyes.)
I awaken my Power of Command to co-create with you now. Together, let us bring more Divine light, love, and power into Earth.
(Close your eyes. Take one slow breath in, hold, breathe out, hold. Then return to normal breathing and open your eyes.)

15. When Bullies "Should" on You, Defend Yourself Deftly

Do bullies strike you as loveable? Actually, they might.

Here at Earth School, bullies don't come properly labeled. Some of the sweetest, kindest, and best-intentioned people you will ever meet… are bullies at the psychic level. This chapter will help you to keep on loving them. And love them without suffering from what is technically known as "psychic coercion."

Releasing Psychic Coercion: WHAT IT IS

On the level of your aura, **psychic coercion** shows up as blobs of gray, life-deadening energy. Some blobs are small, others huge. All those blobs make it harder to know your own mind, your own heart.

The more psychic coercion in your aura, the harder it will be, trying to make contact with the inner you.

Can you recognize your true reactions, desires, opinions, needs? It can be so hard to tell. Guess which person in the following dialogue is, unknowingly, in urgent need of Releasing Psychic Coercion?

Q. **Honey, what do you want for your birthday?**
A. I don't know. What do think I should want?

Q. **Where would you like to go out for dinner tonight?**
A. I don't know. Where would you like to go?

Q. Wow! I thought that lobster dinner was great. How about you?

A. Did I like it? Did I taste it? Was I really here?

Hint: The psychically coerced person's name does not begin with "Q." I like to think of her as "Bambi."

Now, away from the theoretical questions into something more personal: Could *you* have buckets of psychic coercion and not know it?

Lacking any concept whatever about Mystery Ailment, how could Bambi tell if psychic coercion has been limiting her?

Unfortunately, it can be hard to tell. Especially because Bambi is missing something very basic: Simple human self-authority.

That indestructible human faculty can get pretty gummed up by loads of psychic coercion. Ironic, isn't it, how those who suffer from psychic coercion can be the last ones to know?

Bambi's best friend could be crying, begging in kneel-down position, and shrieking at the top of her voice, "Sweetie Pie, please, please, please get a life."

Meanwhile, I can just imagine poor Bambi twisting around, trying to see which poor confused person is being addressed. Because obviously it couldn't be perfect little Bambi.

Resourceful Healer, you can tell when you are being sent psychic coercion. When you fully own skills for Spiritual Cleansing and Protection, psychic coercion shows as plainly as that two-holed, bulb-tipped, sticky-out thing on Bambi's face. (Whatever that's for.)

Just to remind you, unless you are skilled at this particular skill set, you might otherwise miss the problem. You could be a superb acupuncturist, a graduate of the super-prestigious Barbara Brennan School of Healing, plus possess impeccable credentials as a world-class psychiatrist.

You could be a fabulous aura reader, too, yet never notice psychic coercion — or, at least, attribute it properly. Maybe that's just as well, because it wouldn't be terribly helpful to tell a client:

"No wonder you feel so bad. Your aura really stinks from all those globs and blobs of psychic coercion. Plus, did you notice you're suffering from a truly hideous collection of negative thought forms?

"And speaking of awful, disgusting things, get a load of all those stuck spirits.

"Sad! What, you didn't know? Yeah, you have this huge cheering squad of stuck spirits, hunkered down in your aura.

"Congratulations. Now you know. Of course, I don't know how to heal any of this. But isn't it comforting that now you know exactly why you feel so bad?"

No way, Resourceful Healer! In our case, I'm only describing this latest, little-known kind of STUFF in auras because immediately afterwards I am going to teach you exactly how to heal it. Totally!

How Psychic Coercion Lodges in Auras

Of course, it's important to know how psychic coercion gets stuck in the first place. The answer is as simple as $1 + 1 = 2$.

In order for psychic coercion to lodge within, there must be both 1 sender + 1 receiver.

A pretty simple equation, isn't it? (Though not necessarily a *pretty* equation.)

Let's focus first on who qualifies as **a sender of psychic coercion**. Who, exactly, has the mighty power to do this? Must she graduate from the creepy Slytherin House at Hogwarts?

Almost everyone can send out psychic coercion. Alas, almost everyone does… at least before knowing better. Because it is pathetically easy to send someone psychic coercion. All you need do is to tell someone twice, "You should do XYZ." As in:

- "You should cut your hair." And then, the next day, "Really, you need to cut your hair."
- "You should take the bus to work." And then, the next day, "What's wrong with you? Don't you understand? You are supposed to take that bus, not your car."
- "You should have two children." And then, the next day, "When are you going to get started on that family of my grandchildren? I expect twins, remember."
- "Congratulations on those triplets. This is how you should raise them." And then, the next day, "Whaddaya mean, you have ideas of your own? I'm telling you. Your ideas of parenting are so lame. I'll help you. Let's start with whether you should breastfeed or bottle feed."

People are funny. People have opinions. From an energy perspective, all those people have a right to each and every opinion. People even have the right to bombard you with their opinions, uttering each revolting word a short distance from your face.

Once.

Repetitions constitute sending out psychic coercion. Common patterns of sending coercion include the following.

Unsolicited advice.

When such advice is given for the first time, that's fine. Say that loveable Uncle Snuffy grins at you and says, "You've got to learn trout fishing. It's the greatest thrill in all the world."

No problem. That's not sending. Psychic coercion begins with the repetitions. Such as Uncle Snuffy's friendly reminder 10 minutes later, "Really, those trout are waiting for you. Catching them will be the thrill of a lifetime." (For you, presumably, not for them.)

Yes, it counts as "sending" long before the thousandth time, when you want to pick up a fishing pole... and use it to clobber Uncle Snuffy.

Starting right from his second invitation, be it a joke, demand, text, tweet, or email, any such request from Uncle Snuffy would count as sending psychic coercion.

Even a little too much friendly advice, however well meant, constitutes "sending." So, yes, I mean *you* when I suggest that Uncle Snuffy may not be the only one in the family who sends psychic coercion. Up until now, you may have been a bit of a sender, too.

Although our emphasis here is on helping you to deal with those who are sending psychic coercion your way, consider the possibility that you may have been sending out your share.

Unintentionally, of course. Little did you realize how you were transmitting toxic vibes that, once internalized into somebody's aura, would turn into gross, greyish blobs of Oobleck-like psychic coercion.

From now on, when you want someone else to change his life, how about this? Make your request clearly and directly. Just once. Then lay off.

Exceptions include raising a child up to the age of 18, taking care of a dependent who can't think straight, and also doing your job.

For instance, if you teach school, you do have the right to say regularly, "Do your homework." That's different from commanding, "You should all wear baseball caps for the New York Mets, my favorite baseball team. And if you want a really good grade, you had better buy me chocolates."

Nagging.

Darn, and you loved being nagged so much. Can you bear to give appropriate feedback to the nagger? "Stop it. You told me already. Now you're just nagging."

If only nagging were merely annoying. It sends psychic coercion, even if intended as the very friendliest sort of nagging.

Really, how friendly is it for someone to tell you on a daily basis, "Would you please, please, fold your bathroom towel my way?"

Sure, it's only routine, everyday nagging. (Unless it comes from the towel itself, in which case I guess it would count as both a miracle and a really good excuse to telephone Martha Stewart.) Everyday nagging still sends out psychic coercion.

Especially beware the nagging that starts, "You should." As in "You should know by now there is a right way to fold towels and then there is your way. You should do my kind of precision origami folding every time, dagnabit."

Shoulding.

In English, the word "should" always raises a red flag that somebody is sending psychic coercion. "Should" according to who, Uncle Snuffy? Queen Victoria?

Even one sentence containing a "should" means sending psychic coercion. Similar coercive terms are:

- **Supposed to.** As in, "You're supposed to smile when you see me."
- **Must.** As in, "You really must give me this loan."
- **Meant to.** As in, "I am meant to receive money, and you are the one who is meant to give it to me."
- **Duty.** As in, "It is your duty to give me the $10,000 check."

Gossip.

Like nagging and shoulding, gossip is an art form invented by the powerless.

Sure, it can seem like an innocent form of recreation. Maybe it is. Except for all the times that the discussion focuses on what another person should and must do. And why? Allegedly because of being supposed to and having a duty.

Recognize, this is yet more transmission of psychic coercion. Yes, all those earnest discussions about how Lady Gaga should refrigerate her meat dress, etc., do send her psychic coercion.

Pity celebrities who are should-ed by millions. Psychic coercion can, and does, reach them. They *might want to* learn techniques for Spiritual Cleansing and Protection.

Note that I did not say, "They *should* learn techniques for... anything."

Back at your own movie studio, a.k.a. talking on your cell while you load the dinner dishes, it counts as sending if you tell your best friend, "I was just visiting Uncle Snuffy. He really should stop eating all those carbs."

Tell the guy once. To his face. Afterwards you might want to lay off.

As for you, I don't want to alarm you but do you think that, possibly, some of the Uncle Snuffys in your life might occasionally gossip about you? All those fun, secret chit-chats would qualify as "sending psychic coercion," you know.

Happily, releasing psychic coercion does NOT require that you do detective work to track down every sender and take away his fishing pole.

Toxic prayer.

At this very minute, people somewhere are praying. People may also be singing "Kumbaya." Nothing wrong with that... unless they are, basically, using God as a way to boss other people around.

Toxic prayer sends psychic coercion, nicely gift-wrapped with sanctimony. Examples would be:

- "Lord, make them all believe in You." ("Of course, Lord, that means make everyone believe in exactly the same version of You that I believe in.")
- "Dear God, in your great love and compassion, help all Americans to vote for my minister's choice for president."
- "Beloved God of sweetness and light, we know what people should believe about homosexuality, marriage, etc. Smack all confused people upside the head. Or smite them. Do something extreme because they need it, being such idiots."

What, you think prayers like these are ridiculous? Mere laughter doesn't cancel out all the sending being done in your very own neighborhood.

Even if the pious senders don't mention you by name (or know you, personally, at all) that doesn't stop their coercive messages from reaching you.

Knowing about this, please, don't seriously consider fighting back with a prayer. Tempting though it would be to fling yourself down on your knees, clasp your hands, and yell, "God, you just have to make all the pushy, coercive people in this world shut their big yapping mouths."

Advertising.

Sneaky coercion. That's what much advertising is, these days.

Not to alarm you, but forget the idea that the hills are alive with the sound of music. That's just the close-up. In the background, plenty more sounds are echoing 'round those hills. They come from TV and TV crawl, radio, newspapers, magazines, Internet pop-ups, and spam.

Plenty of psychic coercion is sent to you daily through advertising alone.

Internalizing Psychic Coercion

Now you know just how much psychic coercion you have been dealing with. Don't let all that frighten you.

Resourceful Healer, we can make an analogy to germs. They're just about everywhere, too. Germs can definitely make some people sick. But if you have a healthy immune system, germs won't necessarily make *you* sick.

Sure, there will always be plenty of psychic coercion directed toward you. So what? All that matters, for the sake of your own mental health (and healthy aura), is whether or not you take the STUFF in.

That, in turn, depends on whether or not you currently have an active **vulnerability pattern**.

A vulnerability pattern is a very personal way of interpreting problems. It goes deeper than thought forms or their underlying concepts and patterns. It's more a life theme, something that matters to you in a very intimate way. Here are some examples of vulnerability patterns:

- I must make everyone like me.
- Until everyone else is happy, I can't be happy.

- Jesus took on the pain of others. Because I love Jesus, I must do the same.
- If other people knew what I was really like, they wouldn't respect me. So I must constantly live up to my image.

Rational? No. Reasonable? Hardly. But vulnerability patterns go their merry way regardless.

Would you be able to quickly tell if you've got one and, if so, what it is? Not likely.

Vulnerability patterns exist, like other STUFF in auras, within the subconscious mind.

Just one subtle, subconscious vulnerability pattern per person — that's all it takes for psychic coercion to stick to that person's aura.

But how would vulnerability patterns cause a person to take on psychic coercion?

At Earth School, everyone deals with difficulties, disappointments, and delays. Sure, these could count as "your karma" but they could equally be considered "no more personal than gravity."

No matter what you do now, regardless of what you have done in the past, there are bound to be certain Difficulties, Disappointments and Delays.

You knew that life here on earth was 3-D, right? D-d-d-duh!

So what happens when you, someone with a vulnerability pattern, bumps into difficulties, disappointments, and delays?

Picture a little trap door (and I do mean "trap" door) in the back of your head. This symbolizes a vulnerability pattern in your subconscious mind.

Now, let's say that some annoying 3-D thing happens, like when you realize that you just locked yourself out of your apartment. Again.

For one tiny shard of time, before you figure out a solution, it's as though your little trap door opens up. Soon it will close. Briefly, subconsciously, you have a moment of vulnerability. What will enter before that trap door closes again?

Hint: It has been all around you, on the level of energy... every random bit of psychic coercion that has been sent to you recently. Ta ddda!

There it is, hovering around. You could picture it like blobby thought forms or TV waves or radio waves or nasty looking graphics of any kind. Or you could get an idea by imagining the subconscious-level conversation that ensues:

"I'm so angry at myself now. How can I make everyone like me when I do stupid things like this? But maybe if I buy this soap I'll smell so kissing sweet that everybody will like me more. And maybe if I go fishing with Uncle Snuffy, that will smarten me up. And maybe.... And maybe.... And maybe...."

Bam! Much faster than your conscious mind could register this vulnerability-charged thinking, a random bunch of psychic coercion pops in through the trap door, sticking inside your aura.

Spiritual Cleansing and Protection to the rescue! When you do the basic technique for Releasing Psychic Coercion, all those bits of stuck energy will be removed.

For even better results long-term, note the extra ideas at the end of this chapter for healing vulnerability patterns.

Releasing Psychic Coercion: NUTS AND BOLTS

Have you begun to appreciate how helpful it will be to master the skills for Releasing Psychic Coercion? I can think of only one bad part. This technique takes the longest of anything else in our skill set.

Mind you, none of the healing will be hard to do. In fact, most parts of this healing simply adapt skills that you have already mastered.

Besides, doesn't it make sense that it would take a bit of work, removing something as pervasive as psychic coercion?

So don't let the length of this healing discourage you. Personally, I frame it as a triumph over very complicated 3-DDD Earth School grunge.

Part One of the healing is done with help from the impersonal aspect of God, here called "The Holy Spirit." For the rest, you will team up with a personal aspect of God. I'll bring in Krishna.

Krishna, often pictured with his flute, has a presence that's both joyful and expressive. Just the guy if you're game to live more audaciously, free from psychic coercion.

Play with my choices or substitute different names for personal and impersonal forms of God. Just use one consistent choice for each time that you do the particular healing.

(What, you thought I was going to coerce you into naming my personal faves? No way.)

Our nuts and bolts explanation will alternate words of the healing in italics with commentary to follow. Resourceful Healer, I'll provide the usual analysis of why and how each bit of this healing is designed to help you.

Part One. COMMAND A CONNECTION TO THE DIVINE

By now you're a pro at using a preparation process for all techniques of Spiritual Cleansing and Protection. To upgrade your skills, start including Command a Connection to the Divine as a standard part of your preparation process.

That's especially recommended for this particular healing. Psychic coercion is so darned sticky.

Holy Spirit, be here with me now as a super-charged presence. And Krishna, be here with me now in your body of light.

Yes, for this healing, you will need a Cosmic Dynamic Duo, impersonal and personal aspects of God both.

Now the three of you are all dressed up in your superhero costumes. Or whatever. Ready to go!

(Close your eyes. Take one slow breath in, hold, breathe out, hold. Then return to normal breathing and open your eyes.)

I awaken my Power of Command to co-create with you now. Together, let us bring Divine light, love, and power into Earth.

(Close your eyes. Take one slow breath in, hold, breathe out, hold. Then return to normal breathing and open your eyes.)

However much psychic coercion needs to be removed on this occasion, your healing team will be up to the job.

Part Two. REMOVE COERCIVE THOUGHT FORMS

Break the vicious cycle right here. Negative thought forms increase vulnerability to psychic coercion; in turn, added psychic coercion will generate thought forms that cause more vulnerability.

Take this example: "A committed spouse should have no personal needs outside the marriage." That idea could generate negative thought forms and psychic coercion, both.

Why stop to parse the disgusting particulars? Bring on the healing!

I call on The Holy Spirit to shine Your light of truth into all the NEGA-TIVE thought forms here, plus their underlying concepts and patterns.

Remove them from me, this place, and everything in the world that I own, right now.

Sure, you may as well include all those hideous thought forms in your home, your car, your tissue box.

Now I call on The Holy Spirit to shine Your light of truth into all the POSITIVE thought forms, concepts and patterns that have gotten hooked into the dynamics of psychic coercion.

Remove them from me, this place, and everything in the world that I own, right now.

After decades of doing this healing, I had a head-slapper moment. Of course, psychic coercion can spread, taking root in positive thought forms.

Before I had that great big "Hello!" it helped that I had started puttering in a garden.

Somewhat late in life, this native New Yorker learned a bit about how to grow things. What a discovery, that a yard could contain more than dandelions and crabgrass! The skill set called "Gardening" meant that I could actually grow plants on purpose.

Gardening requires weeding, however.

And if you want to move out an aggressive weed, it won't be sufficient to snip off a few obvious leaves. Bring on the heavy duty pruning shears and maybe a grabber tool thingie. (I'm a beginner gardener, not exactly sophisticated yet.) Anyway, I'll use my whatchamacallit tools to dig out that long, pesky root.

Even after removing the first obvious weed, extra search-and-destroy might be needed. Some flowers might even have to be pulled and re-planted because they have grown so darned weedy.

Continuing with our previous example, it isn't enough to uproot obviously negative thought forms, like "Devoted spouse equals happy victim." You might need to temporarily remove some compromised positive thought forms too, such as "I am committed to making this marriage work, no matter what."

Really? Regardless of the personal cost?

Why not clean out a cringe-worthy habit, like "I make this marriage work by stifling my feelings and desires."

Later, when you're acting more like your authentic self, so very nicely cleaned up, then it will be appropriate to install some fresh new petunias. I mean, recommit to your marriage ideals, positive thought forms and all.

With our highly efficient technique for moving out all weeds at once, you won't have to hunt down the specific names of each culprit-like thought form. Co-creating with the Divine, just make your simple request. Then your Cosmic Team-Mates will swing into action.

Together uprooting weedy old thought forms, wow! Brings new meaning to that popular saying, "God is in the details."

(Take three long, slow, deep breaths.)

Resourceful Healer, you might be tempted to skip this part. Not skip breathing for the rest of your life but adding slowness and purposefulness while you breathe three times in a row.

Well, don't. Why cheat yourself out of those productive, long, slow, deep breaths? This silent step of your technique is there for a purpose. Give God and your aura time to complete this part of the healing, okay?

Rushing this part of a healing is like washing the dinner party dishes before your guests arrive. Which might not save as much time as you wish.

Now, Holy Spirit, please create a complete new set of positive thought forms, concepts, and patterns to replace the NEGATIVE ones that were just moved away.

Regarding the old ones that were POSITIVE, reinstall free-standing new versions that will strengthen my free will and self-authority.

Always replenish, right?

(Take three long, slow, deep breaths.)

While you're at it, you might want to take an extra second to wallow in relaxation.

Just how good do you feel now? Because, in some subtle ways, you're probably doing much better already. Speaking of which...

It is done completely. Thank you, Holy Spirit.

Words of closure at the end of a healing will tell your subconscious mind, "Seal the deal." Yes, this part of your healing has been accomplished in full. Excellent!

Part Three. REMOVE BLOBS OF PSYCHIC COERCION

Some psychic coercion looks small, like a tiny speck. Other bits are larger, like medium-sized globs. Still more psychic coercion clumps up so big, I count it as "blob-sized."

(Fortunately, no special measuring tools must be purchased before you get on with this healing.)

I ask Krishna to install violet flames all around me. They will recycle negative energy.

Your Power of Command is enough to co-create the coolest appliance ever. Imagine a softly burning flame in a pleasing shade of purple.

Personally, I like to picture it shaped like the plastic models of soft-serve ice cream cones, those rippling, triangular vanilla treats. And about two inches tall.

Only this is no plastic junk food at the human level. Instead, violet flames are a seriously effective etheric-level cleanup appliance. Energy goes in hot and filthy. Then it comes out clean and cool.

Krishna, please go into my physical body and all my subtle bodies. Find every bit of psychic coercion. Throw it into the nearest violet flame to recycle the energy.

Must you visualize this in great detail? Just the opposite. Be sloppy, since your Divine team-mate happens to be marvelously deft.

The human part of this teamwork merely requires that you use Your Power of Command by speaking out the words of this healing. Ask and it will be done, bringing wonderful results.

Why employ violet flames for this cleanup? One way or another, you need to choose a specific destination for removing the toxic energy. Choosing this destination is no frivolous matter, since coercion-type energy is very real and extremely toxic.

Practical jokes are soooooo not recommended.

(Allow the air to settle down. Or just wait 30 seconds, eyes closed, paying attention to yourself in any way that you like.)

Part Four. REMOVE ASTRAL TIES

How far have you come with this healing? Let's keep track. You have weeded out all the blobs and globs of psychic coercion. Old thought forms no longer contribute to vulnerability patterns. But are you done yet?

Whoa! Won't it be important to do a variation on our familiar Astral Tie Healing? After all, you want to demolish all psychic-level connections between yourself and all those silly senders of psychic coercion.

I ask Krishna to do this healing with me. Krishna, please locate all the astral ties between me and all sources of psychic coercion, be they family members, friends, groups of people I know, groups of people I don't know, whether or not they consciously intend to influence me.

Cut and dissolve all those astral ties now.

Excellent. You're nearly done.

Part Five. REPLENISH

Of course, replenish. Don't you deserve that?

Krishna, fill me and everything I own with new love and light, power and peace.

You could also request that everyone involved in the astral tie removal will receive this nice treat. Generally, I don't bother. Personally, I don't want to facilitate giving coercive people any extra reserves of energy. There is such a thing as being too nice.

Place a gossamer-thin layer of protection around my physical body and each of my subtle bodies in order to repel any psychic coercion sent toward me.

Notice, this is not some big, fat, gross-out, armor-like shield. I've written elsewhere about how counter-productive it is to junk up one's aura with defensive boundaries, fake walls, lurid or sneaky mirrors, etc.

Here you request protection that's thinner than your typical condom. Which works absolutely fine.

Now I call on The Holy Spirit to help me wake up all the healthy circuits that You have given me to know my own heart and mind. I commit to paying attention from now on.

You've heard of anti-oxidants. Just now you have requested anti-vulnerability-oomphies. Yum!

I resolve to stick up for myself. Because my spontaneous desires and emotions, values and ideas, really do matter.

Today's healing can represent a new beginning in your life. Being a Resourceful Healer is one thing. Sticking up for yourself as a human being — that can be quite another.

Many of the healers I have known, self included, have gone through years of being powerful healers for others. However, when it came to our own lives, we were useless at fending off bullies. Maybe even pathetic.

Well, this latest healing can help. Including these final words for Releasing Psychic Coercion:

I affirm my human wisdom. I claim my full self-authority. In every situation, I can know what I want and need. Then I follow through in objective reality, using appropriate speech and action.

Having used Your Power of Command to send forth these words, notice this important technical point. Speaking out the words one time will do the job completely.

This exemplifies the difference between using Your Power of Command versus repeating affirmations.

Personally, I have nothing against affirmations. They're lovely. Also way better than nasty insulting self-talk. Nonetheless, affirmations work very slowly.

Back at our Thought Form Healing, we explored how much more effective a one-time healing would be versus investing hours each day, repeating positive words just to counter-act negative thought forms.

Because I have nothing against affirmations, our latest healing technique actually includes the word "affirm," as in "I affirm my human wisdom."

That is only a one-time use of the word, however, not the same thing as "doing affirmations.

Resourceful Healer, what if you're like me? Somebody who runs around her garden carrying a scary looking grabber tool thingie?

I mean, what if you're also very eager to grow spiritually, willing to do whatever it takes if only you can finally become Enlightened, self-realized, "normal," etc.?

It's so personal, one's term for that most cherished ideal of perfection. Whatever you call it, you have the right to choose your own path, towards that goal.

So remember that, when in the presence of a psychic coercion sender:

- Do something to stop that sending toward you.
- Say something to stop that sending toward you.
- Take advantage of your improved flow of power circuits in life.

Only you know what your next steps of fulfillment would be. Well, pursue them.

Releasing Psychic Coercion: EXPLORE THE RESULTS

Now let's shift into the first-time experience of Releasing Psychic Coercion.

Move into a comfortable seated position. Check that your legs and arms aren't crossed. That way, life force energy can move through you most freely, which will add to your clarity.

Keep pen and paper handy for jotting down whatever you experience. When I ask you to write something down, open your eyes just long enough to grab the paper and do some quick, sloppy writing. Then close your eyes.

With such a complex healing, the sound of your voice can help you learn more easily. Why not make a recording? Go through the sequence of parts and steps. Be sure to leave pauses in-between so that you can follow your own instructions.

Either way, here we go. Do the following steps, one at a time. (Open your eyes as needed to take a quick peek.)

Part One. BEFORE PICTURE

1. Close your eyes. Take three Vibe-Raising Breaths and then return to normal breathing.
2. Notice how it feels *in your body* right now. Ask inside for some words to describe this.
3. Open your eyes long enough to write those words quickly. Immediately close your eyes.
4. Take three Vibe-Raising Breaths. Then return to normal breathing. Notice how it feels to be you *emotionally* right now.

Ask inside for some words to describe this. Open your eyes long enough to write those words quickly.

5. Close your eyes and inwardly say some improvised words of completion, e.g., "Once again this Resourceful Healer is daring to learn something new. I'm so proud of myself, growing faster than dandelions in June. Job done for now!" Open your eyes.

Part Two. DO THE HEALING

Use Your Power of Command to speak out the words for Releasing Psychic Coercion. (Find this in a box at the end of this chapter.)

Part Three. AFTER PICTURE

Now let's find out what has changed for you.

1. Close your eyes.
2. Take three Vibe-Raising Breaths and then return to normal breathing. Notice how it feels *in your body*. Ask inside for some words to describe this. Open your eyes long enough to write those words quickly.
3. Close your eyes again.
4. Take three Vibe-Raising Breaths and then return to normal breathing. Notice how it feels to be you *emotionally* right now. Ask inside for some words to describe this. Open your eyes long enough to write those words quickly.
5. Close your eyes and celebrate this latest completion with some improvised words, e.g., "This time, I went for what I wanted. And it turned out great! Now this healing is complete." Open your eyes.

Part Four. ASSESS RESULTS

Read what you wrote before and after the healing. How do they compare?

Results will be more subtle than nagging. But at least as real.

Which human being is in charge of your life? That's you — now more than ever.

Releasing Psychic Coercion:
HELPFUL USES

Just like all our previous healing skills, Releasing Psychic Coercion has extra uses. Which will appeal to you? Only you know.

- Self-authority speaks to you, if you're auditory.
- Self-authority lights up your truth, if you're visual.
- Self-authority just feels right, if you're kinesthetic.
- Self-authority makes sense, if you are part Vulcan.

One way or another, you can find your way into greater spiritual self-authority. Thanks to this particular healing, you may find it easier than ever to go, "Yes! That's for me." Here are some other long-term benefits.

Increased self-confidence.

Like other forms of astral debris, psychic coercion is not instantly recognizable. So your need for this healing could sneak up on you. It's not as though you will wake up one morning, smell the coffee, and think, "Yecch, I've got astral cooties."

Instead you have some very human ways to recognize this psychic-level ailment, such as, "I don't feel good. There must be something wrong with me. Whatever is it? I don't know."

Maybe you've suffered from awful psychic coercion for years yet never noticed a thing. Then let the results dawn gently, one day at a time... more confidence in yourself, for no official reason at all. Plus some or all of the results described next.

Decisiveness.

People respond differently to carrying a lot of psychic coercion. Some of us develop a mental block around making decisions.

You might have become indecisive about job-related choices. Or love relationship choices. Or which clothes to take out of your closet.

Could this brand of indecisiveness be related to the precise type of psychic coercion you carry? Sure.

Would it then be smart to spend weeks analyzing the cause of your particular vulnerability pattern?

Perhaps, if you're eager to waste loads of time. Otherwise might I recommend that you simply do the healing already?

Spend the 10 minutes it takes, max, once you have the hang of this particular skill of Spiritual Cleansing and Protection. Because many a big intimidating "mental block" is really composed of pathetic little wads of psychic coercion.

Once they're gone, instantly, you're back in charge.

Afterwards, you can read about a lovable fictional nitwit and laugh, but not because she reminds you of you.

Choosing your own religion.

Religion-flavored psychic coercion may seem mild, as in: "Haven't seen you in church lately."

Sometimes religion-based coercion is way more intense, such as: "If you do XYZ, you are so going straight to Hell."

Let's bring new perspective, now that you have freed yourself of psychic coercion. Regardless of your religious affiliation, or lack of it, you have recently gained membership in a new group, "Resourceful Healers Who Have Skills of Spiritual Cleansing and Protection."

RHWHSSCP? Don't even try to pronounce that acronym.

As a member of that free-flowing group, you'd better believe that plenty of psychic coercion is sent whenever somebody nudges or nags you about religion. Sometimes a person like Biff has no idea just how much Hell-fear has influenced him... not until all those blobs of psychic coercion are gone.

This healing can help him, or you, to breathe freely again.

Even scarier than threatening you outright with Hell are the words, "I'll pray for you."

Many a student of mine has lived in fear of a religiously fanatical spouse or parent or child, someone who "generously" volunteers help by means of prayer.

Even worse, an entire congregation or Bible Study Group can be assigned to "Pray for you."

And why exactly? Don't you have your very own direct access to God?

Talk about bossing people around! You do have the right to ask religious zealots to stop playing God with your life. More on that at the end of this chapter.

Meanwhile, on the topic of helpful uses for this healing, using this skill of Spiritual Cleansing and Protection will buy you some energetic breathing room. Even if clearly requested to stop, some religious senders won't take your "No" for an answer. They will continue to send you psychic coercion every long day for the rest of your life.

However, as you have learned, psychic coercion doesn't automatically land inside a person's aura. Whether or not you become a receiver — well, that part is up to you.

What if coercion still slips through occasionally? You'll know. You will start having that familiar experience of being weighed down.

Pause what you're doing, soon as you can, and do the healing. I think you'll soon discover a new kind of freedom.

Trying a tad more tank.

Ever have this problem? You decide to start a project that's going to take a bit of sustained effort, like cleaning out the garage. Great, you're going to do The Project and you're going to do it Your Way.

Only you're so easily distracted. When a problem arises, all motivation vanishes. You feel confused, even unmotivated.

Maybe you procrastinate like crazy before ever returning to that awful project again.

Could be, just the thought of that project turns you into a kind of bobblehead, moaning "I don't know."

One way or another, you never, ever wind up finishing The Project.

Such a horrible feeling of powerlessness! It can feel as though your perfectly fine idea was a great big balloon which popped into oblivion, a bigger mess even than smashed up Humpty Dumpty.

Know what's especially annoying about this? Odds are, some people in your life have ideas that *never* seem to burst like a balloon. These people's ideas are more like a tank.

Aunt Matilda comes to mind, for instance. Once she begins any project, nothing is going to stop her.

Now, you may have zero desire to become exactly like fearsome Aunt Matilda. Except wouldn't it be fun to have just a tiny touch, a tad, of her tank-like ability to persist at whatever she tries? Perhaps you could become a sensitive kind of tank?

Abso-grunting-lutely! Next time your pet project pops into nothing, use Your Power of Command to do the technique for Releasing Psychic Coercion. That just might start your creativity rolling.

Afterwards what if you still feel discouraged? Ask yourself a tank-like question: "What just happened in objective reality?"

- Did your roommate criticize you for cleaning out that garage?
- Did anybody say or do anything recently that belittled your efforts?
- Some kind of problem came up. Well, what was it?

Admittedly it's hard to focus on objective reality when you're stuck with loads of psychic coercion. After this healing, however, you may find more clarity than ever before. Hail this new beginning of effectiveness in objective reality, including new spunk for overcoming obstacles!

With that shinier aura and clearer thinking, you may find it so much easier than before to get your tank rolling.

Horridly holy choices depart.

When Dabney's aura was rippling with psychic coercion, making choices for himself seemed frightening. The future hung before him like a scary question mark. Many times a day, Dabney would ask himself, "Am I really supposed to be doing this?"

By now you know that senders of psychic coercion often use language like "should" and "supposed to" and "have to" and "need to." If receiving happens, whoosh, in come truckloads of psychic coercion. Splat! Right into Dabney's aura and subconscious mind!

What happens after someone like Dabney takes on truckloads of religiously phrased psychic coercion? Most likely, he will internalize the coercion process. Dabney might even glorify feeling so coerced because he imagines God as One Big Holy Sender of shoulds and supposed to's.

Millions of people have been raised to believe in a form of God who is harshly punitive. Such a God uses the tiniest sin as an excuse to cast a sinner into hell everlasting. And apparently be gleeful about it.

What, the tender creator of dewdrops? God as an uncaring vengeful rageaholic? Personally, I don't believe in that version of God for a minute.

Were you taught to believe in this horrid version of holiness? Well, you can change that right now. It's especially easy to use your free will since you have developed such a cleaned up, daisy fresh aura!

Whichever kind of God you believe in, that's exactly the kind of God who will be in your life.

Therefore, Resourceful Healer, feel free to revisit your concept of God. Why not choose a version to match your newfound self-authority? Maybe this is also a good time to reconsider old expectations about determinism versus free will.

If you believe in free will, you can use it. If not, should you believe only in fate, that's another beautiful belief system. Only why bother to do much in life except learn how to be a good sport? You will be stuck with whatever fate brings you.

Of course, you could believe in both fate and free will. I'm partial to this version: "I commit to vigorous use of my free will. And any time things don't work out as planned, that will be gracefully accepted as my fate."

The choice is yours. As with defining God, whatever you choose to believe about free will versus fate will be supported by your current reality.

Apart from the nature of God and the human toggle switch called "free will," don't underestimate the power of your conscious choice. Simple choice influences your subconscious mind and your link to humanity's collective unconscious.

All these hidden portions of you will work differently depending on what you choose to believe at any given time.

In the past, your ability to choose freely could have been crippled by STUFF. If you have carried certain types of psychic coercion, in past years you may have tried repeatedly to believe in a loving God who supported free will. Yet you never could make it stick. Just making the attempt might have made you feel guilty.

Blame old psychic coercion for that, not God. Even better, Resourceful Healer, find out what happens after Releasing Psychic Coercion.

I think you will find that all attempts at self-authority will work far better now. So you might wish to sit yourself down for a brief ceremony where you use Your Power of Command to tell God the kind of relationship you would like to have. Effective immediately!

Releasing Psychic Coercion: TRUE TALES

Ready for a scary story about visiting the dentist? Okay, it was an orthodontist, and I wasn't even getting the work done. The official patient was my son.

I had served as Transportation Fairy. While my big boy's braces were being checked, I sat in the waiting room with other moms, pleasurably absorbed in a tween magazine. (They really do have some of the best makeup tips, you know.)

In the background, a radio was tuned to Washington's classical music station. My son was on his way to nice, straight teeth. Contentment seeped through me until I was nearly napping. Neither I nor anyone else in the waiting room was prepared for what would come next.

Suddenly I leapt from my chair, hollering "Absolutely not. How dare you?"

What was I bellowing about? Search me!

Everyone stared in alarm. Hey, even I was curious. Sitting down, I racked my brain. What had caused that outburst?

Right away an answer was delivered, courtesy of my short-term memory. Just before I stood up and hollered, WGMS had been playing music. Then they segued into a commercial I had never heard before. A suave male announcer had said this:

"Ladies, I know all of you have been thinking about getting liposuction...."

It was the lead-up to an ad from a local cosmetic surgeon. As a certified consulting hypnotist, I can tell you the technical term for what was being broadcast to listeners. It was a great big sneaky post-hypnotic suggestion. That friendly announcer was delivering a really despicable form of subliminal advertising.

Why did I react as I did, since my conscious mind didn't even register those words? For decades I have kept myself clear of psychic coercion, owning a skill set that you now own, too.

Consequently I have developed an ongoing agreement with my subconscious mind, a zero-tolerance policy against all senders of psychic coercion.

Yes, I have become tough that way. All of me says no to coercion, and not just my conscious mind. Which is why I responded as I did:

No. As in, "Absolutely not. How dare you?" A very resounding NOOOOOOOOOOOOOOOOOOO!!!!

Advertisers persuade most effectively when the listener is sleepy or inattentive or reading fascinating tween beauty tips about application of eyeshadow.

That way the advertiser's message can bypass the listener's conscious mind, dump directly into the listener's subconscious mind, and generate "spontaneous" urges to buy, buy, buy.

Once I understood what had happened, I apologized to the other mothers in the orthodontist's waiting room. Then I explained.

Had they heard that commercial? Did they want an advertiser to implant the idea that every woman listening really wanted to pay for a form of vanity surgery that is violent, expensive, and sometimes even deadly?

Okay, those mothers probably listened to me only because they feared for their lives. What kind of maniac would I turn into if they refused to play nice? Would I pull out a gun? (In Virginia, you're allowed — maybe even encouraged — to carry a concealed weapon. Sure, bring along your machine gun to church, to a bar, and definitely to the orthodontist's office.)

Resourceful and Polite Healer, maybe you will never react as strongly as I did, with that zero-tolerance policy against all senders of psychic coercion. Nonetheless, you can enjoy immediate and long-term benefits of Releasing Psychic Coercion.

Releasing Psychic Coercion: TAKE THIS HEALING FURTHER

What if you have received plenty of psychic coercion in the past? How can you quit being a receiver now?

In every social situation, pay attention to what YOU want. Every human soul has personal preferences in life, things that you love versus things that you hate.

Well, listen to those preferences. Then start speaking up.

If you were the tiniest bit of a brat at age two, there is hope for you now.

What else can you do, when bullies should on you? Educate them. Coercers may have no clue what they're doing. I didn't. Back in the day, I belonged to a cult. Righteously I thought it was *helping* people if I pushed them to join.

Sad! However, I didn't know better, not yet. I credit T.I.C. for teaching me about psychic coercion, what causes it and how to heal it. That ended my sending habit. Gone for good! No longer would I nag people because I assumed this was a great way to help them.

These days, I'll bend over backwards to avoid sending psychic coercion. I'll tell my client, "Remember, you are the authority in your life. Whatever I say is just my opinion."

For me, all it took to tone down the sending was learning about psychic coercion in the first place. Before then, it had never occurred to me to question whether or not I had the right to "should" other people.

Years later, I developed a "Tell It Once" rule, as in "Tell Margie about her bad breath just once. Don't try the indirect version, like slipping mouthwash into her tequila."

What will happen if you experiment with a rule like mine? Not everyone will welcome your efforts at education. But you might choose to talk to coercion senders anyway. At a minimum, you will find out how far gone they are into bossiness, fear, etc.

Avoiding coercive threesomes.

Say that your mother constantly nags you about your father's habit of eating potato chips. As if the thought never crossed his mind that maybe he doesn't need to weigh that extra 200 pounds.

In a way, it's cute. Technically Mom is attempting to gain double points at sending psychic coercion. You are being coerced, of course. Will you go forward, representing your mother to further the bullying?

That ought to be worth at least twice Mom's normal points, right? And all of this, seemingly, for Dad's own good.

Yecch!

What do you have to lose, explaining to Mom that you believe in a "Tell It Once" rule? Maybe she'll put her own tongue on a diet.

Regardless, you will have given her your one ethically allowable, crystal clear communication. "No, Mom, I will never, ever again, serve as your Shoulding Messenger."

How to follow up with this experiment? From that day forward, act as if *you* were the one raising a child. Every time that Mom asks you to nag on her behalf, just say no.

Be consistent. Call it a victory for social skills. And maybe smile as your Dad keeps on eating those chips.

When a person is too far gone to honor your wishes about sending coercion, what more can you do?

Because you just might love that silly mother of yours and want to talk to her regularly, despite her obnoxious sending habit.

Behaviorally, hold firm. Whenever Mom sends you coercion, laugh and change the subject. If she persists, leave the room or hang up the phone.

Beyond that, if you have somebody in your life who keeps shoulding you regularly, I would recommend Releasing Psychic Coercion once a week.

Religious Bullies, in a Class by Themselves

Of all the silly ways that people send psychic coercion, isn't "spiritually-superior" coercion the worst of all?

Yes, you have the right to defend yourself against religious bullies. Maybe they will never consider you quite as infallible as The Pope. Nevertheless, you have the right to speak up.

- Speak out your truth once.
- Speak to anyone in your personal life (not your work life, alas, unless you're independently wealthy).
- Speak boldly, no matter how earnest the psychic goop sender and how many scriptural quotations are invoked.

I recommend saying something like the following, one time, to anybody who says "I'll pray for you" or any similar volunteer efforts to fix you:

"I'm only going to tell you this one time, so please listen carefully. You have told me your perspective about religion. Now stop. I happen to have my own personal relationship with God, which is none of your business. If you have been praying for me, or asking anyone else to pray for me, stop that right now. And don't start up again. Ever.

"In the future I won't give you unsolicited advice about religion. I'm warning you now, I won't accept it from you, either.

"We can talk about other topics, if you are interested in having an actual relationship with me. But if you ever, ever bring up this subject again, I will end the conversation immediately. Understand?"

Resourceful Healer, you can practically see the steam rising off these words, can't you? This isn't advance smoke from Hell but annoyance.

Personally, I have had my fair share of encounters with religious bullies. After all, I have lived in the Bible Belt for decades.

In my experience, it's a waste of time speaking politely to religious zealots. The busybody will take your words as encouragement to start a fresh round of bullying.

This is comparable to talking with a telemarketer who figures that prolonging your conversation in any way… just might result in a sale.

Releasing
Psychic Coercion

Part One. COMMAND A CONNECTION TO THE DIVINE

Holy Spirit, be here with me now as a super-charged presence.
And Krishna, be here with me now in your body of light."
(Close your eyes. Take one slow breath in, hold, breathe out, hold.
Then return to normal breathing and open your eyes.)
I awaken my Power of Command to co-create with you now.
Together, let us bring Divine light, love, and power into Earth.
(Close your eyes. Take one slow breath in, hold, breathe out, hold.
Then return to normal breathing and open your eyes.)

Part Two. REMOVE COERCIVE THOUGHT FORMS

I call on The Holy Spirit to shine Your light of truth into all the
NEGATIVE thought forms here, plus their underlying concepts
and patterns. Remove them from me, this place, and everything in
the world that I own, right now.
Now I call on The Holy Spirit to shine Your light of truth into all
the POSITIVE thought forms, concepts, and patterns that have
gotten hooked into the dynamics of psychic coercion. Remove
them from me, this place, and everything in the world that I own,
right now.
(Take three long, slow, deep breaths.)
Now, Holy Spirit, please create a complete new set of positive
thought forms, concepts, and patterns to replace the negative
ones that were just moved away.
Regarding the old ones that were positive, reinstall freestanding
new versions that will strengthen my free will and self-authority.
(Take three long, slow, deep breaths.)
It is done completely. Thank you, Holy Spirit.

Part Three. REMOVE BLOBS OF PSYCHIC COERCION

I ask Krishna to install violet flames all around me. They will recycle negative energy.

Krishna, please go into my physical body and all my subtle bodies. Find every bit of psychic coercion. Throw it into the nearest violet flame to recycle the energy.

(Allow the air to settle down. Or just wait 30 seconds, eyes closed, paying attention to yourself in any way that you like.)

Part Four. REMOVE ASTRAL TIES

I ask Krishna to do this healing with me. Krishna, please locate all the astral ties between me and all sources of psychic coercion, be they family members, friends, groups of people I know, groups of people I don't know, whether or not they consciously intend to influence me.

Cut and dissolve all those astral ties now.

Part Five. REPLENISH

Krishna, fill me and everything I own with new love and light, power and peace.

Place a gossamer-thin layer of protection around my physical body and each of my subtle bodies in order to repel any psychic coercion sent toward me.

Now I call on The Holy Spirit to help me wake up all the healthy circuits you have given me to know my own heart and mind.

I commit to paying attention from now on.

I resolve to stick up for myself. Because my spontaneous desires and emotions, values and ideas, really do matter.

I affirm my human wisdom. I claim my full self-authority. In every situation, I can know what I want and need.

Then I follow through in objective reality, using appropriate speech and action.

16. Prevent Psychic Attack

I get more questions about psychic attack than any other aspect of Spiritual Cleansing and Protection. Now that you have learned a related healing, you're ready to deal more effectively with this frightening problem.

For starters, let's calm down. Some of you may have turned to this chapter first, so great is your fear of this particular form of victimhood. Well, stop shaking and gather your wits. The threat is probably not what you think.

"Psychic attack" is a convenient way to explain a boatload of problems. Convenient but usually wrong! To see what I mean, take the following quiz.

Psychic Attack Quiz

Here are situations where a friend of yours might complain of a problem. Which of the paired answers is the more likely cause?

1. John: "It's hard for me to know what I want. I feel terribly bogged down."

A. Great-Aunt Wanda is giving John the evil eye.

B. Psychic coercion is what gives John the problems; right now he is such a receiver!

2. Jane: "I feel like an external energy is dragging me down, causing me to feel tired constantly."

A. Someone has cursed Jane.

B. Jane could use a Stuck Spirits Healing.

3. Jim: "What's the point of dating? The girls don't seem to like me."

A. Jim's mom has cast a spell on him so that no girlfriend will ever snatch away her darling boy.

B. Jim needs the kind of healing you're going to learn in the chapter after this one.

4. Jenny: "Some kind of energy causes me to feel spaced out, turning every day into a struggle."

A. Sinister forces are attacking Jenny. If this space-out thing continues she will die.

B. Jenny might have a problem involving astral-level imbalance beyond the scope of this book. Although not necessarily difficult to heal, Jenny's problem could require more advanced skills than basic Spiritual Cleansing and Protection. Time to seek out a professional at Energy Spirituality, Energy Psychology, or Energy Medicine. (Should Jenny's struggle persist, then it's wise to seek help from a psychiatrist.)

5. Jo-Jo: "All the things I own feel like a burden, a headache. I'm tempted to leave it all behind and join an ashram."

A. A rival at work has attacked Jo-Jo psychically.

B. Quick, Jo-Jo, do a Negative Thought Form Healing.

Psychic Attack Quiz, Some Answers

Yes, as you may have guessed, B. is the answer to each question here. Yet more answers could have been listed. All five problems in our Psychic Attack Quiz could have causes which wouldn't be fully resolved by either of the answers provided.

There could be a physical illness or a long-term psychological imbalance. Or perhaps the complainer happens to be a drama queen (or king, or prince, or understudy).

Here is what I would tell Jo-Jo, Jim, Jane, Jenny, or John: "If you're worried about psychic attack, start with techniques of Spiritual Cleansing and Protection. It won't take long to do any of these healings, not after you have mastered each skill."

What don't you have to include in your version of happily ever after? Living in fear of psychic attack.

Why Astral-Level Goop Can Feel Personal

Let's clarify more differences between psychic attack and other energetic problems that could be confused with it.

Psychic attack means that another person has the power to send you toxic energy. Popular definitions of this threat include becoming the victim of black magic, having somebody purposely assault your aura, evil people manipulating supernatural forces in order to destroy you, vengeful torturing ghosts, etc.

Hold on. You have already learned how to heal various kinds of annoying, draining astral-level goop. Stuck spirits, astral ties, and negative thought forms — remember them? Annoying but impersonal.

Why call these astral-level problems "impersonal"? Nothing about these stuck energies is connected to the truth of who you are as an individual.

Psychic coercion is trickier to heal since some components are personal. While other components are definitely impersonal.

As you may remember, the *sending* part of psychic coercion can be totally impersonal, e.g., gossip, advertising, busybodies who volunteer to help the Pope become more Catholic, etc.

The personal part of psychic coercion involves being a *receiver* of psychic coercion.

How can you avoid receiving psychic coercion?

Prevention is just as useful as healing. Now that know about sending, you might choose to cut down the amount of psychic coercion being sent to you. Whenever possible, ask people to stop nagging you. Don't read spam. Mute TV commercials.

Your technique for Releasing Psychic Coercion will remove any bits of coercion that slip into your aura regardless.

Over the years, you can develop full spiritual self-authority and heal any vulnerability patterns.

Eventually, no matter how much psychic coercion is sent your way, it will not be received.

All three steps are your business. Don't add the extra job of fearing how other people might damage your aura. Perhaps you know the technical term for that kind of fear: **Energy hypochondria.**

Such an ugly label! At least energy hypochondria is totally optional. It's an over-subjective way of interpreting relationships, plus an insistence on thinking about everything in one's life in terms of energy.

What, this big fan of Energy Spirituality believes there is such a thing as over-emphasizing awareness of energy? Definitely.

Energies are important, including results from Spiritual Cleansing and Protection. However, let's keep a sense of proportion. Energy is just part of life for us humans. Constantly thinking about energy does not mean a person is becoming spiritually enlightened. Instead, it may signal a spiritual addiction.

Being human, you are free to interpret relationships any way you choose. Consider the brilliant title of one of Terry Cole-Whittaker's books: "What You Think of Me Is None of My Business." So what if a few other people don't care for you much? Why interpret that as deeply personal? Why interpret the problematic relationship in terms of energy directed at you?

And if some stuck spirits do like you, that isn't personal either (especially since you know how to do a Stuck Spirits Healing).

Sure, all forms of astral-level debris can *feel* personal. When it lands in your own personal aura, that *location* is pretty darned personal.

I hope you're finding it easy to sort all this out. Still, you may be wondering. Why do so many intelligent people today confuse astral-level debris with psychic attack?

Here's my theory. Many people today are just starting to become aware of energy. These promising beginners haven't yet developed much energetic literacy.

For instance, say that Jo-Jo works with John and she gives him a quick introduction to the concept of psychic attack. She's helpfully sharing as much as she knows. This woman is a caring and sensitive person, very sophisticated as a certified public accountant but still a beginner at energy anything.

So when John complains about feeling bad, Jo-Jo decides to help him. She says, "You feel bad due to an energy problem, not a regular human-type problem." Then Jo-Jo shares the name of the only energy problem she has heard of, "psychic attack."

Blaming all his problems on psychic attack could be very appealing to John, especially if he feels helpless or otherwise has lost a sense of proportion.

Remember the example about the big incense "fire," back in our first chapter? Maxi is the student who told me that once she burned so much incense for protection that her roommates were ready to call fire trucks.

By the end of our workshop on Spiritual Cleansing and Protection, Maxi was doing just fine. Once she learned how to use her Power of Command to heal astral debris, the woman calmed down considerably.

How about you, Resourceful Healer? All you have learned so far about Spiritual Cleansing and Protection has done the same for you, right? Not only has your aura cleaned up nicely. (Excellent job!) You are developing a perfectly appropriate Power of Command.

- Yes, you have learned how to distinguish many different types of astral-level debris.
- Yes, you have cleansed each problem right out of your life, co-creating with Divine help and using Your Power of Command.
- Yes, Spiritual Cleansing and Protection is a practical skill set. If you have been doing the exercises given so far, you own most of that skill set by now.

Phew! Being able to command away forms of astral-level STUFF brings a sense of relief. Compared to before you started developing this skill set, aren't you're less likely to make an energy mountain out of a molehill?

With calmness restored, you're ready to develop street smarts for dealing with… not psychic attack… but everyday problems that can be *confused* with psychic attack.

Human-Level Street Smarts

If you have heard of psychic attack, you have probably heard similar terms as well. Friends like Jo-Jo can warn you to avoid psychic attackers, so-called "energy vampires" or "psychic vampires" or scary "narcissists," "toxic people," etc.

Of course advice like that feels good. How convenient to blame one's bad feelings on an outside source, somebody truly wicked who emits toxic vibes like some mythic fire-breathing dragon.

Over the years, I have encountered more and more clients with energy hypochondria. It made me curious to do some research on Google. Just how popular are some of those fear words related to energy hypochondria?

Below are the search engine hits I found on July 1, 2011, when this book was in production. Search items in italics are strung together with a little narrative (because I couldn't resist):

"How terribly awful is the danger of *psychic attack* (13,600,000 hits).

"Those wicked *psychic vampires* (6,810,000 hits) and *narcissists* (3,780,000 hits) who make me a *victim* (196,000,000 hits). Shame on them! The problems in my life could never, ever be my fault.

"How can I deal with these monsters? Gosh, I'd better educate myself about *toxic people* (147,000 hits) with *toxic personalities* (12,400,000 hits).

"Then I'll studiously *avoid* them. Only then will I be safe."

Just for fun, I decided to add up the hits on this popular form of energy hypochondria. I added up the Google hits on "*Avoid energy vampires*" + "*Avoid psychic vampires*" + "*Avoid narcissists*" + "*Avoid toxic people*" + "*Avoid psychic attack*" + "*Avoid [being a] victim.*"

Well, here are the numbers, Resourceful Healer: 5,380,000 + 1,930,000 + 1,760,000 + 64,100,000 + 3,930,000 + 6,460,000. Total hits: 83,560,000.

How many million? Wow, more than 83 million!

For perspective, let's try some googling on the skills you have learned so far.

"To clean out energy imbalances that could be confused with psychic attack, use skills of *Spiritual Cleansing and Protection* (4,120,000), including *Healing Stuck Spirits* (10,400,000), *Negative Thought Forms* (13,100,000), and *Psychic Coercion* (334,000). Total hits: 27,954,000."

There's a comparison for you: Nearly 28 million people who can use their Power of Command versus 83 million victims.

Just in case you were curious about whether or not you are a pioneer, Resourceful Healer, now you have evidence. People today are way more likely to "empower" themselves with victimhood thinking than by learning to distinguish different types of psychic-level debris. And you, of course, have made it your business to learn how to heal it rather than simply worry about it.

Unfortunately, the harder one tries to avoid "Toxic People," the more one is likely to find them. Everywhere.

Surely life offers us better alternatives than avoidance. In addition to the healings you have learned, what else can help you to feel good energetically?

Here are five alternative strategies for solving the bad-vibe problem by using human-level street smarts. Because most so-called psychic attack isn't astral at all. The unresolved problems are very human.

Telling friends from foes.

Rather than worrying about psychic attack, develop this human-level friendship skill: Learn to distinguish people who like you from those who don't.

Did you know? Within two minutes of a new relationship, you can tell who likes you and who doesn't. To find out, all you need do is quiet down for a moment in private. Ask yourself, "Does Uncle Snuffy like me or not?"

Whatever you discover, don't expect that to change.

Let's use the example of your first-ever conversation with Uncle Snuffy. If he doesn't like you then, it's probably not negotiable. Sure, you can try hard to turn that relationship around. You could offer Uncle Snuffy any and all of the following:

- Beseeching him to notice you via sweet looks and winsome smiles.
- Doing him favors.
- Using his name a lot.
- Secretly copying his body language.
- Doing him more favors.
- Bringing him flowers and chocolates.
- Hey, you could even hand out free money.

Will Uncle Snuffy accept all of your offerings? Probably. That still doesn't mean the man will like you.

Sure, you've seen romantic comedies where the lovebirds begin by disliking each other. They also meet cute. How often have you met cute?

In real life, pursuing a relationship based on dislike is foolish. A gigantic waste of time, actually! For every person who doesn't like you, a hundred others do. At least they would if you met them and talked together for two minutes.

Resourceful Healer, do you know the practical meaning of the word "enemy"? No longer do we live in the era of duels. Therefore, locating an enemy doesn't mean searching for concealed swords and scabbards.

Don't expect a dropped gauntlet to be your clue, either. Practically speaking, for somebody living today, an **enemy** is simply any person who doesn't like you.

So there's a useful distinction to help you avoid feeling that your energies are being drained by others. Maybe you have been pouring way too much of your personal energy, attention, hopes, etc. into somebody who is a poor credit risk, energetically speaking.

Have you been unrealistic about enemies for spiritual reasons?

Perhaps you believe this: "Given enough love and understanding, every relationship can be perfect."

You might also have the habit of worrying about your spiritual evolution. Is your love of God being tested every time you meet a stinker?

Only if you choose to live that way. Common sense suggests that trying to make everybody fall "in like" with you could turn into... a full-time job. An impossible job, at that.

By all accounts, Jesus Christ was a pretty good guy. Everyone didn't like him, however. I've even heard that he suffered a pretty nasty death.

You're allowed to be a nice person, a God-loving person, yet still use decent survival skills. One of them is to minimize your face time with enemies. Not fear them, avoid them, or waste your time labeling the problem in terms of psychic pathology, as in "Which type of toxic personality would Uncle Snuffy be, an energy vampire or a narcissist?"

Way too much work! When you must deal with a non-friend, try something human. Scale your expectations way back. If you must have a conversation, go through the motions. Don't make any non-friend interaction a bigger deal than it has to be.

Struggling to stay friends with non-friends is a far more common drain on auras than so-called "psychic attack."

Spiritual addiction.

I've noticed a pattern in many of my clients, a pattern I know all too well because once I had it myself. "Spiritual addiction" is what I call it. This means putting all one's eggs in one basket — the Woo-Woo Basket.

Spiritual Addiction causes millions of beautiful spiritual seekers to inadvertently shirk their human responsibilities. The imbalance sneaks up on a person who works really hard to be good. Really hard how? In ways like these:

- Praying for yourself.
- Praying for others.
- Meditating.
- Searching for signs.
- Reading people's energy constantly.
- Asking, "What would Jesus do?"
- Trying oh-so-hard to live according to your beliefs.

Seldom do clients come to me complaining of spiritual addiction. Instead they bemoan problems like these:

- Lack of respect at work.
- Lack of a job.
- Lack of money.
- Sex life is sad, at best.
- Not much of a human life at all.
- A stuck feeling about spiritual connection.
- And, yes, feeling attacked by others, belittled, over-influenced, powerless, etc.

Here is what I have learned from combining energetic literacy with depth healing techniques of Energy Spirituality (including Spiritual Cleansing and Protection). Let's revisit your neighbor Mindie-Belle as an example, since she's really a good person although not necessarily friend material.

Like all human beings, Mindie-Belle has parts of her aura about *spiritual striving*. That includes dozens of chakra databanks at her Third Eye Chakra alone.

Currently, hers are mega-huge.

Mindie-Belle also has parts of her aura about *living on earth as a human*. That means hundreds of chakra databanks at the Root Chakra, Belly Chakra, Solar Plexus Chakra, Heart Chakra, and Throat Chakra.

Currently, hers are really, really teensy. Highly spiritual people like Mindie-Belle basically feel like this, "If I fully trusted life on earth, I could be trapped forever. All spiritual values would disappear. I would forget about God completely and become totally materialistic."

Worse than that, what if (like Mindie-Belle) you're a committed Christian? Then your fears could extend to spending eternity in Hell.

Well, here is what have I found, researching hundreds of people with a spiritual addiction. No way does obsessive focus on spirituality make the spiritual parts of life work better.

Just the opposite. Alas, the human parts of life get worse, too. For instance, with spiritual addiction:

- Mindie-Belle becomes spacey and ineffective.
- She develops a massive chip on her shoulder. Contempt for people whose beliefs don't match hers becomes the equivalent of "Give us this day our daily bread (of disdain)."
- Although Mindie-Belle doesn't ignore God, she becomes quite obsessed with God. Is that really such an improvement?

Consider human life a big trust exercise. God put you here, after all. Actually, it's quite possible that you volunteered for this incarnation. Why not trust God enough to *commit* to the human life you have been given?

You could even try an **Official Experiment in Spiritual Trust**. Not for eternity — because that might be asking a bit much. How about trusting your human life for just one week?

What, exactly, would be involved in this bold experiment to heal spiritual addiction? Stop constantly reaching out to the spiritual. Limit all your spiritual activities to half an hour per day.

That half hour can include using skills of Spiritual Cleansing and Protection, as you have been learning to do. Our skill set involves crisply and efficiently healing astral-level debris, not spending all day investigating it. (You get the difference, right?)

Limiting the woo-woo with this Official Experiment in Spiritual Trust, how will you fill the rest of your waking hours? Pay attention to life. You know, as if your human life were actually interesting to you. Results may include these:

Within one week, the balance in your aura can improve significantly. Human life may seem a bit more interesting.

What if you continue the Official Experiment in Spiritual Trust for weeks or even years? That human life of yours can become vibrantly fulfilling. *All* of your chakra databanks can become big and bodacious, not merely the chakra databanks concerned with spiritual seeking.

Speaking of which, the quality of your spiritual life will improve.

Ironic but true!

One more thing... only please don't mention this to people in your life like Mindie-Belle. But between you and me, did you ever wonder? Maybe God prefers when humans beings quit the constant pestering.

Overcoming spiritual addiction brings good results all around. In my opinion, this type of addiction is the #1 cause of so-called "psychic attack." Living vigorously as a human, you won't seem invisible or weak to others in that sad way.

When you grow stronger aurically, non-friends will prefer to pick on somebody else. Perfectly nice people will treat you better, too. And you won't be tempted to call any of the folks you meet "psychic vampires."

Necessary skills for empaths.

As we've discussed earlier, empaths are born, not made. Could you be among the 1 in 20 people with an intellectual, spiritual, physical, emotional, or other life-long gift as an empath? Then beware. Until you become a skilled empath, you're constantly doing unskilled empath merges.

These happen within a split second, usually unconsciously. While in the midst of an unskilled empath merge, you are picking up STUFF from other people. This becomes lodged in your aura. STUFF picked up from others includes *their* negative thought forms, stuck spirits, and psychic coercion.

How hideously this can clutter you up! The draining effect could easily be mistaken for psychic attack, especially when somebody in your life has negative feelings about you. So if you suspect you're an empath, please, get skills.

Learn a skill set for empaths that really works. What would that feel like? Imagine: Your sense of identity is strong. Never do you pick up STUFF from other people just because you stand near them.

This requires energetic resilience. It doesn't come from elaborate shielding or self-analysis. Instead a skilled empath is pretty darned awake inside. You don't pick up STUFF from other people when vibrantly engaged in enjoying your human life. This is a natural kind of empowerment for an empath.

Yes, this way of living is definitely possible. And once you own an effective skill set as an empath, it's yours for life.

Seldom, if ever, will you pick up STUFF from other people. If you do, you will have empath's first aid skills to shake it off quickly. So you will not find yourself confusing this sort of problem with being under psychic attack.

Admittedly, unskilled empaths are less effective in life than non-empaths. But ha ha! Skilled empaths are *more* effective, making this innate talent totally worthwhile.

Cords of attachment to difficult people.

Every cord of attachment contains a push and pull of energy. Technically, then, most of them could be called an energy drain.

If you develop skill for permanently cutting cords of attachment, you can permanently remove one cord of attachment at a time. Doing this, you will gain information about the type of push and pull that was involved. (A problem you no longer have, fortunately.)

Today's knowledge of Energy Spirituality techniques can thus help people to feel a whole lot less victimey.

Meanwhile it makes no sense to fear energetic transactions between yourself and your fellow human beings. Just because you "lose breath" through your nostrils, does that make your nostrils scary?

Other people's negative expectations.

Have you ever found yourself slip-sliding into a different way of behaving, just to confirm another person's poor opinion of you? This is especially likely to happen to **Highly Sensitive Persons** (HSPs). Statistically, that's 1 in 5 people worldwide.

An HSP is sensitive enough to register the subtle cues that people give off about their expectations. Which aren't necessarily wonderful.

Say that Harley is your father-in-law. Unfortunately, he doesn't believe you deserve his perfect child. That silly Harley is waiting so hard for the two of you to divorce, he is practically drooling.

In fact, I hate to break this to you, but Harley thinks you're a nincompoop.

Of course you're not. But let's say that you do happen to be... a Highly Sensitive Person. Unless you know better, you might slip into fulfilling Harley's expectations. So if he expects you to act clumsy, thanks to your magnificent sensitivity, you will get the message. Brilliantly.

When you're around Harley, you just might start falling over your feet. If you don't have enough ways for feet to trip you up, then you might also bump into tables.

Just how bad could this expectation fulfillment thing get? Imagine the shame: Sitting next to Harley at a formal banquet, your fork keeps missing your mouth.

All this would work great in somebody else's hilarious slapstick comedy show. But say that the clumsy behavior is happening to *you*. In your personal reality show! And it seems to make no sense at all.

In the past, you might have considered this psychic attack. Now you know, it's The Revenge of the Forks.

No, actually, I'm hoping you will figure out that the problem is your relationship with Harley and, especially, the fact that you're being more sensitive to his expectations than to your own true self.

To turn this around, build up a stronger sense of identity. First try do-it-yourself. If that isn't enough, consult a professional at psychological healing, Energy Spirituality, Energy Psychology, Energy Medicine, religion, or spirituality.

Three cheers for Harley. He has alerted you to this need for healing. (Not that you ever need thank him to his face. Please don't.)

While you're growing in ways that help you long term, use your regular common sense now. Treat any Harley in your life like an enemy. For instance, give him minimum face time. When you do have to hang with Harley, try sticking forks in *his* mouth. Just kidding about that last part, although it's a tempting idea.

Defend yourself in practical ways against silly Harley. For heaven's sake, don't compound his personal shortcomings by fearing that the silly man knows how to send voodoo.

In this huge Learning Planet of ours, there can occasionally be instances of true, dedicated psychic attack. Fortunately, there are expert practitioners who specialize in this type of healing. I am not this kind of practitioner.

However, I do know how to rule out all the problems in this chapter. On the rare occasions when I make a referral to a specialist at removing psychic attack, it will be appropriate.

Well, you can put yourself in the same resourceful position. By way of analogy, say that you're worried about some puddles on one side of your house. Why rush to replace your roof? Wouldn't it first make sense to check the gutters? The problem could be as simple as a few autumn leaves that got in the way.

And speaking of house analogies....

Broken windows.

Have you ever heard of the zero-tolerance policy toward crime? Sometimes it's called the **Broken Windows Theory**. Zero-tolerance toward crime can be mighty useful, whether you have been elected Mayor of New York City or you're just trying to get a life where you don't feel psychically attacked.

This theory was first developed by Harvard professor James Q. Wilson and criminologist George L. Kelling, author of "Fixing Broken Windows: Restoring Order And Reducing Crime In Our Communities."

How does the fix broken windows strategy work? Say that some local vandals break a few windows in a building. What if those windows aren't repaired? Encouraged by lack of consequences, the vandals may break some extra windows. Encouraged by a continued absence of punishment, the vandals might try their luck as squatters.

Basically, whenever you let people get away with small offenses, larger offenses will follow. But when you routinely fix "broken windows" in your home and life, that's like the proverbial ounce of prevention beating a pound of cure.

As mayor of New York, Rudolph Giuliani decided to implement the Broken Windows Theory by cracking down on petty crimes like jumping subway turnstiles. This led to a drop in the city's crime rate.

Why not elect yourself mayor of your own life? People get away with small stuff whenever they think they can. You can make *them* sweat the small stuff. No need to bring out your sheriff's badge and arrest the wrongdoers, no more than you need to elevate their status in your own mind by calling them "psychic attackers."

Instead, try something simple and civil, like "Excuse me? What did you mean by that?" Use speech and action — objective reality — as a way to solve problems.

That's important because many a Highly Sensitive Person seeks solutions through *subjective* reality instead, such as:

- **Worrying.** What about my vibrations attracted that rude behavior?
- **Over-analyzing.** The only reason I have Harley in my life must be to serve as a mirror. Which lesson do I need to learn?
- **Reminiscing.** Which people from my past does Harley remind me of? How can I resolve my old issues?

- **Wishing.** When I have meditated enough and am fully
  enlightened, I won't ever have to deal with bullies again.

Instead find solutions in *objective* reality. Here and now, choose human
ways to solve problems with good old objective speech and action.

So often, fear of psychic attack becomes an excuse to turn ever
more over-subjective. Wishing, hoping, thinking, and praying won't discourage a squatter. Ironically if you're busy trying subjective fixes, unintentionally or not, you'll be showing total tolerance for creepy behavior.

Zero tolerance is so much more effective. Stand up for yourself.
Speak your mind. Take the most effective action you can in that particular situation. For instance, did you ever try....

Setting Ground Rules

Every personal relationship in your life is governed by ground rules.
These are relationship basics between you and another person. What is
socially acceptable to both of you? What is not?

These interpersonal ground rules aren't usually discussed directly
in a conversation. But they can be. You can initiate that conversation,
where both of you discuss what is mutually acceptable from now on.

Negotiation! Done specifically. Clearly. Out loud.

Even "Agree to disagree" is a kind of ground rule. Which means
there is hope for you to improve relationships with bullies. Even someone as opinionated as Uncle Snuffy may agree to some ground rules.
Find out by initiating a conversation where both of you calmly discuss
patterns in your relationship.

What does each of you need and want? For each of you, what
constitutes "unacceptable behavior"?

Ground rules need not be complicated, but they do need to be
clearly defined. Otherwise, people continue to have their own private
notions about what constitutes "Being helpful." Ideas that can be wildly
different.

Of course, when setting up ground rules for a relationship, they
must be confined to objective speech and actions. You can't legislate how
Uncle Snuffy thinks, nor can he dictate your feelings. Different by far is
which subjects will be considered off limits when the two of you talk.

Can new ground rules enhance your personal power? You bet. All
the old ground rules may have been chosen and enforced by Uncle Snuffy,
back when you didn't know better. Formerly, "Going along" with what

he decided may have been confused with your desire for "Getting along" with the man.

Each of your relationships includes ground rules about which behavior is acceptable... regardless of whether or not these relationship rules have ever been discussed directly. Unless it's a work relationship (and sometimes even then), you have the right to politely request a face-to-face conversation on this touchy topic.

During this rule-setting talk, you can propose definite ideas to Uncle Snuffy, such as:

"Certain topics are not to be discussed from now on, not even one-on-one, and definitely not in front of other family members.

"For me, off-limit topics are my clothing, my weight, and my dog.

"Do you understand? Good.

"Now are there any topics that *you* would prefer for me to avoid when the two of us talk?"

Of course, it's obvious to you that your weight isn't to be announced, down to the ounce, as though you were a bouncing baby boy. Well-meaning Uncle Snuffy may have no clue. What you consider "intrusive," he has considered "caring." So educate him.

Eventually dear Uncle Snuffy may come up with some rules of his own. They might even be reasonable. You have the right to give feedback about all proposed relationship rules. Both of you do.

Compliance.

Once you have ground rules, apply them consistently whenever you're with Uncle Snuffy. Don't be surprised if the man requires a little prodding before he takes any new rules seriously.

Fearlessly, you can become The Enforcer. Disregard any excuses and stick to the straight-and-narrow definitions of acceptable behavior for this relationship.

Should Uncle Snuffy begin picking on your dog, give him one warning. After that, if he persists, terminate the conversation. He'll learn soon enough.

No need to feel guilty about educating Uncle Snuffy. He may never understand your motivation for needing one ground rule over another. Maybe he'll never care about you deeply enough to accept that you could have different ideals, valid sensitivities, and even a mind of your own.

Frankly, that uncle of yours may always be a bully. It's not your job to change him. The appropriate responsibility is to disallow his bullying *you*. In session with clients, I have heard many a story that started with "Help, I'm under psychic attack from Uncle Snuffy," or the equivalent.

When a client like Jim releases STUFF from his aura, he can begin to deal with obvious bullies in his human life. Long before Uncle Snuffy arrived on the scene, Jim didn't inhabit his life very fully. That's the main reason why Snuffy could become such a problem.

Resourceful Healer, has your situation has been similar? Then take heart. All the healings you've learned have made you more resourceful than ever. Not only have you nearly completed the skill set of Spiritual Cleansing and Protection. Now you can develop the skill set called "Setting Ground Rules for Important Relationships."

In addition you can implement other strategies already discussed in this chapter:

- Developing human-level street smarts.
- Ending spiritual addiction.
- If you're an empath, becoming skilled.
- Ignoring inappropriate expectations.

Along with Spiritual Cleansing and Protection, these human-level skills can eliminate most bad-vibe problems.

"But-but-but," some of you may be wondering. "Couldn't there still be some instances of real-life psychic attack?

How Common Is Psychic Attack Anyway?

Out of thousands of personal sessions I've had with clients, how many times has the astral-level problem really been psychic attack? Nine.

All those clients wound up doing just fine, thank you. Regular skills of Spiritual Cleansing and Protection aren't going to be enough to deal with serious psychic-level malice. In such a case you would be wise to bring in a professional with some extra skills.

But first, please, think of these numbers: In my entire career since 1970, out of many thousands of clients, there has been true psychic attack maybe nine times. Most of those instances I've been able to heal by using various skill sets of Energy Spirituality; about five times, I have had to make a referral.

Far more common have been clients who believed they were under psychic attack. Turned out, their biggest suffering was caused by one or more really nasty cords of attachment. Easily healed.

Take the example of one of my clients, whom I will call "Mr. Cutie." He had a grim cord of attachment to his mother, Pearl. Back in the day, she did truly hideous things to him. For instance, when he was a little boy she would punish him by dunking his face in the toilet.

As an adult, Mr. Cutie continued to replay this incident through his cord of attachment to her. The ugly energy dynamics were transmitted 24/7.

This was like having somebody sending Mr. Cutie body odor. But not because an official stink bomb was sent off by a psychic attacker. Simply because he was standing way too close, and way too long, near something really smelly.

We're talking casual stench, like having your dog Fido wander too close to a skunk. Thirty years of suffering after Pearl's death were not from a psychic vampire. More a need for aura-level hygiene.

Removing that cord of attachment for Mr. Cutie was the equivalent of washing Fido in tomato juice.

This kind of cleanup isn't drastic. It brings about the end of the problem, not the end of Fido. Only, in this analogy, many quarts of tomato juice.

Basically, if you hear somebody all worked up about "I'm under psychic attack," I encourage you to think "Tomato juice" rather than "Panic." Astral-level debris happens to be something you are learning how to heal, right?

Cutting cords of attachment is an extremely useful skill set for removing personal kinds of connection that can drain energy. If you decide to learn…

Give the process all due respect.

Cutting even one cord of attachment amounts to major surgery at the level of auras. Sure, you can learn to do it. But don't think you can learn the entire skill set in a few minutes, not if you aim to use a quality method.

You might be able to learn from a book. Look for a how-to that thoroughly explains a quality method. If you prefer to learn from a real-live person, find a teacher with professional-level skills.

Either way, give that skill set the respect it deserves — just as you have been doing here with the skill set for Spiritual Cleansing and Protection.

Avoid the Quickie Method.

According to popular myth, "All you need do is ask Archangel Michael to cut all your cords of attachment." Actually, the Quickie Method for Cutting Cords is a sad variation on a technique you have already learned, doing an Astral Tie Healing.

Think about it. With your skills for Spiritual Cleansing and Protection, you can appreciate why The Quickie Method with Archangel Michael wouldn't even help to successfully cut one astral tie, let alone permanently remove the much bigger energetic structure called a "cord of attachment."

(Hint: After the removal process requested of Archangel Michael in the Quickie Method, what is being put back? Nothing. Now, what happens, after removing any goop at the astral level, if you don't purposely replenish your aura with something good?)

You're ideally prepared.

Resourceful Healer, thanks to your new skill set for Spiritual Cleansing and Protection, you have the ideal background for learning to cut cords of attachment. Ideal why?

Using your Five Cleaning Supplies has helped you to develop skill at paying attention to your inner experience. This can bring you great finesse and wisdom for all skills of Energy Spirituality.

I wish everyone who aimed to cut cords of attachment would also learn our skill set of Spiritual Cleansing and Protection. For one thing, it is often the more appropriate skill set to use.

One of the very first things I do with any client is to check for major problems with astral-level debris. Sometimes we'll devote an entire first session to moving out psychic coercion, stuck spirits, etc. Then, in a follow-up session, I'll be able to facilitate cutting a cord of attachment.

My client Joe supplied a fine example of this when he wrote this comment at my blog:

"I had a good few cords of attachment cut by another healer, and while I did feel different about myself after the cord to the my mother was cut, with the others I didn't sense much benefit until later when I had a session with Rose where she cleared out some astral entities.

"That really helped me experience a different kind of clarity."

Resourceful Healers, you could consider removing astral-level STUFF like preparation for surgery. Before making that first incision, wouldn't you first make sure that the patient's body was clean?

Actually you may find what you've learned to be a beautiful basis for sessions where you use *any* skills for mind-body-spirit healing, such as techniques of Energy Medicine and Energy Psychology.

Defense against the dark arts

Completing the topic of "psychic attack," I invite you to consider our skill set as a kind of energetic "Defense Against the Dark Arts."

You have learned all our major healings by now, except for the last one (coming up in the next chapter). You have buffed up your human-level street smarts, acknowledged that everyone you meet isn't going to be a friend. Ground rules have been explored, too.

By now, you're not just cleaner energetically. You're better equipped to deal with human reality.

Nonetheless, if you're like many of my students (or this teacher), you're still a great big idealist. Every day you wake up with hope in your heart that today will be a really good day. A great day, bringing the sweetest surprises! A day when, somehow, you will serve humanity!

Expectations matter so much in human life. Expect to be happy, sure. But other experiences could matter more for your soul's spiritual evolution, like honesty with your own emotions, service to others, integrity, and compassion to meld with your strength.

How about the resolve to savor your experiences, no matter what? You volunteered to be here at Earth School, remember? Well, now you're equipped with sophisticated skills for cleaning up the joint.

Clean up what you can. Enjoy the rest. That's my advice.

When talking with friends, how can you share this newfound cleaning ability? What if, these days, your buddy Jim's entire lifestyle is based on shielding himself, fearing psychic attack, and avoiding toxic people?

Of course, I wouldn't recommend nagging the man. As you know by now, that would qualify as sending Jim psychic coercion.

But you sure could invite him *once* to read this chapter... which you have just completed.

17. Experience The Ultimate Energy Makeover

This isn't the first book Biff has read for self-improvement. He works hard on himself. For instance, Biff doesn't do any old yoga. No, the classes he takes are more like yoga boot camp.

Biff neither smokes nor drinks nor takes drugs. He does go shopping quite often. To achieve that casual "I don't care" look, Biff shops carefully. Actually his frugal parents would be appalled at how much Biff spends on haircuts alone.

Beyond making sure that he looks good, Biff has done psychological work galore. He has dealt with complex issues, providing employment for many, many talented therapists.

Successful at work, he's athletic, interesting, sexy, and kind. Altogether that Biff is quite a catch. So how come he never scores a second date?

Is life simply unfair? Guess what Biff doesn't know.

He's still got pimples. He smells bad. Nobody cool ever sits near him in the cafeteria. His Social Studies teacher, Miss Mavis, makes life hell for him every single day. High school sucks.

Sure, we know that Biff graduated from high school years ago. He knows this, too. Except for a certain part of his aura. Which doesn't.

Specifically, Biff's aura is carrying around some hideous old facades and belief bodies. They got stuck in him long before he reinvented himself into the cool guy of today.

Mostly Biff has succeeded at transforming that sad high school outcast. Now he just needs to stop sending out those pitiful loser facades from the era of "No girl will ever want me."

In this chapter, Biff can learn to release these sticky bits of his past. You, too, may have been living with obsolete facades and belief bodies. Would you know consciously? Hardly.

Contrast is the simplest way to find out. After this chapter is done, automatically you will begin living without these limiting relics of your past. Discover then how your quality of life changes... thanks to removing those tricky, limiting, hidden, clashing facades and belief bodies.

Healing Outgrown Facades:
WHAT THEY ARE

People are complex, even if you're just viewing them on the surface. To simplify dealing with all those complexities, human beings subconsciously create astral-level **facade bodies**. Each one sends out a quick summary, like a tweet or newspaper headline proclaiming, "This is me."

On the receiving end, when you meet new people, their quick facade summaries are helpful. All of us need a way to sort through the problem of "So many men, so little time."

Think about it. Haven't you developed some conscious habits for sorting through strangers? Some of us specialize in noticing faces while others evolve into proud butt watchers. Label-conscious adults observe clothing. Others prefer to view body language.

Now let's add the hidden factor relevant to Spiritual Cleansing and Protection. Beneath the surface of life, a smarter kind of evaluation is done as well. This happens through **auric modeling**, how a person's aura appears to everybody else.

Auric modeling is completely visible to aura readers (those with full, conscious energetic literacy); otherwise the information will be available only subconsciously.

Socially, the single most important part of a person's auric modeling is... facade and belief bodies. Subconsciously these are worn — and duly noted — whenever two or more people interact.

To picture this, think of the Broadway show "The Lion King." Each character carried a giant, stylized mask. In real life, off-off-off Broadway, your aura carries one mask, or facade body, for every single relationship or social role.

In case you're wondering, that amounts to a huge inventory. What's in your personal collection of facade creations? It could include your *online dating* mask, your *singles bar mask*, and your *eligible bachelor at the bowling league mask.*

A different mask pops out whenever you're with Mom or Pop, Kid or Grandkid, and so forth; plus facades for everybody in your present and past — yes, every single person you have met in this lifetime since Day One.

Each of your facade bodies displays a quick summary of social attributes for that particular role, including:

- Your degree of confidence.
- How much you typically talk.
- Whether you're full of life or full of sloth.
- How wrinkled your clothes look vibrationally (which may, or may not, correspond to the amount of wrinkling on your physical clothes).

Subconsciously, this facade of yours proclaims itself to everybody who meets you. Not necessarily in a subtle manner, either. More like back in the day, when your baby brother would wake you at 6:00 a.m. by blowing a toy trumpet into your ear.

Blaring, glaring first impressions scream out like that — subconsciously, of course — courtesy of your facade bodies. Of course, you're also subconsciously reading similar data from facade bodies about everyone else in your life.

Adding to the merriment, you also have a **belief body** that sprongs out in every conceivable social situation. Picture it like the mask worn by you as you're playing Simba on Broadway.

As an actor, you wear your mask for other characters to see. But won't you still have to look through that mask yourself? What is that like, looking at people through the inside of a mask?

Hey, you should know.

You do it every day of your life, many times each day. Each belief body of yours contains patterns about you on the receiving end of a relationship.

Subconsciously you are fraught with expectations, such as:

- How much love and respect will you accept from that particular relationship?
- Will you be able to take a compliment?
- Compared to the other person, do you consider yourself equal, superior, or inferior?

What if you want to upgrade this old mess?

Unbeknownst to your conscious mind, each belief body exists as something very real on the astral level. Which is why new clothes won't change it at all.

Psychologically based healing techniques may produce a meaningful shift. But working from the human level to impact all these subconscious patterns is a very big deal, requiring slow, painful work to adjust one facade and belief body pair at a time.

Laborious counseling can change this combo, one relationship at a time, one day at a time. But how about fixing the other 500+ hideous facades that remain after the first three are fixed?

Poor Biff thinks he's going out for a "first date." Yet his belief body carries yesterday's expectations of social failure. That sure can limit his interaction subconsciously, ensuring that Biff will definitely *not* get lucky.

Each of us carries a large collection, one for every relationship, present or past. Just do the math: For every single interaction with a person, you will wear one facade body plus one belief body.

What happens to the rest of your collection? It stays stored in your aura like extra socks in a chest of drawers. (Since facades and belief bodies are made of astral-level energy, they can pack down really small, too.)

When you greet somebody you know, out pops the appropriate facade and its flip side, the belief body. Or, for a new relationship, you will spontaneously generate a new facade and belief body combo; this will be based on the rest of your collection.

Must you always wear these astral masks? Yes, since you're human.

Does it make you a phony wearing these things? No, merely human.

No blame here, right, Resourceful Healer? Facades and belief bodies are not the same as putting on an act, an **intentional personality projection** or **fake facade**.

Putting on an act to impress someone else adds a layer atop the regular, human, facade body that has been generated automatically.

Inadvertently these fake façades send a mixed message, contradicting what is already projected through the regular facade body.

For instance, say that Biff plays a role to impress his latest date, like "I'm as suave as James Bond, minus the danger." His suave act may be very convincing.

Yet it will be contradicted by his facade and belief body. They're busily whispering to his new date, "You won't like me, of course. Soon you'll be making fun of me behind my back. The failure of our friendship is only a matter of time. Afterwards I will feel betrayed and alone."

Hearing this explanation is, I hope, consoling. Even if you don't have Biff's particular romantic history!

Finally you can stop blaming yourself for certain social failures in your past, right? Old astral-level facades couldn't leave just because you tried really hard to impress some other person.

Although *fake facades* are optional for human beings (not something I would ever recommend, personally, but optional) astral-level *facade bodies* are about as optional as having skin.

Realistically, here is where your choice lies: Will you keep wearing whatever random old astral masks have been stuck in your aura? Or will you use your skills of Spiritual Cleansing and Protection to give yourself an image makeover?

Some folks do manage to update their facades and belief bodies without studying a thing. It's a knack, like instinctively knowing how to select stylish clothes. For the rest of us, there's the makeover technique in this chapter, Healing Outgrown Facades.

Think you don't need this healing? Think your set of facades and belief bodies couldn't be better? Then you will get no results.

However, most of us get so many results, it's scary good.

Your facades and belief bodies aren't exactly broken. They just probably don't do you justice, especially if you have actively sought personal growth over the years.

Ironic, isn't it? As a fast grower, haven't you been working really hard to improve yourself? Improve what, body language? Tone of voice? Shoe wardrobe? Maybe even the look of your butt?

Now hear this. Upgrading yourself on the outside won't bring the expected results necessarily. Not if, from the inside, you're still sending out Biff-style facades. Beware the mixed message:

- "I'm so cool" proclaims your clothing.
- "You're going to despise me no matter what" whines your facade.
- Uh-oh.

Healing Outgrown Facades:
NUTS AND BOLTS

Using Your Power of Command will be simple, way faster than finding that perfect new pair of blue jeans. Easy but powerful, no wonder I think of this healing as the Ultimate Energy Makeover! So here goes.

As usual, words of the healing will be italicized, then followed by explanation.

Part One. COMMAND A CONNECTION TO THE DIVINE

Father-Mother God, be here with me now as a super-charged presence."

Once again, we're going to Command a Connection to the Divine. For variety, let's use the name "Father-Mother God." (As always, go with my example or substitute any choice you prefer. For this healing, I do recommend choosing an impersonal form of the Divine.)

(Close your eyes. Take one slow breath in, hold, breathe out, hold. Then return to normal breathing and open your eyes.)

I awaken my Power of Command to co-create with you now. Together, let us bring more Divine light, love, and power into Earth.

(Close your eyes. Take one slow breath in, hold, breathe out, hold. Then return to normal breathing and open your eyes.)

Part One is now complete. You're positioned energetically to facilitate a powerful healing. Next part will require that you remove all existing facades and belief bodies. So here goes.

Part Two. RELEASE THE OLD FACADES AND BELIEF BODIES

Father-Mother God, please shine Your light into all my facades and belief bodies.

One benefit of omniscience is how easily God can locate every single one of your facades and belief bodies. Awesome, that God can tell where you leave off and these astral masks begin!

Separate them out from me.

After you make your request, each of your facades and belief bodies will gently be pulled away from your aura and rest nearby.

Immediately fill and surround me with Your healing presence.

Ever feel self-conscious when you take off your clothes? That's nothing compared with how naked you could feel after releasing old personality projections.

How bad could it feel, losing all those familiar (if limiting) versions of being yourself and then hanging out, more than butt naked, for days? Never find out, please.

Doing this healing as taught to you here, Resourceful Healer, you won't have to suffer one bit. God is asked to replenish you immediately.

Each of my current facades and belief bodies was developed for a reason. Send that knowledge to my subconscious mind for storage, in case I ever need it.

Now in my fifth decade of working in the field of personal development, I keep learning more about people and how very quirky they are. Our skill set of Spiritual Cleansing and Protection is, to me, a great example of the mysterious process of self-realization. People take one highly personal growth step at a time.

Already you have witnessed how fast certain types of astral debris can be removed forever. Stuck spirits, astral ties, and psychic coercion — ugh! They are so very not personal. The STUFF is so deeply uninformative. Quick, heal it all and take it away; then fill yourself up.

But what if this facade kind of STUFF might be different? What if facades and belief bodies might prove informative at some future time? Definitely, let's get rid of them when doing this healing, and yet....

When you include this sentence about "storage" in your healing, this could be likened to throwing away your calorie-ridden cake yet having it, too. (Sometime in the future.)

Thanks to Your Power of Command, all of the relevant data can be stored in your subconscious mind.

This part of your healing creates a kind of **Subconscious Facade Archive**. Will that ever be useful? Perhaps at some future time you will wish to understand more about those facades and belief bodies. Where did they come from? What were the chains of causation?

How might that data become useful? A serious kind of STUFF that gets stuck in auras is **frozen blocks of energy** from past events, going back to the womb and, even, previous lifetimes.

This distinctive type of astral-level debris requires a separate skill set for release. Yet one more reason to consult your favorite professionals at Energy Spirituality or Energy Psychology, right?

Should your newly created Subconscious Facade Archive ever be needed to help you heal frozen blocks of energy from your deep past, you will be all set — thanks to this part of Healing Outgrown Facades.

Now move each of my old facades and belief bodies forward through time, evolving them super-fast until they dissolve into pure light. Store the life lessons from them into my subconscious mind as well.

Back to the future! Thanks to this part of your healing, your Subconscious Facade Archive can be available whenever needed. Otherwise you can go free, welcome to ignore the whole thing. Sweet!

I love setting up the Subconscious Facade Archive, feeling the facades and belief bodies vibrating higher, faster and faster, then becoming a blur of moving energy. Next those old bodies morph.into dazzling white light. The process reminds me of time-lapse photography.

Ever see that in a video? Images captured over time are speeded up in a sequence, unfurling like a blossoming rose. Resourceful Healer, I have applied that concept to our healing technique so that all the "images" will be saved in that Subconscious Facade Archive for future reference.

Conveniently, this isn't hard for God to do when moving out STUFF at the psychic level. (Psychologically doing the equivalent for yourself would be way harder, more like personally parting the Red Sea.)

How about an example of what I mean about speeding up facades during this part of the healing. Well, remember Biff? At the start of our chapter, he wore a facade for first dates that was a throwback to his junior year in high school.

This caused the handsome adult version of Biff to send out the mixed message that, despite the current state of his life, he remained a pimply social misfit.

Not everybody stores facades from those acne-ridden days of yore. If you're a psychologist or other professional healer, maybe my example about Biff at the start of this chapter made you stop and think.

Why did this particular guy hold onto this particular facade? An awful lot of teenagers suffer from acne, but surely all of them don't keep reliving those experiences. Most of us move on. Why not Biff?

Questions like these do have an answer. Especially in the case of Biff. (It's easy to know his back story since I happen to have invented him.) One cause of Biff's stuck facade is a childhood trauma that he has long since forgotten... consciously.

Back when he was a newborn, Aunt Francine paid a visit. Baby Biff's face was ruddy and prune-like from his recent journey through the birth canal.

Mom cuddled him anyway. Something about her adoring expression annoyed Aunt Francine. So she joked to Biff's mother, "Cute baby, if only he didn't have that awful skin."

Biff's mom joked back, "Yeah, the girls are going to find him disgusting."

Hearing this affectionate teasing (and, trust me, babies do hear telepathically until they learn how to talk), Biff's subconscious mind stored every bit of that dialogue. His subconscious has no sense of humor.

That's not just Biff's problem. Nobody's subconscious mind has a sense of humor. We store everything that happens around us, down to the exact words.

So let's consider that, subconsciously, Biff remembers a great deal of STUFF about social rejection, frozen blocks of energy from that overheard conversation and similar blocks from womb-time and perhaps even previous lifetimes.

At some point in his development, maybe Biff will decide to release the full set of frozen blocks of energy. Thanks to his Subconscious Facade Archive, Biff will be able to access full knowledge of his past, including all former facades and belief bodies.

Now, continuing to understand nuts and bolts of this healing....

Place a gossamer-fine layer of protection around each one of my bodies, physical and subtle.

You know what it's like to feel vulnerable. Compare the stinging sensation of an opened-up blister to how you might feel right after removing countless facades and belief bodies. Hence this request for healing energy to replenish you while awaiting the new "healthy skin" to grow back.

Incidentally, why make that protection layer "gossamer fine"? For healing at the level of auras, finesse is preferable. Fortunately we can heal delicately because we are co-creating with God. No thick, clunky smear of astral-type Vaseline for us, no no!

Part Three. REPLENISH

Now I call forth my own identity as a soul.

Part Three of this healing starts with my very favorite sentence of the whole sacred facade swapping deal. Allow me to introduce you to somebody really important... somebody who has been with you always. Ironically this somebody has probably been ignored for most of your life.

Say hello to your **soul**. This is your core identity, the you-ness expressed in your life as a human being.

Hello! This distinctive soul of yours matters far more than either nature or nurture, surpassing the importance of your genes, with potential to over-ride every single thing about how you were raised.

Soul has a lasting quality, like fingerprints. Only you have way more to your soul than memories of how you were created long ago. Your soul can help you to follow your bliss right now.

All human beings become happier and more effective when living with soul. Resourceful Healer, even for the purpose of helping others, you will be most successful when strongly expressing that gusto-great part of you.

Vital though it is for self-actualization, your soul can languish for years. Uninvited, ignored, unused, and unrecognized.

Think of Biff's old facades and belief bodies. Which did they represent more, his suffering or his soul?

Most of us express only a fraction of our soul power. Healing Outgrown Facades is going to change that.

So this part of the healing begins to activate the power of your soul for shaping your life. I just love how the healing takes off from this point, like sledding downhill when the snow is just right.

Before now, we did the equivalent of pulling a sled upward to the top of the hill, getting into position. With these soul-related words, we push off and let the thrilling new ride commence.

Soul, help me to hear, feel, and express your presence, trusting my every-day likes and dislikes, thoughts and feelings. Awaken within me fully. I am open to receiving more of your wisdom day by day.

Don't say this unless you mean it. But, really, what do you have to lose? Personally, I wouldn't recommend skipping these words.

Now I charge you to co-create with Father-Mother God. Make me a complete new set of facades and belief bodies. These are to be the clearest expression yet of the true Divine Pattern for my soul, so I can bring more truth, joy, and power into this lifetime.

Such a concept! Imagine how different your life would be if you had been raised in a perfect family, enjoyed the best education money could buy, developed brilliant social intelligence, dressed perfectly for every occasion, and succeeded at every single thing you tried.

Except maybe what happened instead really was perfect, too. Some of your problems may have occurred because, like every incarnation, your life began with a very specific **life contract**.

Very likely, certain assignments were part of the deal you agreed to, back on the Other Side. Perhaps you had a few karmic debts to pay off in the form of "bad" this and that. You've probably done a great job at handling that, too, under the circumstances.

Only what if, like Biff, you have confused one-time karma payback with your lifelong core identity, that Divine Pattern for your soul?

Limited prior versions of yourself may have stayed active in your aura, projected through outdated facades and belief bodies.

Now, Healing Outgrown Facades, you're asking God to collaborate with your soul to create a new version of yourself that will have the highest truth value yet.

Imagine installing this new versions of yourself; it expresses yourself more completely than ever before. You, a uniquely magnificent soul!

(Take a few slow, deep breaths. Stretch your body.)

Resourceful Healer, doing this breath-n'-stretch will integrate your results faster... all the way out to the surface level of life. Which is where you need a congruent expression of your new facades and belief bodies.

Remember the story of Peter Pan and how he first met Wendy? Flying boy had lost his shadow. He asked the cute human girl to sew it back on.

Just substitute *you* for Peter in this story. Substitute *your facades and belief bodies* for the shadow. With that essence of you sewn back nicely, won't it be appropriate to stretch a little, just to make sure things fit properly? And now for some crowing:

I give thanks that this is done. It is done. It is done.

Gratitude is one fine way to end your healing. I'm just delighted if you're willing to give thanks for what you've received.

However, you don't have to give thanks. You could substitute any statement that brings closure. If you like, try "That's all folks," just like the old Warner Bros. cartoons.

Just say something to officially end this latest episode of Healing Outgrown Facades. Back to normal life for you.

Whatever "normal" is. Because of the healing you have just completed, "normal life" could start showing up... way, way better.

Healing Outgrown Facades: EXPLORE THE RESULTS

Now let's shift to your first-time experience of Healing Outgrown Facades. Move into a comfortable seated position. Check that your legs and arms aren't crossed.

Keep pen and paper handy for jotting down whatever you notice. When I ask you to write something down, open your eyes quickly and do some quick, sloppy writing. Then close your eyes.

Want to record this historic event? (And this will be historic every time that you do it.) Use your favorite electronic device for recording. Remember to leave pauses appropriately.

Either way, here we go. Do the following steps, one at a time. (Open your eyes as needed to take a quick peek.)

Part One. BEFORE PICTURE

1. Close your eyes. Take three Vibe-Raising Breaths and then return to normal breathing.
2. Notice how it feels *in your body* right now. Ask inside for some words to describe this. Write those words quickly and close your eyes again.

---

3. Take three Vibe-Raising Breaths. Return to normal breathing. Notice how it feels to be you *emotionally* right now.

4. Ask inside for some words to describe this. Open your eyes long enough to write those words quickly.

5. Close your eyes and think some beautiful words in conclusion language, e.g., "My reality is personally created by me, for me. One more exploration of my magnificent self is complete for now." Open your eyes.

Part Two. THE HEALING

Use Your Power of Command to speak out loud the words for Healing Outgrown Facades. (Find this in a box at the end of this chapter.)

Part Three. AFTER PICTURE

Now let's find out what has changed for you.

1. Close your eyes.

2. Take three Vibe-Raising Breaths. Return to normal breathing. Notice how it feels *in your body*. Ask inside for some words to describe this. Open your eyes long enough to write those words quickly.

3. Close your eyes again. Take three Vibe-Raising Breaths. Then return to normal breathing. Notice how it feels to be you *emotionally* right now. Ask inside for some words to describe this. Open your eyes long enough to write those words quickly.

4. Close your eyes and create some conclusion language, gift wrapped as thoughts, e.g., "Wasn't that cheaper than buying a whole new wardrobe, plus 20 years of psychoanalysis! Now this technique is over." Open your eyes.

Part Four. ASSESS RESULTS

Open your eyes. Read what you wrote before and after the healing.

How do they compare? That contrast informs you about immediate results.

Long term, this new skill of yours will subtly improve how other people respond to you, setting up a cycle that increases your self-esteem.

And maybe you have already noticed the immediate change within you. A more soul-aligned upgrade of your life has been installed for good.

Healing Outgrown Facades: HELPFUL USES

Helping you to feel more like you — that makes such a difference for quality of life. All our skills of Spiritual Cleansing and Protection have been designed to upgrade your inner alignment.

What is special about Healing Outgrown Facades? There are social implications to this particular upgrade. All your facade and belief bodies impact how others treat you. So this particular healing has some amazingly helpful apps.

You lost the weight.

After the fabulous weight loss, you want to show off that svelte new you. Think of all those diet commercials where the proud winner/loser triumphantly holds up a huge pair of jeans that no longer fit. You could be doing the astral equivalent of wearing those oversized jeans every day.

Long after achieving your weight goal, old facades could be projecting habits like these:

- Feeling fat anyway.
- Self-loathing.
- Expecting others to consider you un-sexy.

Incidentally, if you're contemplating a diet, it can't hurt to fix your facades and belief bodies *now*, lose the extra pounds later.

Single again.

After the divorce or the breakup, you're back in the dating game. Ouch! Are you feeling just a little reluctant to learn dating all over again?

Your new freedom could bring great happiness. Especially if you make the most of this "wonderful" new opportunity. Boost your confidence by releasing facades and belief bodies that would otherwise keep you on the rebound.

Admittedly this kind of cleanup is no substitute for cutting the cord of attachment to your ex, which is my single most important recommendation for getting on with one's life after a breakup. You may be amazed what a difference that makes. Meanwhile, healing facades and belief bodies can provide an easy, quick fix. Implications for your happiness are huge because all your facades and belief bodies are related.

By analogy, think of your past experience with your love-life as if it were a color scheme. Newly single, it's as if your entire collection of facades and belief bodies has been painted like stained army camouflage. New ones would be spontaneously generated to match.

So color ALL your facades and belief bodies right now. Color them astrally beautiful.

But you don't want a divorce or a breakup.

Say that you're not single now. Far from it. What if you're in a love relationship that you cherish?

Excellent! But doesn't that love relationship have any troubling history at all? Events from your past can't be changed. At least the leftover energies can.

Sure, it is entirely possible to change your energetic holdovers from the past. Keep the life lessons but move out old pain, fear, etc.

Don't just expect "Time" to heal things. That passive approach only works for people whose standards are really, really low.

Again, I would recommend cutting your cord of attachment for a depth healing. But it's also vital — and easy — to update your facades and belief bodies. You deserve that new beginning.

And now that you own this latest skill set, doesn't that bring you extra confidence? Upgrading your old faces on demand… could become a great gift for your relationship, something to do every Valentine's Day.

Stuck, ironically.

Despite working hard to gain skills for self-improvement, what if you still feel stuck?

Working so hard, you deserve better. Changing habits can take a long time for one particular astral-level reason. One that you can guess.

For instance, consider the plight of my student Vonda, an empath who wanted to become skilled.

She had succeeded brilliantly at turning her empath gifts OFF, waking herself up from the inside. No longer would Vonda do those silly automatic unskilled empath merges, picking up STUFF from random strangers.

Whew, what a relief that Vonda finally had developed skill as an empath! Yet she kept walking into a room and projecting what to others? What???

"I will always be there for you. Incidentally, what do I expect in return? The usual nothing."

What??? That sure stinks.

In reality, Vonda is now a skilled empath. Still, at the level of auras she sends a mixed message.

- Mostly, through her auric modeling: "I'm strong and free, a skilled empath."
- But also, through her old facades: "I'm the sweetest little philanthropist/martyr/nurse in all the world."

Time to change that, right? And you know how, Resourceful Healer.

Whatever skill sets you are developing for self-improvement, now you can supplement them with appropriate facades and belief bodies. Otherwise it could take years before you live the full results.

Step 13 for your 12-step program.

How hard a struggle it can be, recovering from a dysfunctional pattern. You want to be a better person, yet change can seem painfully slow.

Say that you're in a 12-Step program, bravely in recovery as an alcoholic. Say that you have been clean and sober for three long years.

During that time, you have made new friends. You have learned so much. Really, you have grown enormously. Yet something may be exactly the same (and I think you know which something I mean).

Just how much good will it do you to carry around facades and belief bodies from your drinking days?

And what else could you be projecting to others? Only three years' worth of facades from those seemingly endless days in most painful recovery. In those old energy bodies what did you broadcast?

"Hi there. Nice to meet you. I'm an alcoholic in recovery. I commute from Hell."

Come on, don't you ever want to graduate from having your whole life centered around recovery?

You know, in the future you might occasionally revisit that 12-Step community as a fully recovered person, receiving just a wee bit of support as needed and sharing fellowship with your community.

Or you could return six days a week for the rest of your life, perpetually carrying the same old facades of misery that you wore to your very first meeting.

After you've dropped the stinking thinking, your next step could be to fumigate those facades.

Finally complete that mid-life crisis.

Or 20-something crisis. Or Male Menopause.

Heck, so what if there is no officially recognized crisis name for whatever you're going through right now? It still could be real.

A nasty patch in life comes up for most humans every 10 years.

Knowing you, Resourceful Healer, if you're going through one of those nasty patches, it is a class act. You're coping beautifully, doing the very best you can. Deep down you know that eventually you will feel great.

Well, how can your new skill set help? Any time you complete a tricky phase in your life, upgrade your facades and belief bodies. That way they'll reflect who you are in your new, improved state.

You know how old folks can reminisce, starting off with the words, "Back in my day..."? Let *now* be your day.

That choice will be far more convincing if older, less evolved, versions of you have been upgraded. Sure you can change all the way down to your aura and subconscious mind. Resourceful Healer, you even know how to do this *easily*.

You believe in The Secret.

Do you have Big Plans for your Success and Prosperity? Excellent!

Suppose that daily you strive to use the Law of Attraction in order to manifest what has been pasted onto your dreamboard.

Inconveniently, some additional forces are being projected into the ethers. Like it or not, you are going to attract responses to your facades and belief bodies. They are part of your auric modeling, whether you read auras consciously yet or not.

Law of Attraction works most powerfully on the level of who-you-be, your auric modeling. Don't send the Universe a mixed message, not unless you want nightmares to come true along with your dreams.

In less time than it takes to fashion a decent dreamboard, you can master this chapter's healing to use for the rest of your life.

Or you just hate having your picture taken.

Everywhere you go these days, folks are busily snapping pics and making YouTubes. Gak! Not all of us are thrilled about this. Being photographed can make some of us squirm.

"That face and body! No way is that me. Something about this is so... horribly... very... not me."

Ever feel that way? Then consider. The problem may not be how you look physically. It's that each image contains a facade and belief body. Sensing them could make a perfectly healthy person want to hurl.

It's so easy to forget what you show others. Normally, you're not introducing yourself to yourself, so why would you notice?

The bad news is, you can't go back to your old photos and Photoshop those outdated facades and belief bodies.

At least you can change yourself from now on, which will greatly improve all electronic images automatically.

Get new pictures after this healing. Go forth and rebuild your wall on Facebook. Why not?

Healing Outgrown Facades: TRUE TALES

Meredith is a long-time client who first came to me while in medical school. Now she's a resident, a psychiatrist-in-training. For the first few years of our working relationship, I helped to heal her aura by using all the healings in this book, also using other skills of Energy Spirituality.

Eventually we moved into research, reading auras that Meredith encountered while dealing with other doctors at the hospital. If you're interested in what makes people tick, you really can't beat this kind of research.

No wonder this psychiatry resident joined me for dozens of research sessions with Stage 3 Energetic Literacy.

Especially delectable was reading Meredith's facades with different staffers. Let's use the example of that very prestigious psychiatrist, Dr. Biff. (What, I never mentioned that apart from all his other qualifications as a desirable bachelor, Biff is a psychiatrist?)

Every aura contains hundreds of chakra databanks, all of which can be researched. With an advanced form of energetic literacy, we could pull out of Meredith's aura some of her **energetic holograms** from whenever she interacted with Dr. Biff.

(This type of aura-level storage happens automatically and was my inspiration for the Subconscious Facade Archive you have learned to create.)

During our research sessions, Meredith and I would research certain chakra databanks as a baseline. Then I would delve into what about Dr. Biff changed while he was in contact with Meredith. For instance, we would research:

- Dr. Biff's *presence in the room*
- Dr. Biff's presence with Meredith
- Dr. Biff's *power dynamics* with psych residents in general
- Dr. Biff's power when with Meredith
- Dr. Biff's *communication patterns* with psych residents in general
- Dr. Biff's communication when with Meredith
- Dr. Biff's *emotional connection* to psych residents in general
- Dr. Biff's emotional connection to Meredith

What did we learn from this research? Psychiatrists can be at least as crazy as anyone else. Sure, Meredith and I already knew this in theory. Discovering details was the fun part.

Meredith relished the validation when I described aura patterns that matched exactly how these doctors spoke and acted.

Most fascinating of all, we discovered that Meredith's facade would change depending on the particular doctor. There was a lock-and-key fit. Her facade with that doctor would smooth the relationship, given that doctor's own personality quirks.

For a supervisor who was brainy, emotionally detached, and always had to be in control, Meredith's facade spontaneously emphasized being brainy, emotionally controlled, and respectful of authority figures.

For a fellow resident who was emotionally curious, power seeking, and insincerely friendly, Meredith's facade morphed into emotional curiosity, being easy to work with, and slight friendliness.

Amazing! How did she do it?

The changes were instant, effortless, and brilliantly appropriate. Yet Meredith never used her conscious mind to figure out which facade to create for each person. It happened automatically.

Automatically, yes. But it certainly helped that Meredith had moved out enough STUFF over the years so that her auric modeling, her who-you-be was squeaky clean. Plus she had learned the complete skill set for Spiritual Cleansing and Protection and used the healings as needed.

Having great clarity in her aura, Meredith could adapt appropriately to every new relationship. That is my wish for you, Resourceful Healer, even if you never wish to become a psychiatrist.

Healing Outgrown Facades:
TAKE THIS HEALING FURTHER

How often is it wise to do this healing?

- If you're a fast grower, do it every two months.
- If you're a slow grower, do it every six months.

Either way, Healing Outgrown Facades will allow you to upgrade your appearance to others whenever you like.

What a difference it makes, gradually increasing your soul's truth-value in every relationship. As you develop new friendships and work relationships, this can be a way to make them superb in ways you can't even imagine, not yet.

Bring on more and more relationships where you express the true Divine pattern for your soul!

Healing Outgrown Facades

Part One. COMMAND A CONNECTION TO THE DIVINE

Father-Mother God, be here with me now as a super-charged presence.
(Close your eyes. Take one slow breath in, hold, breathe out, hold. Then return to normal breathing and open your eyes.)
I awaken my Power of Command to co-create with you now.
Together, let us bring more Divine light, love, and power into Earth.
(Close your eyes. Take one slow breath in, hold, breathe out, hold. Then return to normal breathing and open your eyes.)

Part Two. RELEASE THE OLD FACADES AND BELIEF BODIES

Father-Mother God, please shine Your light into all my facades and belief bodies. Separate them out from me.
Immediately fill and surround me with Your healing presence.
Each of my current facades and belief bodies was developed for a reason. Send that knowledge to my subconscious mind for storage, in case I ever need it.
Now move each of my old facades and belief bodies forward through time, evolving them super-fast until they dissolve into pure light.
Store the life lessons from them into my subconscious mind as well.
Place a gossamer-fine layer of protection around each one of my bodies, physical and subtle.

Part Three. REPLENISH

Now I call forth my own identity as a soul.

Soul, help me to hear, feel, and express your presence, trusting my everyday likes and dislikes, thoughts and feelings.

Awaken within me fully. I am open to receiving more of your wisdom day by day.

Now I charge you to co-create with Father-Mother God. Make me a complete new set of facades and belief bodies.

These are to be the clearest expression yet of the true Divine pattern for my soul, so I can bring more truth, joy, and power into this lifetime.

(Take a few slow, deep breaths. Stretch your body.)

I give thanks that this is done. It is done. It is done.

18. Let's Party

Celebration time! Bring out that wine bottle from your cellar, the prize of your collection. My, those tuxedo-wearing waiters do look fine.

Hold on, such accoutrements aren't absolutely necessary. (Not that I'll complain if you supply them.) Really I just want to give credit where it is due. Resourceful Healer, you deserve a party, fancy or not.

Congratulations on learning our skill set for Spiritual Cleansing and Protection. Now you're free from so many types of astral-level STUFF:

- Pesky astral ties.
- Confused, energy-draining stuck spiritsl
- Icky antique facade bodies and belief bodies.
- Blah-inducing thought forms in all kinds of unexpected places, not only within you but stuffed into all personal possessions, even the bristles of your toothbrush.
- Also, you used to suffer from the most common form of astral debris on the planet. Not nearly as well known as the name of "Harry Potter" or even "dementor," that former type of STUFF that you used to have was the joy-sucking, astral-level goop known as "psychic coercion."

So, welcome to a squeaky clean, new improved everything about yourself, your relationships, and all that you own in the world. Now, while we're at it, let's acknowledge another change beyond these immediate benefits, something that could prove really significant long-term.

Have you begun to notice benefits from using your Five Cleaning Supplies? They are so essential to your skill set for Spiritual Cleansing and Protection. More about those cleaning supplies will be celebrated soon.

I'm assuming you *did* the "Let's Explore" sections that were provided for learning each healing. If you skimmed past them, no worries. You can always go back and do those exercises later... whenever you're ready for a giant step of personal growth.

However, if you have done the full training in Spiritual Cleansing and Protection, including "Let's Explore," you have all the more reason to party.

Permanent Healing, Not Just "Clearing"

Spiritual growth isn't only about removing STUFF. Just as important is what you add afterwards.

Exploring our many healing techniques, you have applied that principle time and again. Well, the same goes for the very process of healing that you have employed.

Resourceful Healer, remember your wake-up experiences during Part One of our journey together? How about those subtle but important Aha!s in our "Let's Explore" sections?

These super-important parts of each healing were designed to wake up your faculties for spiritual self-authority. In the process of *removing* astral-level debris, haven't you been *improving* your trust in yourself as a human-type spiritual healer?

That's a big deal. Your whole life long, you have had the potential to become that confident kind of healer. And now you have used this vital kind of spiritual trust for the first time. Or else you have advanced the extent to which you use it.

Resourceful Human Healer, you are a magnificent type of lightworker envied throughout the universe, a quickly evolving master of energetic change here at Earth School.

Five Cleaning Supplies — that's the essence of your human equipment as a spiritual healer. Over the decades, I have experimented with many ways of teaching Spiritual Cleansing and Protection, plus I have personally used this skill set to help clients on six continents.

Based on what I have learned so far, I'm convinced that the process itself is important. It can make a huge difference for you long term, claiming all five of your cleaning supplies, especially Your Power of Command.

This new skill set of yours has a context that I call **"Energy Spirituality."** That means a system of spiritual development where you use deeper perception plus healing skills to wake up from inside.

Energy Spirituality aims to bring you an amazing life, moving forward faster on your personal path to enlightenment. Here I would like to give you an overview of the complete system.

- Just as math is the language of science, energy is the language of higher states of consciousness and holistic healing. Anyone who can do regular Gutenberg literacy (reading this page, for instance) is "special" enough to do the other kind of literacy just as well.

- Some students of Energy Spirituality care mostly about developing skills of energetic literacy — Aura reading, face reading, skilled empath merges.

- Other students of Energy Spirituality are mostly interested in permanent healing of STUFF, emotional and spiritual garbage that limits life. Techniques for doing that include Empath Empowerment skills plus cutting cords of attachment.

- Another core skill set for Energy Spirituality is what you have just learned, Spiritual Cleansing and Protection.

Each one of these skill sets within Energy Spirituality depends on using your Five Cleaning Supplies. Comfortably using consciousness, physical self-awareness, etc., allows you to say with conviction, *"I trust my truth. My inner experiences really do count."*

Self-authority can include all Five Cleaning Supplies.

Learning to trust your inner truth can develop gradually. One new chunk of trust emerges and becomes fully integrated. Then you're ready to open the next chunk, and so forth. With each chunk of trust, you will give slightly different answers to these two big questions:

1. *Do I always have the right to use all five of my cleaning supplies?*

2. *Can I trust what I feel, know, see, hear, think, etc.?*

When exploring something "spiritual," don't leave your humanity behind. Trusting your human faculties is basic spiritual self-authority.

This self-authority is your birthright, helping you to evolve most rapidly at the human level.

Your self-authority is the guest of honor at our party. Sure, this aspect of yourself deserves to be celebrated. So how about joining me in this toast at our party:

Here's to my own thoughts, feelings, likes, dislikes! Everything about my subjective reality is true.

Here's to very strong self-respect about my own truth! Always. No exceptions.

A toast like this won't make you conceited. Simple self-respect doesn't mean having crazy, grandiose notions about knowing everything.

You didn't just toast an ability to supposedly decide what is true for everyone else, or pontificate about what must be true for all time.

Instead you simply acknowledged that, as a sane person, you are allowed to value your personal truth.

Combining this subjective self-authority with objective skills of speech and action, you can upgrade your effectiveness as a person.

Spiritual self-authority deserves a toast... and more. Trusting your own truth is the ultimate human resource. You are definitely allowed to use this every day of your life, not just when partying and not only while doing healings for Spiritual Cleansing and Protection.

As entertainment at this party, join me for a fresh perspective on the relationship between self-authority and your human life.

Earth School Heroes

Here at Earth School, every person you meet is a hero. For starters, it was an act of spiritual bravery when you signed up to live here. This is a hotshot, challenging, spiritual learning academy, you know?

Before signing up for this human incarnation, you lived as an angel. You were the happy inhabitant of an astral world. What did you give up, making the choice to become human for a while?

- Instead of feeling 100% connected to God, you would lose the connection. (At a minimum, temporarily. Possibly for the entire lifetime.)
- Instead of feeling 100% connected to your fellow angels, you would experience yourself as separate. (Even lonely, some-

times. Because no amount of Facebook friends comes close to the old angelic Oneness.)

- Instead of living in a state of eternal bliss, you would deeply identify with your physical body.

(Ask random strangers at the mall, "Do you believe that your body is a very, very important aspect of who you are?" Most will answer "Yes." Many will tell you, "My body is *the most important* aspect of who I am." Crazy but true!)

So it's a big sacrifice, signing up inhabit a cute Earth School body. After a few years into the lifetime, you start identifying with that body. Like the typical toddler, you gradually outgrow your angelic sense of safety.

Eventually you oblige your parents by feeling scared when you cross the street... and plenty of other times, too.

Identifying with your body and surroundings, with each passing year a child finds loads of additional reasons to feel frightened. Gone are the free room and board you were used to back at your celestial home. Hellooo! Most human adults do have to earn a living.

By the time you're an adult, if money doesn't scare you, something else will. Between wars and famines, overweight and bad breath and sexual weirdness of one kind or another, every human adult deals with fear. Should you manage to evolve beyond personal fears, you still have to cope with fears belonging to all the people you love.

We're talking rampant fear, right? Not just in humans, either. Earth's animals and plants live in constant fear of destruction. It's a fish eat fish world. Everybody must kill in order to eat, either that or have somebody else do the killing for you. Gentle vegans, you can't escape this. Even cauliflowers scream when being pulled from the garden.

Fear is essential to how Earth School works. Should you overcome fear most of the time, another useful earth illusion may instruct you: Pain. Physical pain. Or psychological pain. Oy veh!

How human suffering shocked you during your first five years of life. Do you have any recollection at all? Suffering like you wouldn't believe! That's why you might need hypnosis to drag out all those repressed screams and sobs from childhood.

You know how children sometimes fear the monster hidden underneath the bed? Sometimes that could be stuck spirits, which you now know how to heal. (Useful skill that, if you're a parent.)

What's an even more common reason for this bedtime fear? I believe it is becoming human in the first place.

That turns each child into the scary monster *in* the bed.

Yes, I suspect that when kids fear those monsters, the most common cause is adjusting to their own human frequencies.

A pure angelic soul, recently sent down from heaven, begins to identify with the comparatively gross, disgusting vibrations of being human. The child goes back and forth about "Who am I?"

Especially at night, fears emerge about monsters. Translating this fear into words, and assisted by discussion with a certified grownup, a handy idea emerges: The problem is a scary, separate monster lurking nearby, possibly *underneath* the bed.

That's just a theory, of course. What's true for sure? No matter how many human incarnations you have had already, becoming human again takes plenty of getting used to. Compared to your former high-pitched tinkliness in an angelic body of light, your human body is so low-note on the cosmic piano.

What kind of school is this, anyway?

Hey, you sacrificed angelic comfort in order to learn, or evolve, or do something else really good here. Whatever big plans you had on The Other Side, it's likely that included plenty of noble intentions.

As a learning academy, Earth School is brilliant. Each soul gets to bring loads of talent into a new incarnation. Plus, you came here with a plan.

Because you have constructed a **life contract** which includes all significant people and major events for the first 21 years (or, if you are really ambitious when designing your life contract, for the first 28 years). Plus there is some loose structure for all the years that follow.

Life contracts mostly ease up after those tightly scripted first decades. Your life contract contains a set number of life breaths, some optional exit points for early escape without having to commit suicide, and the occasional big karmic event after age 30, drama that seems to "come out of nowhere" (such as a marriage that quickly turns sour, giving birth to a child who never really likes you... or winning the lottery).

These seemingly random meant-to-be's, at any stage of life, are carefully planned and quite non-negotiable.

But any discussion of life contract would be incomplete without considering a most precious resource.

This will help you only if you decide to use it, but help you it can. Your **free will** is that optional resource, of course. Most events and relationships can be improved by the use of your free will, a sacred ability to choose beliefs, interpretations, speech, and actions.

Only the first 21 (or 28) years of a life contract tend to be strongly determined; usually this time period is designed to include the lifetime's biggest payback of bad karma. These particular clauses in a life contract can't be stopped by free will.

Even then, however, free will matters. Although you can't *prevent* the meant-to-be, strongly scripted, events in your contract from happening, you sure can choose how you *respond* to them. Those free willish choices will shape subsequent relationships and life events.

Through the years, your free will matters more and more. In summary, life contract items can be the framework on which to design your 3-D masterpiece in this precious lifetime.

And, of course, your free will functions more freely if you use skills of Spiritual Cleansing and Protection.

Another aspect of Earth School design is pure genius. Every thought, word, and action produces consequences. These consequences don't materialize quickly and obviously, as happens at the psychic level.

Instead manifestation for humans is slow. It's also complicated, due to illusions like time and space, plus the intersecting impact of other people's free will as they share objective reality with you, e.g., Human time and space, laws of the land, interest rates, gravity.

Especially confusing about consequences is the **Huh? Factor.** Consequences from previous lifetimes can come back to bite you anywhere, any time.

How nice it would be if Earth School involved simple manifestation — like life at the astral level. Someone could teach you The Secret or The One True Religion.

Supposedly that would neutralize everything about how earth really works. No Huh? Factor. No silly interference from other people's impact on objective reality.

Except here on earth, even that old-time religion won't necessarily last a whole lifetime. Not for many people living these days. People today are evolving faster than during centuries past. Most spiritual seekers alive today experience **virtual reincarnation**, packing the equivalent of many lifetimes into one human identity.

Haven't you already gone through many belief systems, for instance? That's common now, as people try to solve their ever-changing problems at Earth School.

Talk about change, within seven years each human body changes so much that every single cell has been replaced at least once. Thus, even on the surface level, your body is ever-changing. If it weren't for the power of earth's illusions, you wouldn't believe that your baby body or teenage body belonged to the same person as who you are now.

Except one faculty remains constant: Spiritual self-authority can guide your free will.

Many hymns call self-authority a "still, small voice within." When learning skills of Spiritual Cleansing and Protection, this has been called "Your Five Cleaning Supplies."

Whatever it's called, that inner you is available for consultations. You have been learning to trust it. And the better you trust it, the more powerfully you can use your free will.

Of course, one additional factor complicates the effective use of free will.

Your Angel Committee

Meet your Guardian Angel. Or don't. Either way, he/she/it will serve you faithfully.

Even before birth, you chose a starter pack of angels: Guardian Angel plus a couple of Angelic Guides.

They promised to help you, whispering guidance into your subconscious mind. Angels mostly stay in the background unless you specifically ask to speak with them.

The one exception is their intervention whenever an accident threatens to claim your life prematurely. No doubt you have heard miraculous stories of these angelic rescues.

Over time, your personal Angel Committee will expand. Some leave because vibrationally you have become more evolved than you used to be (and more evolved than them).

More celestial helpers will join your personal entourage. Which angels and guides, exactly? That depends on:

- Which choices you make
- Which jobs you undertake

- Which rhymes refuse to break
- Just kidding about that last part.

Ever study Reiki, for instance? Every initiation, you get a healing angel. (Not that your Reiki master necessarily announces this to the class.)

Initiations from any religion or spiritual movement can add to your Angel Committee. But there's more... as they say in infomercials. Choose a new job? Volunteer to help people? Dedicate the rest of your life to producing infomercials?

Based on your commitments, you may receive a new spirit guide or animal spirit or angel, etc. Whether or not you name him-her-it, you get all the celestial help you need. By the time you reach age 30, your personal Angel Committee might number 150 or more.

So you have a lot to be proud of, plenty of reason to party. And if you're really curious to know more about your merry cheering squad in their astral bodies, you can take a course in psychic development that emphasizes meeting your personal Angel Committee. Or else get a reading.

Regardless, here comes the single most important fact about your personal Angel Committee and how it relates to free will and self-authority....

Who Is Your CEO?

Chief Executive Officer of the Me Corporation — that's you. You even have employees. All those angels and guides in your Angel Committee work for you. Each one has volunteered to inspire your life at the human level, keeping you safe, helping you to succeed.

So who sets the standards being supported? Who decides which type of success matters most? Of all the beings in your Angel Committee, which one is the big boss?

You. You are the boss. Nobody in your Angel Committee matters more than you and your free will, directed by your spiritual self-authority.

Even the wisest guides don't run you. Their job is to love and support you.

Students of psychic development can sometimes forget that. Some even make a religion of consulting a favorite angel to the point where the CEO stops making decisions and acts more like a trusting supplicant.

Say that this happened to your friend Vonda for a while. There you are, having dinner with her at a lovely restaurant.

You ask, "What do you want for dessert?"

Vonda closes her eyes. She consults with her favorite spirit guide, Sam.

Smiling, she opens her eyes and announces, "Sam tells me I want the chocolate layer cake."

Truly, there are worse ways to experiment while you're here at Earth School. For instance, Sam could have told Vonda to order the Jello.

Actually, many people live in the Vonda way for years or decades. Vondas may believe they're doing the ultimate in spiritual evolution.

Why? Consulting your favorite angel would definitely be preferable to making decisions based on somebody else's favorite angel. Or "Why don't I get stinking drunk first? Then I'll decide."

Still, Vonda has neglected someone important. (And I think you know who that someone is.)

Resourceful Healer, as the CEO of your Angel Committee, your free will matters enormously. For instance, you can choose to seek self-actualization. Perhaps your first priority would be a closer relationship to God. Serving humanity at the highest level could be another great choice. Maybe you would like to become a healer, helping suffering humanity to become a more happy humanity.

Aspirations like these require that you train your human-level consciousness to co-create at the spiritual level. What a fast way to evolve! And your Angel Committee will support that.

Another choice might involve seeking other human types of success. More money! More sex! More power! Or you could simply strive to be a good, responsible human being who is effective in the world.

These, too, are highly evolutionary spiritual paths. And your Angel Committee will support these worldly pursuits, even if never consciously consulted for guidance, not even once.

Unfortunately, many goodies at Earth School are addictive. So it's easy to get hooked on earth's flashier rewards, the money and sex and power. Millions of folks, consciously or not, follow in the footsteps of Alexander the Great or Hugh Hefner.

Still, that's going to be a fine, educational experience here at Earth School. Why not spend one of your lifetimes pursuing something so very human?

Another interesting choice for you as CEO might be to emphasize psychic-level experiences. This choice is fun. It's flashy. Furthermore it is also very fashionable in certain New Age circles. You can find loads of friends, and even more products.

Yes, entire industries have sprung up around selling angel cards and angel pictures. Online you can find loads of teachers who encourage you to depend on advice from astral beings, begging them for flashy signs and wonders and synchronicities. I call this idealization **"The Romance of the Astral."** And I'd like to warn you about it right now.

Great teachers of psychic development don't encourage this kind of imbalance, of course. They help their students to keep their human heads. So their students evolve at a brisk pace.

Vonda might wish to learn how to do psychic readings or mediumship or channeling at her favorite frequency. With a well-balanced teacher, Vonda could pursue psychic development while staying beautifully balanced as a human being.

However it can be very tempting to glorify astral-level beings and practices. If Vonda's human life seems to be stuck, she might spend more and more of her time seeking guidance, as if trying to peek ahead at the answers in her math textbook.

When the woo-woo interests grow bigger than human interests, uh-oh. It's The Romance of the Astral, championed by many a New Age crowd.

Remember our earlier look at the three worlds? Astral experiences are, by definition, flashier than what is merely human. Sure, astral flash is appealing. But watch out. Falling for The Romance of the Astral can begin like a crush but end more like a love addiction.

Vondas can become so infatuated with The Romance of the Astral, they forget about human life or spiritual life. These pale by comparison with flashy psychic-level entertainment.

How would that dependency show? Over-dependence on astral-level flash can manifest as:

- Trusting angels more than people.
- Constantly seeking guidance from energies or spirits, rather than paying attention to objective reality.
- Feeling way more interested in psychic phenomena than human relationships.
- Relying on predictions more than living in the present.

- Confusing external validation with one's personal path toward enlightenment.

Frankly, living for The Romance of the Astral may not be the fastest way to evolve spiritually while living on earth. Anything that causes you to lose interest in "ordinary" human relationships is iffy — whether bourbon, online pornography, or angel porn.

You chose to be here for this lifetime, correct? Ever since birth, this has been *your* lifetime, aided by your personal Angel Committee. Why act as though it's the other way around?

Far as I know, if a soul wants to evolve, attaining a human incarnation here at Earth School is one of the very best gigs in all the universe.

Even a really crummy lifetime counts spiritually. Like Fred Flintstone's sad existence, where he incarnates into poverty, witnesses constant violence from dinosaurs, fails to live up to even the most unambitious goals. Finally he dies a slow, muddy death.

Afterwards, however, such rejoicing in heaven!

At Fred's life review he discovers how much he has evolved spiritually, achieving distinctive learning that his soul will keep forever.

All brave Earth School volunteers can achieve immense spiritual growth, even a Rodney Dangerfield, someone who seemingly gets no respect whatsoever.

By contrast, how exotically glamorous is astral life, anyway? After your current lifetime ends, you're going to live in an astral body again, no human add-ons. You will go to the appropriate psychic-level world (a.k.a. "Heaven"), be surrounded by astral beings at your level of consciousness (a.k.a. "Other angels"), and enjoy astral life together for as long as you wish.

Except for future brave experiments where you incarnate at a learning academy such as Earth School, you will live eternally in a body of light. Which means that once again you will feel totally connected to God and all that is. Once again, you will feel so much bliss, it practically oozes out of your wings.

Returned to a psychic-level body, you may sign up for the very same kind of volunteer work that your personal Angel Committee has been doing for you here: Serve and advise, support and love. Jobs like these can be delightful. Just one catch.

Although you can learn, you won't evolve.

Angels, fairies, beautiful spirit guides with flowing hair, ancestors who stay "dead" by not yet incarnating elsewhere: What do all of them have in common (aside from a relatively blissful life)? None of them evolves spiritually.

Flashy ways to get stuck.

The psychic realm contains more layers than a croissant. Higher levels can seem way glamorous when you live at one of the layers below... especially since the astral level contains more variety than the human level.

Remember our cosmic piano analogy from Chapter 9? Most of the 88 piano keys count as astral.

Human life certainly contains many layers of vibration. In our piano analogy, remember, human frequencies contain a full octave, seven white keys, plus five black keys.

Sure, there is huge variety in the consciousness of your fellow humans. Think about the contrast between your life, as someone who reads books for fun and profit, compared to someone who never reads, neither for fun nor profit.

Frequencies of earth energy vary wildly. Higher levels of intelligence, athletic ability, or physical beauty, can be immensely attractive. Enjoying Earth School, sometimes people grow addicted to the glamour of high-level *product*, such as diamond jewelry, luxury cars, and handbags with four-figure price tags.

Yet all that allure seems puny by comparison with what is available at the astral plane. Compared to anything human, psychic flash means experience that is more, bigger, shinier. Think Taj Mahal plus the Sistine Chapel plus Yellowstone National Park; sprinkle in some Disneyland and then add a lot more glitz.

Astral anything is higher-vibed than the human equivalent, even at the very lowest astral frequencies. Getting hooked on all that allure brings on The Romance of the Astral.

Even when we emphasize just being human, certain activities can charm us because of a hidden astral dimension. For example, did you know? Getting drunk moves consciousness into an astrally dominated experience.

That's why a substance that chemically depresses the nervous system can feel so good. When tipsy enough, one's hearing and vision change. Human senses shift into a version of our surroundings that's more like what a spirit experiences. No wonder certain drinks are called "spirits."

- Different types of liquor create linkage to different astral experiences, so a red wine high corresponds to a different astral high than bourbon.
- Smoking pot moves consciousness a bit higher than alcohol does. No wonder it's called "getting high."
- Cocaine, heroin, and other hard drugs temporarily move consciousness into an even higher astral realm. No wonder they are called "even more addictive."
- Sexual acts can shift consciousness into lower astral planes. Another term for "pornography addiction" could be "The seductive pull of a lower astral vibration." Low or not, these vibrations are seductively higher than ordinary human vibes. Simply because they are astral rather than human.

Astrally-tinged experiences like these will temporarily change a person's aura. And not for the better.

Subjectively, it's a matter of flash. Astral-flash experiences may be highly addictive. A person can lose the taste for human-level experience. By comparison, "merely human" could appear deadly dull.

Nonetheless, free will rules while we're human. A courageous, persistent ex-addict can move fully into recovery. Reinvesting in everyday human life, every good human attribute can come alive again, even that very human privilege of finding unexpected joy.

Regarding recovery, a shining inspiration is First Lady Betty Ford. Having used energetic literacy to analyze her aura from comparison photos, I discovered immense evolutionary change. By her death at 93, the founder of the Betty Ford Center had attained spiritual enlightenment. (See related articles at my blog, www.rose-rosetree.com/blog.)

Overcoming addiction is glorious for everyone who manages it. Pleasant, though? Hardly! Let's take the example of Cousin Buddie. Normally his idea of heaven is a hot game of blackjack at a Las Vegas nightclub, brightly lit at 3:00 a.m.

After losing all his money, Buddie returns to his modest apartment, a place with far lower wattage. "There's no place like home," he grumbles. Because it really feels like "no place," unbelievably blah and boring.

But let's say that his family stages an intervention. Soon Cousin Buddie decides to stop gambling, once and for all. A few weeks into recovery, Cousin Buddie still feels resentful and grumpy. Yet he starts noticing interesting little things about his apartment, like differences between one room and another.

Eventually, such a home could feel like a palace.

For anyone in our human kind of body, when addictions are gone, the human level can start feeling like the spiritual treat it is: Comfortable, sacred, with extraordinary and ordinary all mixed up together, a thrill ride for the spiritually ambitious.

From a spiritual perspective, a humble home like Cousin Buddie's is anything but. Living in a physical home with a human body brings precious opportunities for spiritual advancement. Not only can human-level reality become fascinating. When one is willing to treat human life as though it actually mattered, rewards come lavishly.

The Romance of the Astral seems to support human life but actually undermines it. Fascination with psychic-level experiences can be just as addictive as gambling, smoking weed, or drinking whisky.

Resourceful Healer, let's take another look at the importance of committing firmly to human life, avoiding addictions of any kind, and celebrating the precious opportunity for evolution you have by virtue of living on earth.

Attracting stuck spirits.

If you pursue psychic development, be discerning. Choose your teacher very carefully.

Never think you're economizing by being cheap with your personal development. The Internet offers a great deal of free and useful information at the human level, but no reputable teacher of psychic development will teach skill sets that way. Esoteric, powerful techniques require quality control and individualized coaching.

In England there's a glorious institution known as "The College of Psychic Studies" with a careful selection of well-trained instructors.

In America, there are superb teachers of psychic development including Michael and Raphaelle Tamura, Kathryn Harwig, James Van Praagh, Nancy Clark, Becky Walsh, Sonia Choquette, Barbara Y. Martin. That's just the start of a very long list.

However, some less savvy psychics will advise you to open up to "whoever." That's inviting problems, whether in pursuit of mediumship, channeling, or other forms of psychic development.

Having done the Stuck Spirits Healing, you're aware that earth houses free-floating stuck spirits galore. You also know that an opened-up aura invites anyone in the neighborhood to latch onto your energy field.

Saying, "I'm open to whoever comes" may seem like sweet surrender to spirit; in reality it's sweet surrender to *spirits*, a different matter entirely.

What, if anything, could be worse for your friend Vonda than carrying around thousands of entities in her aura? That would be daily channeling of whichever low-level astral beings happen to hang in her neighborhood.

Plenty of channelers do that inadvertently. That's like hiring a bum off the street to advise the Microsoft CEO.

Taking questionable advice.

Are dead people wiser than the living? Sometimes.

Perspective from the psychic level can have practical uses. A mid-range astral being could do great work at finding lost objects or locating a parking space. Or maybe he might be qualified to give medical advice, like Roamin' Ralph Waldo. (*"That's Dr. Ralph Waldo,"* he might tell you, via the medium. *"I worked as a physician for 16 years before my death."*)

And this ghost might do grand work for you now, diagnosing physical ailments and making recommendations for treatment.

Except between you and me and the medium, psssst. How good a doctor was Roamin' Ralph Waldo in the first place?

Sensible human beings don't just pick any doctor who happens to work in the neighborhood. Does it make more sense to trust that any random dead doctor will do a grand job?

All we really know about stuck spirits is that they have a different perspective due to living at the psychic level.

Say that your friend Jenny channels an entity who offers medical help. This would mean taking advice from a being outside her own personal Angel Committee, a group that has been carefully screened by Jenny's own Higher Self.

What doesn't Jenny know about the being she channels? Only everything.

Let's say that Jenny asks the astral being his name and is told, "Albert Schweitzer."

This Albert could be an eager young soul, like a promising first grader. Not necessarily The Great Albert Schweitzer.

If Jenny's soul development is like that of a high school freshman, why would Albert's advice be terribly helpful? It won't be, apart from The Romance of the Astral.

Ironically, underachieving.

The Romance of the Astral causes people to aim lower than they need to. When it comes to personal growth, no, Jenny doesn't have to settle for spiritual guidance from:

- Some random cute young angel.
- The nearest stuck spirit in her neighborhood.
- The deva of her washing machine (now broken, at the dump).

Really, I understand the appeal of "Whoever is available." I still remember the first time my mother sent me grocery shopping. Her assignment was to buy two pounds of potatoes.

At the vegetable bin, I started feeling sorry for some of those potatoes. Several were misshapen and ugly, not too fresh-looking either. A few of those lonesome potatoes had begun to sprout sad little eyes.

"Whoever will want to buy them?" I thought. So I scooped up the very worst ones as if they were unloved orphans and proudly took them home.

Only you can decide if, as a resourceful adult, you need make it your job to carry out rescue missions to enhance self-esteem for psychic-level beings.

Earth is loaded with volunteer opportunities to help people, plants, animals, the environment. Is it really more important to help astral beings? Choose your volunteer work wisely.

CEO as weathervane.

What first caught my attention about The Romance of the Astral? Some people I knew began acting like slaves to astral beings. Only instead of feeling used, these otherwise smart individuals felt as though they had been chosen as spiritually special.

Witness a story that I heard from super-committed spiritual seeker Jason:

"While vacationing in Hawaii, I was looking for a rock to take home as a souvenir. One rock called to me from the beach. I mean, it actually called to me.

"'Pick me.'

"Of course I obeyed the call. For the last two years, it has lived in my bedroom, where it often gives me advice. Recently my sacred rock told me, 'You're supposed to go back to Maui.'"

Proudly recounting his story, Jason shrugged. "I just bought my ticket. One way. I don't know what I'm supposed to do when I get there but I have faith that further instructions will follow."

Sure they will follow. But instructions from whom? From God? I don't think so.

Although stuck spirits usually attach to people, sometimes they will choose physical locations like a gambling casino, hospital, or beach.

Other times, a stuck spirit will inhabit a rock, a pendulum, a piece of jewelry, etc.

Here is what I advise, if ever a rock should speak to you. Give yourself credit for having perception at the psychic level. Then immediately do the Stuck Spirits Healing. (This healing can clean up your rock, your house, etc., along with you personally.)

Resourceful Healer, don't confuse an astral presence with The Will of God. Otherwise, for the rest of your life, you could spin around like a weathervane.

Tricky tales.

Tales from the astral won't help you grow faster than other stories. Compared to reading romance novels, real-life ghost stories could possess way more allure. Yet this flashier kind of narrative might have an unfortunate kind of staying power.

No matter how much you adore that Harlequin paperback, reading it will take just a few hours. Then it's done. By contrast, the stuck spirit on your ghost tour can keep you entertained with stories for as long as you're willing to listen.

Some methods of healing stuck spirits emphasize The Romance of the Astral. Supposedly the healer needs to learn an entity's complete tale, down to the color of his bedroom slippers.

Yet you know how to heal stuck spirits beautifully by now. This dependable method doesn't demand that you spend weeks listening to anyone's stories.

Personally, I believe that every moment of human life is precious. Today's top business executives make appointments every 10 minutes. Your time is just as valuable, each golden minute.

Enjoying human reality.

Question the Romance of the Astral. Could it be shaping your lifestyle right now? If you have gone from CEO of your Angel Committee to being treated like the errand boy, there's a clue.

Does this kind of power shift seem far-fetched? It has happened to plenty of people who went wild over woo-woo.

Max, for instance, told me, "My guides wake me up at 3 a.m. to bring me messages."

"Why do you have to be on call like that? You could always tell them to go away," I suggested.

"It worked. They did go away," he told me the next day, surprised.

Why surprised?

If angelic guidance matters to you as much as it does to Max, consider setting up an office hour. Maybe an office half hour.

Choose a time that is convenient for you, the human in charge. Tell your guide how you want things to be. Discover how well this relationships works on *your* terms.

Usually it will work well, anyway.

Why wouldn't a person have control over his own spirit guides and angels? Most likely, Max's "guide" wasn't chosen by his soul at all. Instead of being a member of Max's Angel Committee, this volunteer was a stuck spirit with attitude.

That entity quickly learned that Max was so star struck about astral anything... that Max could be used as the entity's puppet.

Suppose that Max tells his guide who appears at 3:00 a.m., "This isn't working for me. Let's meet up every day at noon. Save up your messages for then."

If it's really a soul-selected guide, he/she/it will honor Max's request. If not, that guide is more likely to seek someone else, someone more easily dominated.

You are in charge of your mind. If you want to be. And why wouldn't you want to be? "Ordinary" human reality can be such a thrill!

Owning your own life, your own body.

Ready for another glamour tale? Bob was taking my seminar on Spiritual Cleansing and Protection. Just as I taught you earlier about Five Cleaning Supplies, at one point I led course participants through an exercise to awaken Physical Self-Awareness.

Next came Q&As, much as we did in Part One of this program. Maybe you wonder, what kind of Romance of the Astral-type problem could a person have, paying attention to his own physical body? Bob announced scornfully, "I don't choose to pay attention to my body."

Turned out, Bob had become thoroughly hooked on The Romance of the Astral. He would rather pay attention to some fourth-rate shyster, now deceased, than to his own nose.

Of course, direct feedback from Bob's long-suffering body isn't as thrilling as tales from the astral. But if Bob wants a glorious human life, he might want to develop an interest.

What is the modest price that Bob — or any of us — must pay for a glorious life? Merely giving attention to our own human-level lives. (You know, the lives we felt so excited about... while drawing up life contracts on The Other Side.)

An "ordinary" human body is miraculous, really. It will amply repay you for any conscious attention paid to it. Which is more than can be said for random astral-level beings.

And, of course, it is important to remember that, if you want to read auras, you can do it by studying energetic literacy. You don't need to study aura reading as a form of psychic development.

Spiritual development (including energetic literacy) and psychic development (as taught by a highly skilled teacher) can both be wonderful paths. It's just wise not to confuse them. Study one or study the other, not both at once. As for the skill set we're celebrating now, Spiritual Cleansing and Protection can support either path of development.

Experiences both nauseating and optional.

Maybe you remember my promise early in this book to comment on Fabiola's puzzling experience with Archangel Michael:

"I was in a workshop where the leader asked Archangel Michael to take over. Afterwards I think everybody in the room felt nauseated. I did, anyway. Now I'm scared to even *think* the name 'Archangel Michael.'"

What happened? That workshop teacher channeled someone but it sure wasn't Archangel Michael. This Divine Being doesn't make people nauseous. But low-level astral beings sure could.

Say that Melissa claims to channel a high spiritual being. Says who? The spirit? Hey, God talk is cheap. In India, you can find plenty of storefronts with names like "Krishna." That doesn't mean that the blue-skinned deity personally works at each cash register, taking your rupees.

Similarly, plenty of channelers claim to connect with Archangel Michael or other Divine Beings. Maybe Melissa just made a beautiful wish and assumed it came true. Maybe a stuck spirit claimed to be Archangel Michael.

If you are interested in channeling, I recommend that you study with a reputable teacher. Most notably, I recommend Teaching of the Inner Christ, www.teachingoftheinnerchrist, where you can safely experiment with conscious channeling as taught by experts.

Otherwise, just say no to The Romance of the Astral.

A Powerful Law of Attraction

For those who care to actively use free will, earth becomes a place to evolve fast. Life can become enormously fulfilling. Great choices for directing your human consciousness include the following ideas:

Seek direct experience of the God of your understanding. Follow organized religion or choose disorganized religion. Or choose the honorable path called atheism. Whichever you choose, the Universe will honor your choice and keep on loving you, no matter what.

Study energetic literacy, if you like. This won't bring on a spiritual addiction, nor will it add STUFF to your aura, no more than learning regular Gutenberg literacy — which you're using right now to read these words.

Choose any Divine being you like to help you each day. For most balanced human beings, it's plenty to check in briefly once or twice daily.

Neither your personal evolution nor a healthy relationship with God demands that you outsource your life. Not even a favorite version of God must demand your constant worship.

If it interests you, experiment with getting to know your guardian angel or other spirits in your personal Angel Committee. Study psychic development if it fascinates you. Just remember that you are the CEO. These beautiful beings are in your life to serve *you*.

Whatever your chosen path, emphasize taking responsibility for your human life. My research on the spiritually enlightened suggests that after human life is really mastered, and all STUFF is cleansed from that person's aura, that individual spontaneously feels one with God.

Note the order. Outsourcing one's human life to God brings spiritual addiction, not enlightenment.

Your spiritual path could simply require that you keep yourself reasonably clear of astral debris and otherwise you simply emphasize making the most of your human life.

With self-authority, you get to choose. That's the point. Choose and then the Law of Attraction will bring experiences to you from whatever frequencies you favor.

Now you can more fully appreciate the words you have learned to use to prevent stuck spirits getting stuck in your aura:

I close off my aura to all but my own Higher Self and those beings of the highest vibration who are with me at the choice of my soul.

Tough talk! Yet it's appropriate, coming from the CEO of your life, you, the Resourceful Healer.

Nothing in all the world can compare to the delight of your human life, one golden moment at a time. Both the Divine and astral worlds are at your disposal, not merely available to you but so very responsive to your sacred Power of Command.

You, The Guest Of Honor at this Party

One of my favorite sights in all the world is to watch a baby being pulled along in a comfortable stroller. Nicely tucked in, surrounded by blankets and toys, how that baby glows.

A loving caregiver is gently providing that ride. Keeping the baby safe. Providing everyday tenderness. Sending love.

Meanwhile that tiny tot looks for all the world like a king or queen. Just sitting there in the sunshine, gliding on by.

Amazing, being a baby, isn't it?

That's what it is our whole lives long, spiritually. We grownups are so beautifully taken care of, long term. We begin as angels. We end as angels. In between, we can enjoy a lovely, evolutionary ride.

Next time you see a grownup, consider: That grownup is just as adorable spiritually as when a baby. The kind with the silky skin… and maybe a semi-bald head… and such a goofy, innocent, drooling smile.

That grownup is much more adorable, really. Because any adult on this earth has had a chance to advance so much spiritually when compared to the babyhood years.

Oh yes, you might also wish to remember — that adorable kind of grownup is definitely you.

Acknowledgments

This book has been all about teamwork, human, celestial, and Divine.

Starting with the human lineup, my gratitude goes to TIC founders Ann and Peter Meyer, plus my original TIC teachers AlixSandra Parness and Rich Bell. Thanks go also to the current generation of leaders at Teaching of the Inner Christ.

Bill Bauman, Ph.D., is the best human teacher and healer I have known in this lifetime.

More very human thanks go to my husband Mitch Weber and our son Matt Weber. Lavish thanks also go to Amy and Doug Patton, Marilyn Cooley, J.P. Fernow, Jeffrey Chappell, Eda Warren, Judy Lavine, Melanie Matheson, Dana Wheeler.

When not using my Power of Command, I seldom talk in public about the Divine and celestial beings in my life. But I sure talk *with* them early each day, and sometimes other times, too. You'all know who you are, especially those who helped most with this book. It's easy for you to know how very grateful I am for your dependable, vast inspiration.

In a category of her own is an angel of the very human kind, my foreign rights agent Deanna Leah of HBG Productions, who has brought my work to readers in so many countries. Impeccable Deanna deserves thanks in many languages.

Final acknowledgments go to you Persistent Students, Wise Interpreters from Japan, and Intrepid Clients from six continents. Most strongly in my heart now is Karen Kline, making her transition back to angel as this book is being typeset. Such a hugely evolved being as my "student" this lifetime, how hilarious is that?

As for you, Resourceful Healer, if this book has touched your heart, if any of the silly jokes has made you laugh, if any of our Q&As gave you exactly what you needed, you might want to thank these great people most. Because they taught me how to teach.

Glossary

Astral Attachments. This sinister-sounding term means the same thing as ghosts, discarnate entities, or stuck spirits. Our Stuck Spirit Healing takes care of this problem, whatever you call it.

This core skill of Spiritual Cleansing and Protection helps everyone concerned. Demystifying the process, the technique offered here can save time for the healer and provide easy protection, including helping you to avoid The Romance of the Astral.

Astral Beings. Light-filled beings at a range of frequencies can all be called "astral beings," yet their range of vibration is enormous. At one extreme is the loving, helpfulness of beautiful guardian angels. At the other extreme are low-frequency beings whose latest earth experiences emphasized cruelty or violence, being drunk, drug addicted, or bound to pornography.

Human auras include astral-level bodies. So, in a sense, we humans could also be considered astral beings.

Astral Level. Reality comes in three flavors vibrationally: Human, Astral, and Divine. The astral level contains worlds that could be called heavens and hells, each "world" populated by beings at an appropriate level of vibration.

However, astral-level frequencies are also built into human experience. Your aura, for instance, contains astral frequencies.

Skills of Spiritual Cleansing and Protection remove troubling forms of STUFF at the astral level… in order to clean up human experience.

Astral Tie. Miniature energy drains, these psychic-level ties are like strings that connect you to other people. Commonly confused with cords of attachment, astral ties can be healed much more easily.

Learning to remove them is excellent preparation for the more complex skill of permanently removing cords of attachment. Efficiently doing an Astral Tie Healing is a core skill of Spiritual Cleansing and Protection.

Aura. The human energy field, full of information. Many bodies overlap each person's physical body. Collectively they are known as an aura.

Astral-level debris, such as psychic coercion, gets stuck within a person's aura. Moving out this STUFF is essential for mind-body-spirit healing. For best results, holistic healers supplement their other skill sets with the aura cleansing techniques of Spiritual Cleansing and Protection, or the equivalent.

Aura Reading. This kind of reading involves perceiving and interpreting the information in a person's energy field. Identifying the presence of astral-level debris is an important part of the skill set of aura reading. Also available to a skilled aura reader is information about Divine-level gifts of the soul.

In addition, the full skill set of aura reading includes detailed reading of chakra databanks and can be done from regular photographs as well as in person.

Two very different approaches exist for researching the human energy field. See more at two separate terms in this glossary, Energetic Literacy and Psychic Development. Equally important, they are as different as physics and chemistry.

Auric Modeling. Whether or not a person has developed skill at reading auras consciously, subconsciously everyone does it. People busily gather that data in every conversation, every relationship. Because aurically each person's presence rings loud and clear. How does this show? Auric modeling.

Resourceful Healer, this Glossary is continued in the Online Supplement to this book.
Find it at **www.rose-rosetree.com.**

Index and
You Saw It Here First

A very full index is supplied online as part of our huge Online Supplement at www.rose-rosetree.com.

Here I'd like to flag some terms that aren't well known yet in the context of personal development, spiritual development, or psychic development. Yet all these items in our index can make a big difference for your quality of life.

You can definitely find them, and more, in the Index on the Online Supplement. Follow that language!

- Astral Ties
- Energy Sandwich
- Facade Bodies
- Negative Thought Forms
- Power of Command
- The Romance of the Astral
- Spiritual Addiction
- Yecch Factor

Resourceful Healer, maybe you and I will never be germ free. Maybe we won't even try.

But moving out astral-level grime is both possible and smart.

May techniques of Spiritual Cleansing and Protection help you take your rightful place as a leader here at Earth School.

How to Order
Rose Rosetree's Books

It's easy to order these life-changing books
directly from the publisher.
We appreciate your business and will give you quality service.
Within the U.S. and Canada, call tollfree 24/7: 800-345-6665.
For secure ordering online, click on www.Rose-Rosetree.com.

Use Your Power of Command for Spiritual Cleansing and Protection

Practical techniques are thoroughly explained. Resourceful Healer, now that you have completed this skill set, **big congratulations**.

Spread the word to any friends who might benefit. Just tell them once, of course — no sending psychic coercion!

Magnetize Money with Energetic Literacy

Manifest more of what you desire. Learn about the hidden connection between your chakra databanks and what you really attract.

This bold how-to includes detailed profiles of Esther Hicks, Rhonda Byrne, Brian Tracy, Bill Gates, and more. See amazing illustrations that reveal how chakra databanks are different for enlightenment versus spiritual addiction.

Cut Cords of Attachment

Use this as a how-to and/or a consumer guide for healing significant, deeply felt imbalances in your emotional and spiritual life.

You know, Resourceful Healer, that means STUFF removal. Learn the only trademarked system in America for cutting cords of attachment. You can learn to do this effectively, efficiently, and permanently.

Read People Deeper

Body Language, Face Reading, and Aura Reading from regular photos — use leading-edge techniques to investigate 50 practical areas of life, including confidence, truthfulness, sexual stamina, loyalty, chemical addictions, intelligence, and more.

Aura Reading Through All Your Senses

Discover the easy-to-learn method of Aura Reading Through All Your Senses®. This international bestseller honors your personal gift set, rather than demanding that you be 100% clairvoyant. Your personal gift set can become the basis for superb, effortless aura reading.

Become The Most Important Person in the Room

The most practical book yet for becoming a fully skilled empath! Do it in just 30 days, one short chapter a day plus an easy 10-minute homework assignment.

Turn your empath gift(s) OFF and enjoy your life so much more. Also included, for the spiritually ambitious: Complete instructions for safely turning your gift(s) ON to perform brief Skilled Empath Merges.

Empowered by Empathy

The first book for empaths in the English language! Explore a complete system to use *consciousness* to turn your inborn gifts OFF or ON at will.

This unique approach, Empath Empowerment®, has won acclaim internationally, bringing life-changing results. Both Print and Audiobook Editions are available.

Let Today Be a Holiday

Add new skills that allow you to powerfully co-create with God. You'll find over 450 techniques, plus thought-provoking ideas based on direct experience of reading people with full energetic literacy. One uplifting chapter for every day of the year!

The NEW Power of Face Reading

Practical skills can open your heart to new kinds of human perfection.

Rose Rosetree

Rose Rosetree pioneers systems of energetic literacy. Using skills of Spiritual Cleansing and Protection, she gauges results by reading auras all the way down to the level of chakra databanks. In a typical year, Rosetree spends over 1,000 session hours helping clients.

Her how-to books (including a national bestseller in Germany) are available at www.rose-rosetree.com and 800-345-6665. Join the lively conversation at Rose's blog, "Deeper Perception Made Practical."

Corporate clients include Long & Foster, Canyon Ranch, The Food Marketing Institute, George Washington University, The College of Psychic Studies in London, and VOICE in Japan.